A Shared Space

Folklife in the Arizona-Sonora Borderlands

Volume 1 in the series

Folklife of the West

Series Editors

Barre Toelken,
Departments of English and History,
Utah State University

Sylvia Grider,
Department of Anthropology,
Texas A & M University

William A. Wilson,
Department of English,
Brigham Young University

A Shared Space

Folklife in the Arizona-Sonora Borderlands

by James S. Griffith

Utah State University Press
Logan, Utah
1995

Utah State University Press
Logan, Utah 845322-7800

Typography by WolfPack
    Cover design by Michelle Sellers

Cover photographs:
    Juan Soldado, from a postcard; photograph by David Burkhalter.
    The finish line of the race between Relámpago and el Moro, copied
    from a photograph in the posssession of the Romero family.
    Cleaning a grave for el día de los muertos; photograph by David
    Burkhalter.
    Three Yaqui cascarones; photograph by James Griffith.
    A San Ramon frame by Jesús Leon; photograph by James Griffith.
    The entrance to the Panteón Nacional; photograph by James Griffith.

Library of Congress Cataloging-in-Publication Data
Griffith, James S.
  A shared space : folklife in the Arizona-Sonora borderlands /
James S. Griffith.
      p.   cm. — (Folklife of the West series)
  Includes bibliographical references and index.
    1. Arizona—Social life and customs. 2. Sonora (Mexico : State)—Social
    life and customs. 3. Folklore—Arizona. 4. Folklore—Mexico—Sonora
    (State) 5. Arizona—Boundaries—Mexico—Sonora (State) 6. Sonora
    (Mexico : State)—Boundaries—Arizona.
  I. Title. II. Series.
  F815.G75 1995
  306'.09791'7—dc20   95-4388
                              CIP

Contents

vii .. Acknowledgments

1 .. Introduction: A Fence in the Desert

13 .. Chapter 1. Respect and Continuity: The Arts of Death in a Border Community

35 .. Chapter 2. The Magdalena Holy Picture: Religious Folk Art in Two Cultures

55 .. Chapter 3. Cascarones: A Florescent Folk Art Form in Southern Arizona

67 .. Chapter 4. El Tiradito and Juan Soldado: Two Victim Intercessors of the Western Borderlands

87 .. Chapter 5. The Black Christ of Ímuris: A Study in Cultural Fit

109 .. Chapter 6. "The Mormon Cowboy:" An Arizona Cowboy Song and its Community

123 .. Chapter 7. Leonardo Yañez and "El Moro de Cumpas:" A Borderlands Horse-Race Ballad and its Composer

147 .. Chapter 8. Baroque Principles of Organization in Contemporary Mexican American Arizona

165 .. A Few Final Words

169 .. Notes

191 .. Bibliography

199 .. Index

Illustrations

xi .. Map of the Arizona-Sonora borderlands
12 .. Cleaning a grave for el día de los muertos
20 .. The entrance to the Panteón Nacional
23 .. A double grave decorated with cut flowers
40 .. Jesús León at his booth at the Magdalena Fiesta
42 .. Olga Ruiz painting a frame outside her house
42 .. Framed picture of Our Lady of Guadalupe
43 .. Composite picture by Anastacio León
45 .. Altar of the Tohono O'odham chapel at San Luis
47 .. Cross in the "combed paint" style
62 .. A cluster of Santa Cruz Valley-style cascarones
63 .. Three cascarones
70 .. El Tiradito from the east
76 .. Chapel by the grave of Juan Soldado
76 .. Postcard with multiple, hand-tinted images of Juan
     Soldado
82 .. Printed prayer card to Juan Soldado
129 .. Two famous horses, Relámpago and el Moro
129 .. The finish line of the great race at Agua Prieta
132 .. Leonardo Yañez, "el Nano"
146 .. Mission San Xavier del Bac from the south
150 .. The retablo mayor of mission San Xavier del Bac
156 .. A yard shrine in South Tucson
158 .. A grave marker in the Casa Grande cemetery
158 .. A low rider car display at the Pima County Fair Grounds

Acknowledgments

The essays in this book are the result of over twenty years of experiencing, seeing, doing, and asking. None of this was accomplished alone. My old friend and colleague Bernard Fontana has been companion on many field trips and provider of excellent ideas and data. Richard Morales has taught me much about his cultural traditions, including the meaning of the word *respeto*. My wife Loma and my children Kelly and David have all shared in much of the learning process. Loma accompanied me on numerous field trips in Arizona and Sonora, and read and commented on the manuscripts several times in a highly constructive way. Debbie Boecher made the fine map, working well on short notice.

The essay on the arts of death in Ambos Nogales was originally prepared to accompany an exhibition at the Pimería Alta Historical Society in Nogales, Arizona. The director of that institution, Susan Clarke Spater, was and is an extremely supportive friend and colleague. Teresa Leal O. and Alberto Suárez Barnett, both of Nogales, Sonora, were helpful in the original field work and have remained good friends in the intervening years. The trustees of the Pimería Alta Historical Society, the original publishers of the essay along with the Southwest Folklore Center, have graciously permitted its republication here.

I have been interested in the reverse glass painting tradition of Magdalena de Kino since the early 1970s. Many people have accompanied me on my collecting and data-gathering trips. Among these, Richard Morales stands out. Excellent travelling companion, thoughtful friend, and concerned colleague in the recording and understanding of his own regional traditions, he has had a hand in much of the work that resulted in this book. Pack Carnes, Bernard Fontana, Donna Howell, Keith McElroy, John P. Schaefer, and Dr. Felipe de Jesús Valenzuela have all accompanied me in the field over the course of this work. Robert Quinn provided information on the European tradition of *Hinterglasmalerei*. Special thanks must go the *pajareros* themselves: the late Jesús León and his son Anastacio, Álvaro Moreno, and Olga Ruiz, who taught me about their artistic traditions.

My work on cascarones also started with an exhibition, this one at the Tohono Chul Gallery in Tucson. Vicki Donkersley of that institution is an extremely talented and enthusiastic curator, and always a pleasure to work with. Cascarón makers Lou Gastelum, Virginia Islas, Feliciana Martínez, Ángela Montoya, and Ernesto Quiroga all consented to interviews concerning their cascarón-making traditions. My daughter Kelly Aserappa introduced me to Egg Bonkers. I am indebted to Venetia Newall of the *International Folklore Review* for permission to publish revised versions of this essay and the following one on El Tiradito and Juan Soldado, which were first published in that journal.

Once again, Richard Morales was with me in the initial stages of the study of Juan Soldado and has provided help and ideas all the way through. Randall Legler recalled for me what El Tiradito looked like in the 1920s, and the late Jim Elliot introduced me to some early written descriptions. Cate Bradley, Jim Clark, Renee Haip, Maggie Harris, and José Quijada accumulated much useful historical and contemporary information on El Tiradito during their coursework at the University of Arizona in 1989. Alan E. Bernstein of the University of Arizona Department of History introduced me to Jean-Claude Schmitt's fascinating book *The Holy Greyhound* and thus indirectly to the account of St. Martin of Tours and the spurious Christian martyr. Celestino Fernández, Macario Saldate, and Arturo Carrillo Strong provided information regarding Jesús Malverde.

James E. Officer of the University of Arizona helped me understand the historical account of the Black Christ of Ímuris, while various individuals named in the essay contributed other insights and narratives. Arquitecto Jorge Olvera of Mexico City led me to much information concerning el Señor del Veneno.

Many people contributed to the study of "The Mormon Cowboy." David Fisher and Norma Kelsey first suggested the idea and put me in touch with Norma's aunt, Blanche Hill. Mrs. Hill (widow of "Teet" Hill, "the Mormon Cowboy" himself) granted me an interview. Carl T. Sprague wrote, telling me what he knew concerning the song. Cliff Edwards offered tantalizing recollections of a possible earlier version. Colleagues Barre Toelken and William A. Wilson sent me useful information, and Hal Cannon, Michael Korn, and Pack Carnes discussed problems of interpretation and presentation with me. John Fitch of the University of Arizona School of Music transcribed the melody of the Sprague version and made helpful comments on matters of style. Finally, the following present and former Gila County residents took the time to respond with valuable information to a newspaper appeal: Paul Blumer, Don Haines, Jack Henderson, Mrs. Nash Jones, Larry Kellner, Helen Lard, Robert F. McCusick, Phil Meadows, "Old Timer," Charlie Saunders, Mrs. Loretta Shepherd, and Mrs. Carl Vance. Paul Wells, editor of the *John Edwards Memorial Foundation Quarterly*, in the last issue of which the article originally appeared, gave permission to republish it here.

Jim Officer accompanied me on my first visit with Leonardo Yañez, "el Nano," and put me in touch with Ralph Romero Jr. and Arnold Elias, both of whom contributed important information. Officer was also with me on my visit to Rafael Romero Sr. Celestino Fernández was with me on most subsequent visits to "el Nano," as well as to Trini Ramírez. Many other individuals have shared their thoughts and memories of the famous race and its aftermath with me. Kathleen Sands accompanied me to a race that didn't happen in Phoenix, while Donna Howell was with me at one that did in Pitiquito, Sonora. Donna Howell also translated the corrido texts which Leonardo Yañez so kindly prepared for the Southwest Folklore Center. These translations were checked and commented upon by Celestino Fernández and Lorraine Varela. I am indebted to the Yañez family for their gracious permission to publish the texts of don Leonardo's songs.

Robert Quinn introduced me to the joys and fascinations of the Spanish colonial baroque style in Mexico back in the 1960s and has since acted as mentor and friend. His comments on the manuscript have provided helpful insights and a broader perspective. Arquitecto Jorge Olvera has remained a constant source of ideas and information. Richard Morales added his understanding of his culture to this, as he has to all the other projects. The late Robert K. Thomas and Bernard Fontana accompanied me in the field and discussed the project with me.

David Burkhalter, a sensitive documenter of the borderlands, took some photographs for me, allowed me to use his own prints, and printed some of my negatives. Helga Teiwes and the patronato San Xavier generously permitted me to use Helga's photograph of the retablo mayor of San Xavier del Bac. I am grateful to both these artists for their assistance.

All the people mentioned here and elsewhere in this book have contributed greatly to the various projects; I reserve to myself the responsibility for whatever errors of reporting, understanding, and interpretation might be in the essays.

Finally, special and heartfelt thanks must go to the various tradition bearers of the Arizona-Sonora borderlands. It was they who created and preserved their traditions, they who lived the lives I comment upon, they who have so graciously welcomed me into their midst with my camera and tape recorder, my sometimes odd enthusiasms, and my questions. Quite obviously this book would not exist without them.

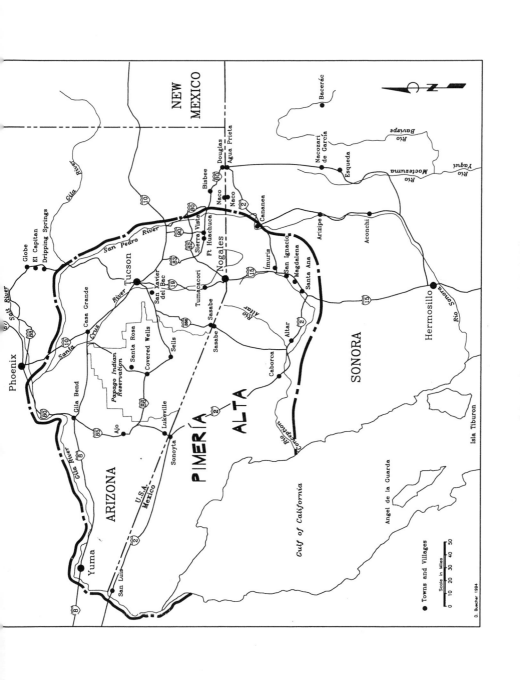

NEW MEXICO

ARIZONA

U.S.A.
Mexico

PIMERÍA ALTA

SONORA

Yuma
San Luis

Phoenix
Gila Bend
Ajo
Lukeville
Sonoyta

Gila River
Salt River
Gila River

Globe
El Capitan
Dripping Springs

Casa Grande
Santa Rosa
Covered Wells
Sells
Santa Cruz River

San Pedro River

Tucson
San Xavier del Bac
Sasabe
Sasabe
Tumacácori

Papago Indian
Reservation

Río Altar

Caborca

Río Concepción

Gulf of California

Angel de la Guarda

Isla Tiburón

Sierra Vista
Ft Huachuca
Bisbee
Naco
Naco

Nogales
Imuris
San Ignacio
Magdalena
Santa Ana
Altar

Douglas
Agua Prieta

Cananea

Arizpe
Aconchi

Nacozari
de García
Esqueda

Bacerác

Río Bavispe
Río Moctezuma
Río Yaqui

Hermosillo

Río Sonora

● Towns and Villages

Scale in Miles
0 10 20 30 40 50

D. Buecher 1994

Introduction

A Fence in the Desert[1]

Southern Arizona is border country in a number of ways. In the first place, its southern boundary is also an international border, shared with the Mexican state of Sonora. The borderline, as well as the broader cultural zone of the border, are basic realities of life in southern Arizona and northern Sonora. But southern Arizona is itself a multicultural region with its own system of what one might call internal borders. It is home to several Indian nations: the Quechans (formerly the Yuma), Cocopah, and Tohono O'odham or Desert People (formerly the Papago Indians) who have lived here for time out of mind, and several communities of Yaquis, descended from nineteenth-century political refugees from the Yaqui homeland in Sonora, Mexico.[2] Each of these groups has its own reservation. There is also a large Mexican American and Chicano population, some families of which have been in the region for two centuries.[3]

These cultures interact with each other and with the dominant Anglo American society. This latter group started arriving in the 1850s, gained an almost exclusive hold on political and economic power in the 1880s and 1890s, and continues to grow through birth and through immigration from elsewhere.

The term Anglo American, or Anglo, as it is used in the American Southwest, really means anyone who isn't Hispanic or Indian. Thus, Chinese Americans, African Americans, and even Serbian Americans, all of whom have had an important presence in southern Arizona since the late nineteenth century, are somehow all Anglos. Even without taking into consideration these ethnic differences, the dominant society carries within it what might be described as its own series of internal borders. Catholics, Protestants, and Latter-day

Saints; miners, farmers, and cowboys; urban, suburban and rural dwellers: all these distinctions have long been important ones in the Arizona-Sonora borderlands, as indeed they have all over the American Southwest.

This cultural complexity is paralleled to some extent in the neighboring state of Sonora, Mexico. O'odham live and claim a homeland in northern Sonora just as they do in southern Arizona. Northern Sonora holds no Yaqui communities, to be sure, but Yaquis travel through the region on their way between the Yaqui communities in Arizona and southern Sonora. Magdalena, Sonora, sixty miles south of the border, is an important Yaqui pilgrimage focus. Anglos interact with Mexicanos in Sonora as they do in Arizona, albeit on different terms. And northern Sonora enjoys an increasing variety of ethnic groups, religions, and traditional occupations, as thousands of people from all over Mexico come to the border in search of economic opportunity.

The international boundary between Arizona and Sonora was established as a result of the Gadsden Purchase in 1853. In its simplest conception, it is a dividing line on a map, running from New Mexico northwest to California. On the ground, it takes the form of a fence. It runs over hills and through valleys, through a countryside that shades from the Chihuahuan Desert on the east through a zone of grasslands and oak-covered hills to the Sonoran Desert, which starts near the border city of Nogales. From Nogales, the line travels through an increasingly dry Sonoran Desert until it reaches the Colorado River and California.

There are six ports of entry on the Arizona-Sonora border. With the exception of the westernmost town, each community has a counterpart on the other side of the line. From east to west the paired border towns are: Douglas/Agua Prieta, Naco/Naco, Nogales/Nogales, Sasabe/Sasabe, and Lukeville/Sonoyta. San Luis Río Colorado, Sonora, the sixth port, has no corresponding town in the United States. Connecting these clusters of population stretches the border fence, marked as well with cement monuments so placed that each one can be seen from those to the east and west of it. The fence runs mostly through lonely country, more frequented by four-legged than by two-legged animals.

Where it traverses true desert (and deserted) country, the fence is made of several strands of barbed wire. In more settled stretches it changes to chain-link. The fence serves as a barrier to human traffic but only to a degree. Shoppers crossed daily in the 1980s through holes in the Nogales chain-link fence, while a rural international market has for years taken place on weekends at a gap in the fence where it runs along the southern boundary of Tohono O'odham Nation (formerly the Papago Indian Reservation). This permeability is changing; as I write in April, 1994, steel strips have replaced the chain fencing in San Luis and Nogales, and there are plans to install them in Naco as well.

The fence itself is featured in local Spanish. One illegally enters one country from another *de alambre*—through the wire. A person who does this is an *alambrista*, a "wireist." Not all informal crossings are above ground through the wire, however. In the late 1980s, customs officials discovered an elaborate tunnel leading from a warehouse in Agua Prieta, Sonora, to a similar structure in Douglas, Arizona. Powerful hydraulic lifts had been installed at either end, and the whole set-up was capable of handling considerable quantities of goods. At least two *corridos*, or Mexican ballads, about "El Túnel de Agua Prieta" have been written, recorded, and issued on commercial cassettes.[4]

El túnel doesn't stand alone as an underground path across the border. Tucson and Nogales newspapers in March, 1994, were full of accounts of young criminals who lived in trans-border drainage pipes and robbed people who tried to use these pathways to cross the border. And tunnels from the 1920s and 1930s, reputedly used to smuggle liquor or Chinese or both, figure in Nogales oral traditions.

The fence serves other, more social purposes from time to time. During the 1980s, international volleyball games were regularly held near Naco. Each team played in its own country, with the chain-link border fence serving as the net.[5]

To the east of Naco, in Agua Prieta, Sonora, match racing between selected horses has long been an important form of recreation. In 1957, an Agua Prieta horse named *Relámpago* (Lightning) won an important race and became the instant target of many challenges.[6] One of the challengers was *Chiltepín* (named after the fiery local wild chile), from Pirtleville, Arizona, a small town near Douglas. Hoof-and-mouth disease regulations made it impossible for either horse to enter the other's country for the race. The match was finally held, however, following a suggestion which is said to have been made by the chief of U.S. Customs in Douglas. A level stretch of border fence was chosen, and each horse ran in its own country.[7]

The Border as a Cultural Region

The border is more than a boundary separating one country from another. It is also a cultural region which extends for many miles into each nation.

I am often told that a border town such as Nogales, Sonora, "isn't the real Mexico." That is perfectly true, of course, just as Nogales, Arizona, "isn't the real United States." Each is a border community, a place of cultural negotiation. Each attracts residents and visitors from the other side of the line. Folks cross the border daily in both directions to shop, to work, to socialize. Each town has taken on some of the character of the town on the other side of the border. This border zone actually extends for many miles on either side of the border towns themselves. For the traveller from Michigan, U.S.A., or from Michoacan, Mexico, the foreign flavor starts long before one arrives at the boundary line between the two nations, and reminders of home persist long after one has crossed over into the other country.

The society of the border communities is to a great extent bilingual and bicultural. Thus equipped, individuals can successfully negotiate between the two languages—and the two worlds—which come together along the border. The existence of these two worlds—the fact that the individual is coexisting with a system which may not be perfectly understood but which has the power to affect one's life—can lead to a certain amount of anxiety. Very often in human society, jokes cluster around such areas of anxiety, and the border is no exception. A whole body of bilingual, bicultural jokelore exists all along the U.S.-Mexico border. Some of the jokes follow traditional one-liner formulas, like the following:

> Knock-knock
> Who's there?
> Kelly
> Kelly who?
> *¿Qué le importa?* (What difference does it make to you?)

Or the toast,

> Here's to Mexico, where the sopa's not soap and the *ropa's* not rope, and the butter's meant to kill ya.

This joke does two things: it plays with two false cognates (*sopa* is Spanish for "soup," and *ropa* means "clothing"). With the pun on the Spanish word for butter (*mantequilla*, roughly pronounced "meant to kill ya"), it also reminds the listener of the unsanitary stereotypic burden borne by Mexican food.

A longer narrative joke suggests the advantages of speaking two languages:

> A man robbed a bank in Tucson and fled for the border, hotly pursued by the FBI. He got to the border first and slipped across, while the FBI had to get permission to cross and get their papers all in order. When they finally crossed the border, he was long gone. But the FBI always gets its man, and so they caught him, way up in the hills, in the little village of Bacadéhuachi, Sonora. When they caught him, he didn't have the money with him. He spoke no English and the FBI guys spoke no Spanish, so the agents hired an interpreter.
>
> The first thing the head FBI guy asked the interpreter was "Tell him to tell us where he hid the money."
>
> The interpreter turned to the prisoner and said: "Dice el señor que ¿dónde está el dinero?" (The man wants to know where the money is.)
>
> The prisoner responded: "¿Dinero? Claro que había dinero, y debe que estar por alguna parte, pero no me acuerda precisamente que dónde está." (Money? There sure *was* some money, but I don't remember just where it is now.)
>
> The interpreter turned to the FBI agent and said "He says he's forgotten where he put the money."
>
> The FBI agent drew his pistol, cocked it, and laid it against the prisoner's head, saying, "Tell him that if he doesn't remember where he put it in two minutes, I'm going to blow his brains out."
>
> The interpreter turned to the prisoner and said, "Dice el señor que si no te acuerdas que dónde está el dinero entre de dos minutos, te va a dar un balazo por la cabeza." (The man says that if you don't remember where the money is within two minutes, he's going to put a bullet through your head.)
>
> And the prisoner answered, complete with gestures, "Pues en este caso, está el dinero atrás de la casita de mi

hermana. Es una casita blanca, en ésta mera calle, dos cua-
dras de aquí, al lado izquierda de la calle. Atrás de la casa
hay un arból muy grande, y diez pasos al norte del arból,
hay una piedra blanca. Abajo de la piedra blanca, allí está
enterrado el dinero." (Well, in that case, the money's at my
sister's little house. It's a white house, on this very street, on
the left side of the street. Behind the house is a big tree,
and ten paces north of the tree is a white stone. Under the
stone, that's where the money is.)

The interpreter turned to his employers, removed his
hat, and said, "He says he's willing to die like a man."

As this story makes plain, power lies with the bilingual individual
who can manipulate both sides. Incidentally, I first heard the joke in
pretty much the form I have given it here. I have since heard the same
story set in East Los Angeles and another telling set in sixteenth-century Mexico, as a conversation between Cortez and the Aztec, Cuauh-
temoc, with Cortez's famous Indian mistress, Doña Marina, also
known as La Malinche, in the role of interpreter.

In recent years bilingual border jokes have spread beyond their
original bicultural context. Since the 1950s I have heard the tale of a
monolingual from Mexico who was looking for a pair of socks—*un par
de calcetines*—in an American department store. After being shown a
wide selection of clothing by an increasingly frustrated monolingual
English-speaking salesman, he finally pounced on the first pair of
socks he saw, exclaiming *"Eso, sí que es."* ("That's what it is!") The
clerk responded: "You dumb Mexican, if you can spell it, why can't you
say it?" In 1993, this bilingual pun was used in a radio commercial
advertising a nationally-distributed brand of Spanish language
instruction tapes.

Although other scholars have suggested different functions for
this kind of joke,[8] the genre in my experience serves to celebrate a special sort of person on the border—the bilingual. In Texas they may be
primarily Chicano in-group jokes; I don't think they are on the Arizona border. I have collected them from Chicanos and Anglos alike—
bilingual Chicanos and Anglos, that is.

The Pimería Alta, A Binational Region

The central Arizona border region is made more complex by the presence of two Native American tribes. The ancestral home of the Tohono O'odham stretches on both sides of the international border from the Altar Valley west almost to Sonoyta. On the U.S. side, the O'odham live on Tohono O'odham Nation, the second largest reservation in the United States, stretching from the border to just south of Interstate 10, and from the Baboquivari Mountains west to a line just east of Ajo. Although most Sonoran Papagos have moved to the United States within the present century, a few villages of O'odham still exist in Sonora. The O'odham have no Sonoran reservation lands, however, and the Indian communities are being encroached upon by Mexican ranchers and agriculturalists.

It is an article of faith among Tohono O'odham that the international agreement establishing the border also established O'odham rights to move freely from one side of their ancestral territory to another, without necessity of passports or other papers. I am not aware of any historical documents substantiating this belief.[9]

One occasion on which O'odham do in fact cross the border in great numbers is the annual Fiesta de San Francisco, held in Magdalena de Kino each October 4. This is the major folk Catholic event of the year for many O'odham, Mexicans, and Mexican Americans and is discussed at greater length elsewhere in this volume. Suffice it to say that the devotion to San Francisco is a highly complicated regional phenomenon involving a saint who seems to be a composite of St. Francis Xavier (whose statue it is), St. Francis of Assisi (on whose day the feast is celebrated), and Father Eusebio Francisco Kino, S.J. (the pioneer Jesuit missionary in the region, whose bones are on view in the Magdalena plaza in front of the church). Although each of the three cultural groups involved conceptualizes the saint in a different way, all participate in his annual fiesta and pilgrimage.[10]

The importance of San Francisco to Arizonans, as well as Sonorans, points to another aspect of the central Arizona-Sonora borderlands. This part of the border is a cultural region in its own right, even though an international border runs through the middle of it. Jesuit missionaries in the late seventeenth century referred to the area as the *Pimería Alta*, the "Land of the Upper (or Northern) Piman Speakers," to distinguish it from other areas to the south which were occupied by speakers of a related language. (Pima is the term used by Spaniards and others to refer to the people who call themselves O'odham. Piman traditionally includes the Desert People—the Tohono O'odham—as well as the River People—Akimel O'odham—of the Gila and Salt River Valleys.)

Today, over 300 years since the first permanent contact between natives and Europeans in the Pimería Alta, the region seems to be culturally distinct even though it reaches into two nations—Mexico and the United States—that did not exist until over a century after Kino's day. The presence of O'odham culture, the devotion to San Francisco, even the distribution throughout the region of a unique style of giant tortilla made of wheat flour, all attest to the persistence of the old Pimería Alta at the close of the twentieth century.

Cultures in Contact

It is important to realize that the Mexican Americans, O'odham, and Yaquis of Arizona all maintain their cultures in some relationship to dominant Anglo American society. Anglos have been in social, political, and economic control of southern Arizona since at least the 1880s and the arrival of the transcontinental railroad.

Anglos participate in the older traditions of the Pimería Alta in a number of ways. They consume selected cultural items such as the regional food locally called "Mexican food, Sonora style."[11] They purchase piñatas and cascarones, and either use them for their intended purposes as things to be destroyed while adding to the festive atmosphere of a party or place them in their homes as regional decorations. Some attend the Magdalena Fiesta, not as much out of a devotion to San Francisco as out of an interest in regional traditions.

In other words, many Anglos have begun to use items of traditional regional culture as symbols of the region itself. They display bits of traditional art and folklore physically or verbally as they assert their place in their adopted home. Anthropologists have long noted that items of culture can change in many ways as they move across cultural boundaries; this process can be seen over and over in the Pimería Alta.

Many Anglos living in the Pimería Alta conceive of themselves as living in a much larger cultural region—the American Southwest, or simply, the Southwest. It's a real region, of course: the southwestern corner of the United States, distinguished physically by its dryness and culturally through its long history of influences from the Valley of Mexico. Ever since the late nineteenth century, when the Fred Harvey Company needed to convince travellers on the Santa Fe Railroad to stop at its hotels in New Mexico and Arizona, the Southwest has been marketed to Americans from other parts of the United States.

So it is that this area of diverse natural settings and traditional cultures has become in the minds of many Anglo Americans a unified region, taking much of its color from its hub of fashion, the area around Santa Fe, New Mexico. And so it is that aspects of a very real group of traditional cultures have been transformed into colorful accents in the lives of Anglo American immigrants.[12]

This can be seen in the various strategies used regionally to market salsa. The Spanish word *salsa* simply means "sauce"—any kind of sauce. (Worcestershire Sauce, for example, is called *salsa Inglés,* "English sauce," in Mexico.) As a loan word in English, salsa has come to mean a particular kind of Mexican-style sauce containing chiles of some kind. In traditional Mexican culture, this kind of salsa is used as casually and as commonly as ketchup is in ours, and for the same purpose: to give extra flavor to one's normal meals. In Anglo American culture salsa appears either as an accompaniment to a specialty cuisine called "Mexican food" or as something in which to dip tortilla chips at a party or before a meal. Mexican-based salsa companies tend to advertise their products either with representations of the ingredients or with some visual symbolic statement of the condiment's hotness and regional character. Some Arizona companies use symbolic visual statements of the product's Mexican character, often images of women wearing regional Mexican costume.

Still other Arizona companies, aiming for a wider Anglo American market, use images—cattle brands, kachina masks, adobe houses, saguaro cactus, and mesas—that are evocative, not of a particular cultural tradition but of the American Southwest as a whole. Salsa in this context is no longer just a daily accompaniment to meals, or even part of a specialized kind of Mexican cooking. It has become part of a Southwestern lifestyle. It adds flavor, not to one's bacon and eggs, but to one's life as a consumer in an exotic region of the United States.[13]

In summary, the southern Arizona-northern Sonora border country is a culturally complex area in which the process of cultural negotiation has a long history. If we are to credit the work of archaeologist Charles Di Peso, traders and missionaries from central Mexico, based near present Casas Grandes, Chihuahua, brought new goods and ideas into the region as early as 1000 A.D.[14] More recently, Salado, Hohokam, and Trincheras cultures coexisted in the area covered by the essays in this book. With the arrival of Father Kino in 1688, a permanent European presence (including Spaniards, Mestizos, Basques, Catalans, and Jesuits from all over Europe) was established. The cultural makeup of this European presence has grown more complex over the years, with the addition in the nineteenth century of Anglos, Asians, and African Americans. The essays in this book examine in detail some of aspects of the folklife of this complex cultural region.

The Essays in this Volume

The first chapter treats various forms of cemetery art in the twin cities of Nogales, Arizona, and Nogales, Sonora, in an attempt to define some of the processes at work in this border community. Chapters Two and Three describe regionally important forms of folk art and discuss their iconization when they enter the dominant culture. Chapter Four describes a particular kind of supernatural being common to many parts of Mexico. A shrine in Tucson dedicated to one of these spirits has also been iconized by Anglo Americans.

The next two essays deal with the non-iconic reinterpretation of borrowed or shared cultural items. The narratives explaining a black crucifix currently in the church at Ímuris, Sonora, vary depending upon the group for whom (and by whom) the narrative was created. So do narratives concerning the Children's Shrine, a sacred place on Tohono O'odham Nation, depending on whether the story is being told by O'odham or local Anglos. Moving north in Arizona, the ballad, "The Mormon Cowboy," seems to belong to both Gentiles and Mormons in Gila County. Both groups have claimed authorship of the song. The text remains fairly constant in both cultures, but the meaning of the text seems to change depending upon what group is interpreting it.

While the essays so far mentioned deal with cross-cultural matters, the last two in the book are confined to material within a single cultural tradition—material which in each case gives the regional culture some of its distinguishing flavor. Leonardo Yáñez of Douglas, Arizona, was a lifelong professional musician and a nationally famous composer of corridos, or Mexican ballads. Some of his compositions deal with horse match races, one of the most important topics for regional corridos.

Also important locally is the set of organizational principles normally associated with the baroque style of eighteenth-century architectural decoration. Deeply rooted in Mexican (and indeed Aztec and Spanish) culture, baroque organization was firmly established in what is now Arizona in 1797 with the dedication of the mission of San Xavier del Bac, twelve miles south of present-day Tucson. The church is an example of a way of organizing one's surroundings that appears to remain vital in contemporary Mexican American culture.

A word about mechanics is in order. Although I feel it important to present detailed texts and descriptions of the material under discussion, such details have a way of impeding the flow of the text. Therefore, I have frequently resorted to appendices in order to supply such data. Finally, the notes to each chapter serve a dual purpose: to present my source material to my fellow scholars and to present peripheral ideas and details that, while important and interesting, should not intrude upon the main text.

Deciding which names to assign to groups of people can get complicated. The people who for years were called Papago Indians have formally changed their name to Tohono O'odham. I have used the latter name in contemporary descriptions; the former when dealing with the past. Their reservation, politically defined as Tohono O'odham Nation, is still the Papago Indian Reservation on maps. I have used both terms. Mexican Americans live in the United States; Mexicans in Sonora. I have used "Anglos" for participants in the various non-regional streams of United States culture, even though I wish there were a better term.

Cleaning a grave for el día de los muertos, Panteón Nacional, Nogales, Sonora, November, 1989. Photograph by David Burkhalter.

Chapter 1

Respect and Continuity

The Arts of Death in a Border Community[1]

This first essay deals very specifically with the border, both as a line of demarcation and as a cultural region in its own right. Cemeteries in Nogales, Arizona, are different from those in Nogales, Sonora. Yet they are coming to resemble each other in important ways, as manifestations of a border culture that partakes of but differs from the patterns to be found in the heartlands of each of the two nations involved. Like all the traditions discussed in this book, the cemetery arts of these twin border cities are dynamic, changing as the population changes, and as new possibilities arise.

Introduction

Nogales, Arizona, and its twin city of Nogales, Sonora, lie along the international border approximately 60 miles south of Tucson. Founded in 1880, Ambos Nogales (Both Nogaleses), as the two cities together are frequently called, comprises the most important border community between El Paso/Ciudad Juarez to the east and Calexico/Mexicali to the west. With an estimated population of 200,000, Nogales, Sonora, is by far the larger of the two. Its rapid growth is fueled by the various opportunities for personal advancement presented by the inequalities of the two economic systems that meet along the border. In addition to normal traffic of people and goods, there are the *maquiladoras* (assembly plants) for U.S.-based manufacturing companies. These take advantage of the less stringent labor, insurance, and pollution laws of Sonora, as well as the relatively cheap labor available on the Mexican side of the line.[2] Although Nogales, Arizona, is much smaller with an estimated 18,000 population, it, too, is growing, both as an international trade center and as a Sun Belt residential site.

Nogales, Sonora, has had an influx of immigrants from many regions of Mexico who bring with them their own traditions and worldviews. Likewise, Nogales, Arizona, is constantly growing by the arrival of individuals and families from many parts of the United States who bring their own regional characteristics. So the cultural dynamic of Ambos Nogales, perhaps like that of other border communities, is a complex mixture of accommodation and polarization, of stability and change. In each city a binational regional culture is constantly evolving while being continually influenced by a wide variety of other regional cultures from both nations.

A knowledge of this background is essential to understanding the material presented in this essay. In the same manner as this region has developed its own distinctive traditions of cookery, based on the historic importance of beef and wheat raising, as well as upon the traditional native crops of the region,[3] so it has evolved its own ways of dealing with that great inevitability, Death. But just as one finds McDonald's Golden Arches in Nogales, Arizona, and Guadalajara-style birria restaurants in Nogales, Sonora, so too are the national approaches to death on both sides of the border modifying the broad regional picture.

Permanent Grave Decorations

In any cultural tradition, one frequently finds that creative activities center around certain foci. Death is such a focal point for many Mexicans and Mexican Americans. It seems logical that a culture which places such a strong emphasis on the family as does traditional Mexican popular culture would evolve ways of expressing the importance of family members who are no longer living. This is indeed the case. Perhaps the most dramatic expression of this concentration of arts and traditions comes each year on *el día de los muertos* (the Day of the Dead) or All Souls' Day, November 2. As the connection between death and traditional creativity is not limited to a single holiday, however, it is appropriate to begin with the cemeteries themselves and the permanent markers which they contain.[4]

There are four public cemeteries in Ambos Nogales. The Nogales Cemetery on Bejarano Avenue in Nogales, Arizona, was established around the turn of the century. The oldest cemetery in Nogales, Sonora, is Panteón Rosario, begun as a family cemetery in 1892 and opened to the public in 1894. Panteón Nacional, situated like Rosario close to the international border, was a military cemetery during the Revolution and became public in the 1920s. It is the largest cemetery in Nogales. Panteón Héroes, formerly a family burial plot, became public in 1918. Now all three Sonoran cemeteries are seriously overcrowded, and the need for more space is a topic frequently discussed. Meanwhile, Panteón los Cipreses, a private cemetery, has opened on a hill above Panteón Nacional.

In all four cemeteries, locally made grave markers mingle with those which have been imported from outside the area. Imported markers, affordable only by wealthy families, give us an indication of the ways in which people in Nogales have responded to nationally changing fashions in grave markers. Some of the locally made markers reflect these same stylistic currents. Thus, several older graves are surrounded by elaborate neogothic cast-iron fences which were made around 1900 in foundries as far away as St. Louis, Missouri, and Cleveland, Ohio. They were available throughout the United States by mail order and were shipped to Nogales, Arizona, by railroad. There are also locally made, wrought-iron fences, in which the imported style is imitated to the best of the craftsman's ability.

However, many grave markers don't seem to follow national fashions or styles in any way. These are folk monuments, similar to many found in Mexican and Mexican American communities throughout southern Arizona and northern Sonora.[5] They reflect the artistic tastes and resources of the communities in which they were erected. They come in two basic forms: the cross and the *nicho*, or free-standing niche. This latter is designed to hold a sacred image and may take on a wide variety of shapes. American-style tombstones with inscriptions are found, to be sure, but are not as common as a visitor accustomed to Protestant cemeteries in the eastern United States might expect. This is a community of the image rather than of the word.

Most crosses are of metal and usually have a nameplate in the center where the horizontal and vertical elements join. The shape of the nameplates may vary widely, this being one area where traditional creativity is often brought to bear on what is basically a simple form—the Latin cross. Information appearing on the nameplate is usually restricted to the name of the deceased, his or her birth and death dates, and some such formula as R.I.P. (*Requiescat in Pace*) or Q.E.P.D. (*Que en Paz Descanse*)—Latin and Spanish respectively for "Rest in Peace." Sometimes the family relationship of the person or persons erecting the marker to the deceased will be added. Rarely does a funerary poem or some other statement appear. Lettering is frequently elaborate and may have been done either by a family member or a professional sign painter.

The arms of the cross may end in some sort of finial decoration—another instance where a multitude of options is open to the craftsman. The cross may be further embellished (and its stark angles obscured) with decorative iron scrollwork. Filigree ornamental ironwork is a long-established Mexican tradition with roots in colonial times and the baroque age. Two outstanding examples of this work in early southern Arizona are the eighteenth-century crosses on the dome and west tower of the Mission San Xavier del Bac, just south of Tucson. Today, this kind of work is done to order at a number of shops on both sides of the border, as well as by private individuals with metalworking skills. Local smiths also make the fences that surround many of the cemetery plots in both Arizona and Sonora, as well as the *rejas*, or arrangements of bars that appear over so many doors and windows in the area.

Blacksmith shops are not the only places where traditional grave markers are produced. There are also *marmolerías*—shops where monuments are cast from *mármol*, a white composition material. The *marmoleros* (mármol craftsmen) specialize in a wide variety of nichos. These may be quite simple or extremely elaborate. Perhaps the most striking are the free-standing copies of church facades whose towers can soar up to seven or eight feet in the air. The statue inside the nicho usually represents some saint or member of the Holy Family to whom the deceased had a special devotion. Sometimes the statue had actually belonged to the person who now lies in the grave. The dead person's rosary is often enclosed in the nicho or looped over the top of the monument.

Permanent decorations on the graves are not restricted to the markers. Many graves are delineated or outlined with a cement curb, or covered with either mounded dirt or a slab of some sort. (The piles of rocks which, in many rural Arizona cemeteries, serve to protect the graves from coyotes and other predators seldom appear in these urban cemeteries.) Graves may be surrounded by a wrought-iron fence with a gate at one end. This fence provides yet another opportunity for the decorative artist. The four corner posts of the fence may extend upward to provide support for a corrugated metal or plastic roof over the grave. These roofs, or *techitos*, are found mostly in graveyards in Nogales, Sonora, and are a fairly recent introduction to the area. Finally, a very few families on both sides of the border have erected small chapels or mausoleums for their dead.

The setting in which all these graves appear deserves some mention. Public cemeteries in Ambos Nogales are surrounded by either fences or walls and are provided with formal entrances, complete with wrought-iron gates. Within the enclosure, the graves are arranged in rows, all facing the same way. In contrast to many Catholic cemeteries of southern Arizona, including Nogales, where the graves are arranged with their heads to the west, the grave orientation varies in the Sonoran cemeteries. This is probably because two Sonoran cemeteries are on fairly steep hillsides, which dictates the grave orientation in each case. With the exception of parts of the Nogales, Arizona, cemetery, there is no grassy expanse of the sort associated with the memorial parks of the United States. Rather, bare earth is the rule, and planting is left to individual families. Italian cypresses and irises are quite popular, as is a variety of vinca locally called *cobre tumbas* (it covers tombs).

Furthermore, these folk cemeteries are not static places. In the first place, individual graves frequently change over time. Monuments, once erected, may be replaced or augmented when the family can afford the expense of something more elaborate. The walls of at least one Nogales, Sonora, marmolería are hung with wrought-iron crosses which were left there after being replaced by new, more elaborate cast monuments. A grave may be marked with a simple wooden cross at first, then over the years acquire a covering slab, a metal cross, fence, and techito, and finally a composition monument. These additions are usually made either on one of the deceased's anniversary dates or on All Souls' Day. When the family of the deceased dies out or moves away, the grave may fall into disrepair. In at least one Sonoran cemetery there is a move afoot to level these abandoned monuments to make the much needed space available to other families.

Much of the change that takes place in the cemeteries of Nogales operates on an annual cycle centering around November 2, All Souls' Day in the Roman Catholic calendar and The Day of the Dead—*el día de los muertos*—in Mexico.

All Souls' Day in Ambos Nogales

Casual Anglo American visitors to a Mexican or Mexican American graveyard during the summer rainy season might get the mistaken impression that the cemetery is neglected and uncared for. This is seldom the case. In fact, cemetery maintenance patterns are not the same as in the Anglo world. Although larger cemeteries may have a resident caretaker, it is the job of the individual families to maintain their own graves. Little attention is paid to weekly or even monthly care of graves. The major effort for almost everyone is concentrated on the days immediately preceding November 2.

All Souls' Day is the day on which the Catholic world remembers and prays for its dead, many of whom, according to Catholic belief, are in Purgatory and can be aided by the prayers of the living. This is the holiday which forms much of the basis for the American Hallowe'en, as well as for the Day of the Dead in central Mexico. The former celebration is almost totally secularized; the latter owes much of its nature to pre-Hispanic, Indian heritages. The day prior to All Souls' Day in the Roman calendar is All Saints' Day, when the saints, who have already joined God in heaven, are remembered.

Mexican folk belief has elaborated this sequence of days. Nogales residents have told me that October 30 is for people who died accidental deaths; October 31 is for unbaptized children; and November 1 for *angelitos* and *angelitas*—baptized children who died while still at an age of innocence and who therefore are in the presence of God. Some say that the original angelitos and angelitas remembered on this day are the innocent children slaughtered by King Herod in his attempt to destroy the infant Jesus.[6] November 2 is for adults.

El día de los muertos—the Day of the Dead as it is celebrated in much of central and southern Mexico—involves a remarkable blending of Catholic and native beliefs and observances. In addition to honoring departed members of the family (frequently in the belief that they actually come back and visit their graves or the scenes of their life on this day), many people approach the concept of death itself in an almost playful manner. Markets are filled with such items as candy skulls (complete with names) and small statues of skeletons engaged in such everyday acts as playing music, celebrating weddings (and funerals!), and riding skeleton horses. Poets and artists participate in a long-standing tradition of preparing *calaveras*, "skulls." These are printed verses accompanied by cartoons, satirizing the events, customs, and personages of the day by presenting them in skeleton form. The great Mexican popular artist José Guadalupe Posada is perhaps best known for his calaveras satirizing Mexico City society of the early 1900s.[7] Thus the Day of the Dead in central Mexico is a true popular celebration combining the sacred and secular realms and touching in one way or another most of the societal groups and classes of contemporary Mexico.[8]

El día de los muertos in Nogales is quite different. Traces of the mainstream Mexican observances may be seen, to be sure, but most have been recently introduced to Nogales either by immigrants from further south or by members of Nogales's intellectual community. Local observances are focused much more on family continuity, with little attention being paid to death itself. Family members gather to clean, refurbish, and decorate their family graves, and perhaps spend some social time together with their dead. Recently arrived families who have no dead buried in Nogales may adopt one or more unmarked or untended graves.[9] Although the final visual result of all the activity is at its most striking on November 2, preparations begin long in advance.

By September, the women who make paper-flower arrangements for All Souls' Day are taking orders. One must have flowers with which to decorate the graves; although cut flowers are used, they are far outnumbered by artificial ones. The most popular arrangement is a wreath or *corona*, although sprays and crosses are also used. The most old-fashioned artificial flowers are made of paper.

The entrance to the Panteón Nacional, November 1, 1984. Stacks of sugar cane may be seen to the right, along with paper coronas awaiting purchasers. The crowd entering the cemetery gives some notion of the volume of people who go to the cemeteries just before All Souls' Day. The carts in the foreground contain *paletas*, or ice cream bars. Photograph by James Griffith.

Working with tissue paper has been an important traditional Mexican craft since colonial times. Yet little that has to do with the origins of Mexican folk customs is as simple as it seems. Elaborate paper cut-outs in contemporary central Mexico seem to have pre-Columbian antecedants. It does appear, however, that the roots of Mexican folk colored tissue paper work lie in East Asia. The popular name for tissue paper, *papel de china* (Chinese paper) may reflect the fact that the skills involved in working with this sort of paper were brought across the Pacific in colonial days from East Asia and the Philippine Islands. The dictionary name for the paper is *papel de seda* (silk paper). It apparently came to Mexico from the Orient via the annual treasure fleet and subsequently became a part of the national folk art repertoire.[10]

Although families on both sides of the border create their own paper flowers, many part-time professional paper-flower makers are at work, especially in Nogales, Sonora. It is difficult to estimate their number. There must be well over a hundred working to order for florists and individual citizens or producing flowers and coronas to sell at the cemeteries. Nor is the activity restricted to Nogales residents. Craftswomen from as far away as Santa Ana, Sonora, some eighty miles south of the border, sell paper coronas through Nogales florist shops or at the gates of the cemeteries themselves.

Individuals ordering wreaths may choose the color of flowers according to the gender of the person for whom the wreath is intended. Pastels and white were mentioned by some informants as being suitable colors for women, while strong blues and purples were considered appropriate for men.

At the same time that the paper-flower makers are at work, professional florists on both sides of the border are beginning to assemble coronas, sprays, and crosses of commercially manufactured artificial flowers. Made of silk or plastic, most of these come to Nogales from Southeast Asia via the United States. Although the flowers and greenery are factory made, the arrangements are done by hand, reflecting the tastes of both the people who assemble them and those who purchase them.

Other activities slowly gain momentum during the second half of October. About 40 miles south of Nogales, in the area between Ímuris and San Ignacio, Sonora, fields of flowers are slowly maturing. They are planted in the spring with All Souls' Day in mind and after being picked will be shipped as far away as Nogales, Hermosillo, and Ciudad Obregon, the latter about 300 miles distant. Picking starts towards the end of October; in 1984, the last flower fields were cleared by October 31. By then trucks could be seen parked near the cemeteries of Nogales, Sonora, with bunches of white and yellow blossoms for sale. By far the most common flowers grown for this purpose are the *zempasúchiles* (yellow marigolds). The name is from the Aztec language, and the flowers have been used for offerings for the dead for time out of mind in Mexico.[11]

Activity at all the cemeteries increases from October 30 through November 2. People arrive and clean and refurbish their family graves. Some will sit quietly for a while by the graves. Other individuals provide goods and services. Small boys compete to be hired to clean the graves. Outside the gates, vendors (a small village of them at the Panteón Nacional) set up stands to sell all sorts of traditional foods. Sugar cane seems especially appropriate for this day—it was featured prominently on the Mexico City-style altar that was erected by a local baker to show me how things were done in his home region. Coronas, cut flowers, and ready-made wrought-iron crosses are all available for purchase at the cemetery entrance. Here is a description of the Panteón Nacional from my field journal for November 1, 1984.

> A lot of action was going on inside the cemetery. Hundreds of people were there, cleaning, repainting, mounding earth, scrubbing slabs, applying flowers. One man was chiselling something off one tomb, while another was lettering a nameplate which has recently been painted black over light blue. "Ricardo" was as far as he had gotten when I watched him. He was seated on a grave slab, holding the 12" by 16" metal plate in one hand while with the other he painted blue block letters.
>
> The central pathway was the scene of a steady procession towards and away from the gate. Men and women were carrying shovels, brooms, hoes, coronas and crosses, bunches and pots of real flowers, paint buckets and brushes, pails and tin cans and plastic milk jugs of water. Small boys chased each other, carried pails of water, and offered their services cleaning graves. A balloon vendor strolled through the cemetery. People visited, worked, ate sugar cane and corn on the cob, drank sodas. There was little noise—no radios, no musicians—except for the loudspeaker of a car in the street advertising the headlines of a local newspaper, which involved a drug killing in Calle Buenos Aires. Outside the gates, vendors sold sodas, *carne asada* (grilled beef), corn on the cob, *churros* (sugar-coated, fried dough strips), yellow and white flowers, home-made paper wreaths. Small groups of people walked up the road from town, some carrying wreaths and flowers . . . past the blacksmith shop where men were welding in the yard and newly painted wrought-iron crosses shone black in the afternoon sun, past the dusty marmolerías where composition grave markers were being made, past the rows of trucks from Ímuris and La Mesa, each bearing its owner's name and home town painted in elegant, shaded letters on the door, each backed to the street to display white margaritas, yellow zempasúchiles, and coronas of home-made paper flowers. And this, I was told, was nothing compared to the crowds that would be here tomorrow on November 2, *el mero día de los muertos.*

A double grave decorated with cut flowers, Panteón Nacional, Nogales, Sonora, November, 1989. The statue represents the Sacred Heart of Jesus. In addition to the coronas on the crosses, the spray to the left, and the flowers in tin cans, there is a row of *zempasúchiles* around the edge of the curb. Curb, statue, and crosses appear to have been repainted for the occasion. Photograph by David Burkhalter.

Public cemeteries of Nogales, Sonora, are comparatively empty of the living by November 3, but they show evidence of the intense activity of the previous days. Graves have been weeded, raked, swept, washed, and cleaned. New markers are evident; others have been repainted. Iron crosses and fences glisten with new coats of black, white, or even bright blue paint. Holy statues have been repainted in brilliant, lifelike colors or in a solid wash of some bright shade. Stakes have been driven at the four corners of some graves, and multicolored ribbons are woven around and around the perimeter thus formed. Cut flowers are in profuse evidence—some in built-in containers on the tombs; others in tin cans; still others are laid in rows on the graves. Here a grave is covered with yellow zempasúchil petals, with a cross of whole blossoms in the center. There the bare, mounded earth has been raked, swept, and dampened as a background for the owner's initials, formed with orange-yellow blossoms. At yet another grave a simple cross of plumber's pipe has a zempasúchil stuffed into each of its three ends. All these natural colors mingle with the brilliant paper, ribbon, silk, and plastic of the coronas and other arrangements of artificial flowers. Crosses and other monuments are festooned with coronas which range from one to three feet in diameter. Another grave has its techito and supporting fence covered with large paper flowers of every imaginable color. And if each separate grave presents a riot of color, the total effect has to be seen to be believed.

The profusion of independent detail, the color and intensity of the scene match perfectly the diversity of the activity that preceded it. The aesthetic impulse behind the scene seems to reflect the spirit of the seventeenth and eighteenth centuries much more than it does any contemporary fashion. Profusion of detail; richness and complexity of color, form, and meaning; a fascination with miniaturization, movement real and implied, and dramatic contrast—all these remind the viewer that the people of Mexico have not yet abandoned the baroque style that served them so well in the days when Mexico was New Spain.[12]

One of the pitfalls open to an outside observer of any cultural event is the assumption that what was going on at the time of one's visit represents some sort of norm, that things have been this way forever, and that any change will represent a departure from "the way things are." Of course this is not and never has been the case. What I was able to see and experience in Nogales during my brief visits in 1983, 1984, and 1985 was simply a superficial view of one stage in a continuous process of change. Things were undoubtedly different in

1974, and they will be different again in 1994. I shall now discuss some of the changes that seem to be taking place in the traditions clustering around death in Ambos Nogales.

Impulses from the South

I have mentioned that the Day of the Dead is celebrated very differently in central and southern Mexico than it is in Nogales, Sonora. As Nogales grows as a border town, many individuals from those two regions move in, bringing their cultural traditions with them. For example, Ignacio Castaneda Estrada, a professional baker, moved from the central Mexico area to Nogales in the mid-1960s. Establishing his bakery, *La Panadería Catedral* (The Cathedral Bakery), he proceeded to bake the breads which in central Mexico were appropriate to the various seasons. There is a long-standing tradition associated with el día de los muertos of baking *pan de muerto*, or "dead man's bread." This is a special, rich bread which is used both for feasting and for placing as offerings on altars to the dead.

Sr. Castaneda's pan de muerto is a very rich egg bread with sugar and cinnamon sprinkled on top. He forms it into round, rectangular, cruciform, or human-shaped loaves, with small dough "bones" arranged on top. As Sr. Castaneda tells the story, the first year he displayed his pan de muerto in Nogales, people who came into his bakery wanted to know what it was. The custom was unknown at the time in Nogales, at least among his clientele. Now, due perhaps to a combination of his efforts and continuing immigration from further south, he makes and sells pan de muerto in considerable quantity. In 1984, in addition to stocking his bakery shelves with pan de muerto, he sent his son into the nearby streets with more, displayed in a glass-sided bread box mounted on a large tricycle. In a typically Mexican play on words and ideas, the name of the mobile bread-vending unit (which belonged to the Panadería Catedral) was *la capilla*, "the chapel."

At least one other baker was producing pan de muerto in 1984. Round, egg-glazed loaves with a molded dove shape on top were being sold from a cart at the entrance to the Panteón Nacional on November 2.

It was Sr. Castaneda who assembled what he described as a typical Mexico City-style *ofrenda* (altar to the dead) for me to see and photograph. An ofrenda of this sort features candles, candy skulls with names (presumably those of the family's deceased) on them, pan de muerto, zempazúchiles, and sugar cane. I heard of at least two similar ofrendas being planned for November 2, 1984. Both were to be sponsored by members of the intellectual community of Nogales, Sonora; one was scheduled to be erected in an experimental theater. I was unable to visit either of these ofrendas so cannot say whether they were erected.

Members of this same intellectual community, many of whom are also involved in one way or another with radical politics, are perpetuating yet another mainstream Day of the Dead custom—the political calaveras with their cartoons and satirical verses. The calaveras I saw in Nogales, Sonora, in 1984 were accusatory rather than satirical and were directed at corrupt politicians, brutal police, and similar institutional targets. They were published anonymously.

These are the major ways in which the classic Day of the Dead observances of mainstream Mexico are present in Nogales, Sonora. There are other ways as well. For instance, a couple was selling model houses outside the gates of the Panteón Nacional on November 2, 1984. These were made in the region around Guadalajara and are said to be popular additions to grave decorations in that part of Mexico. A small number were purchased and brought to Nogales to see if they would sell. As far as I could determine, they did not.

Immigration from elsewhere in the Republic and a desire on the part of the intellectual community to participate in what it perceives to be a uniquely Mexican institution: these are the two major means by which Day of the Dead observances in Nogales, Sonora, seem to be coming closer to those of mainstream Mexico. At the same time, other influences are arriving from the north. It is to these that I now turn in order to round out the picture of the traditional arts associated with Death in Ambos Nogales.

Impulses from the North

In much of our discussion so far I have concentrated on Nogales, Sonora. However, Ambos Nogales is a border community, with cities both in Mexico and the United States. What goes on in Arizona and how is it different from the Sonoran observances? In the first place, the apparent religious uniformity of Sonora's cemeteries does not hold true across the line. The Nogales, Arizona, cemetery has a section dedicated to that community's long-established Jewish population. (The founder of Nogales, Arizona, was a Russian Jew named Jacob Isaacson, and Jewish merchant families have always played a prominent role here as in other border communities.) A large boulder cut through with the Star of David stands at one corner of the grassy plot, and the individual graves are marked with small, flush-to-the-ground slabs.

There is no formal Protestant section in the main cemetery, but several monuments follow Protestant traditions of eschewing such directly religious visual imagery as crosses and representations of God, the Holy Family, or the saints. A greater number of engraved tombstones are found here than in Sonora. On the other hand, the epitaphs and funerary poems of the Anglo American nineteenth century are few and far between. So are their contemporary counterparts, gravestones engraved with pictures illustrating the occupation or hobbies of the deceased. This is in contrast to other southern Arizona cemeteries, where I have found stones bearing pictures of cowboys at work, bulldozers in operation, hunting scenes, and even a customized Harley-Davidson motorcycle![13]

Among the few local examples of these mainstream Anglo American approaches to funerary monuments are the following. One stone bears the inscription "KILLED WHILE TRANSPORTING CONTRABAND. IN WHAT FOREIGN SKIES DO YOU NOW FLY AMIGO?" This is almost the only reminder in this cemetery that the traditional, stereotypical violence of the western borderlands is not only historically real but still part of life. Another grave, whose Scandinavian-surnamed owner was a non-commissioned officer in the U.S. Army, features a realistic-looking pair of free-standing, sculpted cowboy boots.

Wrought-iron crosses and fences are in great evidence in Nogales, Arizona. Most are in the same baroque style as those of Nogales, Sonora. An occasional piece, however, suggests that additional, more modern models were and are available to customers and craftsmen in Arizona.

The intensity and general flavor of All Souls' Day as celebrated in Nogales, Arizona, is different from the scene in Sonora. Professional florists prepare and sell coronas of plastic flowers, just as the florists do in Sonora. However, the colors seem more restrained in the shops on the Arizona side of the line. (Artificial coronas of all kinds are taken across the border in both directions.) Arizona families make coronas of paper flowers as well as of such contemporary materials as styrofoam egg cartons and plastic six-pack holders. Some grow their own marigolds for the occasion or decorate their graves with potted marigolds which they will later plant. The great profusion of cut blossoms on some graves in Sonora is not duplicated on the Arizona side. Lacking, too, is the commercial activity at the entrance to the cemetery that is so striking at the Panteón Nacional. In fact, activity of all kinds is decidedly muted in Arizona.

Moreover, in Nogales, Arizona, the Catholic Church played a greater formal role in public observances than it seemed to in Sonora. After dark on the evening of November 2, a procession marched from the Sacred Heart Parish Church to the cemetery, several blocks away. The procession consisted of about 35 people with candles, led by the parish priest and three altar boys. They were joined in the cemetery by many more people, and Mass was said to a congregation of well over one hundred. This is a standard Catholic practice in many communities; it was revived in 1984 in Nogales, Arizona, after having been allowed to die out a few years before.

Another public observance was under consideration for the next year. Plans were being made to organize a procession of children, each dressed as a favorite or patron saint. The children would go from house to house, asking for donations of canned and preserved food for the needy. This was considered to be a revival of an old custom, proposed as an alternative to the totally secularized Trick-or-Treat Hallowe'en activities of mainstream Anglo America.

Conclusion

So it is that the inevitability of death as a separator of family members serves as the focus for a great deal of traditional creative activity in the border community of Ambos Nogales. Family dead are remembered through a partnership between patron and craftsperson, each functioning as a bearer of tradition. Families create a social event around the Catholic holiday of All Souls' Day, honoring and remembering their dead. Professional and amateur craftspeople create vast quantities of artificial floral arrangements. Graves are cleaned and decorated. And the result of all this activity is a series of scenes of striking beauty which can be—and are—shared by a much wider community.

But as in the case of much folk art, the tangible, photographable results, impressive though they may be to outsiders such as myself, are really not what is of paramount importance here. That so much beauty is created and available to all who come by is indeed exciting and should be given due notice. The objects and their creators deserve our respect and understanding. But the visitor should keep in mind that these arts would flourish if no outsiders ever came to the cemeteries of Nogales. What I have been describing in the course of this essay is really nothing more or less than a complex act of keeping faith. Keeping faith with departed family members; keeping faith with the great baroque impulses of the colonial period; keeping faith with that complex amalgam of cultural traditions and ideas of both American and European origin that is contemporary Mexico.

There is nothing antiquarian about these arts, these scenes. They are constantly changing. In 1984, six-pack rings and egg cartons provided raw materials for some makers of artificial flowers. A few years later, flowers were made of colored plastic shopping bags. Who knows what contemporary objects will be recycled as floral offerings in the year 2000? The superficial materials keep changing and will continue to do so. But it is my hope that the vital impulse to celebrate family continuity and to express a cultural heritage will persevere as it has for so many years.

Appendix

The Grave Markers of Ambos Nogales: Patterns and Variations

The four public cemeteries of Ambos Nogales contain thousands of grave markers, many of which are complex assemblages involving a number of elements. This is neither the time nor the place for a definitive statement concerning them and the various art styles and time periods they represent. However, the following impressions may serve to indicate some of the patterns which impressed this viewer over the course of several visits.

Crosses

Most crosses are of wood or metal, although some have been cast from cement or mármol. The wooden crosses are often formed of two sticks nailed together and are the simplest, least expensive form of grave marker used. Metal crosses may be of pipe or wrought iron. Most all are Latin crosses; that is to say the vertical member is longer than the horizontal one. A sheet-metal nameplate is often attached to the center of the cross. Common shapes for nameplates include squares, rectangles, circles, lozenges, and stars. I have found a few six-pointed stars on both sides of the border; they are probably simply stars rather than Stars of David, as most do not have the correct orientation for the Jewish symbol. The Sacred Heart of Jesus and other heart forms also appear as name plates. A few older plates have pairs of doves cut out of their upper edges. These frequently appear on children's graves.

The arms of the crosses often end in decorative finials. Wrought-iron crosses usually have the ends of their arms worked into decorative finial patterns. Flattened points are popular, as are ends where the iron bar has been split into two or three points, with the outer points curled back. Finally, decorative filigree metal work may appear on and between the arms of the crosses. Although this work appears to have the potential for an almost infinite variety of patterns, in reality a small basic repertoire of shapes is used. These include straight bars, straight spiral bars, C curves, and S curves.

Nichos

Nichos appear in a bewildering variety. The simplest are made of concrete, probably by the family or friends of the deceased. They often consist of arches with rear walls. Those made at the local marmolerías may feature pointed arches or may be extremely angular in shape. Most elaborate of all are the miniature church facades and the neoclassic domes held up by rings of columns. These are frequently part of a larger ensemble, with a slab over the grave, a nameplate, often in the shape of a book (a motif, sometimes called in English "the Book of Life," that may have been borrowed from the Protestant world), and perhaps component flower containers. With many of these more elaborate monuments, as with the large, forward-curving crosses which are produced by the same marmolerías, we are moving away from folk styles in the direction of a contemporary, nationwide, middle-class fashion. Any nicho, no matter how elaborate or simple, may have a wrought-iron grille or gate protecting the statue within.

Curbs, Slabs, and Fences

Many graves are set off in some way from the ground about them. The earth is mounded over them, or they may be surrounded by a cement curb, or covered by a slab. These slabs, or *bóvedas*, may be flat or arched. It has been suggested that the bóveda is a twentieth-century development from a large, box-like mausoleum, which appears on many of the graves from the end of the last century in Panteón Rosario.[14] One mausoleum in the Panteón Rosario is a box-like affair fully two feet high. It has a vase at each corner and is incised on the sides with Gothic-arched doors and windows, making it resemble a church building.

There is frequently some permanent provision for placing cut flowers; this may be in the form of vases built on the slab or holes (often lined with tin cans) cut into it. A nameplate is often a feature of the slab, sometimes in the form of an open book.

Many graves are surrounded by fences. With older graves, these are quite often cast-iron fences which were made elsewhere and were purchased through mail order. The wrought-iron fences provide yet another setting for baroque, curved ironwork. Once again, a surprising variety of patterns develop from a very few basic shapes.

Recycling

Visitors to Nogales's cemeteries are constantly confronted with ordinary materials which have been recycled into use as grave decorations. Most commonly, a cross has been made of four pieces of plumber's pipe joined at the center with a four-way joint. One such cross in the Panteón Nacional has a name plate made from the lid of a gallon paint can. Cross and lid have been painted silver. The finials of many of these pipe crosses are themselves recycled objects. I have seen doorknobs, oil cans, and the finials from curtain rods used for this purpose. Ready-made screen doors often are provided with S curve strips of thin metal as decorations along the horizontal center divider; these are occasionally used to decorate metal cemetery crosses.

Finally, some ephemeral decorations placed on the graves may be made of recycled materials. I have seen flowers with petals made of aluminum tabs from drink cans and with bottlecap centers. Wreaths of artificial daisies made from plastic soda straws are sold at cemetery entrances as the Day approaches. And I have also seen plastic six-pack rings used for coronas. Among the most fascinating of these artificial flowers are the several varieties which are reproduced by cutting up and reassembling bits of molded styrofoam egg cartons.

Artificial Flowers

One professional paper-flower maker whom I interviewed takes orders in September, starts to work about September 25, and is finished by October 15. In 1984 she made about 40 arrangements, both coronas and *ramas* (branches). She makes flat, daisy-like flowers using a metal stamp and forms other blossoms from tissue paper by means of a number of techniques. The stems are sticks wrapped in green paper, while the leaves are cut out of paper, painted green, and dipped in melted wax after drying. A rama in 1984 cost slightly less than $5.00 U.S. Several different flower varieties were represented in each arrangement.

This is not unusual; another craftswoman I visited told me that she knew how to reproduce 16 different kinds of flowers, while a third distinguishes five different stages of rose blooms alone! It took this woman less than five minutes to go from a sheet of red paper to a finished, partly opened rose. This artist produces a greater volume of coronas than does the first woman I mentioned, and sells to customers as far away as California and Texas. Her prices are somewhat higher than those quoted above.

Each florist shop that produces and sells plastic flower coronas appears to have a readily identifiable style. These styles are partly defined by color combinations and partly by the use of ribbon twists (locally called *picos*, "beaks") and bows which alternate with the artificial flowers. When I visited cemeteries on November 3, 1984, after a week of visiting and photographing in florist shops, I had no trouble identifying the individual sources of most plastic coronas I found there. At least one of the larger florist shops also sells individual artificial flowers, greenery, and styrofoam rings to those who wish to assemble their own coronas.

Most of the florists I visited use styrofoam rings as bases for their wreaths. One man who operates a temporary booth near the entrance to the Panteón Rosario assembles coronas on foundation rings of wrapped wood fiber. Many paper-flower makers use bent wire coat hangers as foundations for their coronas.

Color

Even after the artificial flowers of early November have faded in the sunlight, the cemeteries of Ambos Nogales remain colorful places. To be sure, the predominant color is the glaring white of the mármol used in the cast monuments. An occasional exception, in yellow or blue, provides an accent of color. Most of the wrought iron is painted a glossy black. Here and there, however, white or even bright blue has been used for fences and crosses. Saints' statues are often painted in bright but naturalistic colors, or they can also be given a single, brilliant shade. Markers and fences for children's graves can be blue or pink, according to the familiar color code. And there is always the possibility that a cement slab or monument will be inlaid with colored tiles, stones, or even bits of colored glass.

Chapter 2

The Magdalena Holy Picture

Religious Folk Art in Two Cultures[1]

The annual fiesta de San Francisco draws thousands of people each October to the mission town of Magdalena, Sonora. O'odham, Yaquis, Mexicans, and Mexican Americans all pay their respects to a composite Saint Francis who is widely regarded as the patron of the Pimería Alta. After their devotional activities are finished, the pilgrims relax, visit, eat and drink, and purchase goods of all sorts. Among the objects offered for sale are small, elaborately painted glass frames for holy pictures.

These frames are made by people locally called pajareros, "birdcatchers"—members of a Sonoran underclass that maintains a wide range of traditional beliefs and activities. The frames are offered for sale publicly, but purchased most frequently by Tohono O'odham from the United States, who charge the pictures they contain with spiritual power and place them on altars in their home communities. In recent years the frames have come to the attention of Anglo Americans, some of whom collect them as folk art. Like the fiesta de San Francisco and the composite saint whom it honors, the glass paintings touch the lives of many of the groups who occupy this particular stretch of border country.

When I first saw these picture frames in the early 1970s, I was captivated by their brilliant colors and shimmering quality. On annual trips to the fiesta I would visit the makers' booths, chat a while, and purchase a few frames. I followed a fairly standard pattern of learning: first I concentrated on the frames themselves and the technology of making them. I charted the ways in which their form changed over the years. I then became concerned with the people who made them and the very different people who used them. Much later I became conscious of the fact that, by drawing the attention of mainstream Anglo society to the frames, I was changing them and their context in several ways.

The Fiesta

Magdalena de Kino lies just off Mexican Highway 15, about sixty miles south of the Arizona-Sonora border. It was transformed from an O'odham village into a mission community by Father Eusebio Francisco Kino, S.J. An Italian Tyrolese by birth, Kino joined the Jesuit order after a serious illness during his student days in Hall, Austria. He subsequently came to Mexico, and in 1687 became the first missionary to work in the area of the Pimería Alta. He died in March, 1711, and was buried in Magdalena. When his remains were discovered by a binational archaeological team in 1966, the honorific *de Kino* was added to the name of the town. Kino's bones are on view in the main plaza of the town where he labored, died, and was buried.[2]

Although this essay concentrates on folk practices that focus on Magdalena, it is important to realize that the town is in many ways a modern Mexican population center. It serves as a center for agricultural activity in the surrounding countryside. International road and rail connections tie it with the outside world. The late Luis Donaldo Colosio, the Mexican presidential candidate who was assassinated on March 23, 1994, was a Magdalena native. The folk cultures discussed here function independently of much of Magdalena's and, indeed, much of the Pimería Alta's society.

Magdalena has long been the site of an important annual pilgrimage which culminates on October 4, the feast day of St. Francis of Assisi in the Roman Catholic church. The image that is the focal point of this pilgrimage, however, is not that of St. Francis of Assisi at all, but rather a reclining statue of St. Francis Xavier, the great Jesuit missionary saint and patron of all missionaries. This confusion probably reflects the fact that the Jesuit-founded mission program in this part of New Spain was continued by members of the Order of Friars Minor—Franciscans—after the Jesuits were expelled from the Spanish Empire in 1767. As if this weren't sufficiently complex, popular belief has injected elements of Father Eusebio Francisco Kino into the composite San Francisco, so that in the minds of some worshippers, the reclining statue in the church represents the man whose actual bones are on view in the plaza. Throughout the rest of this essay, I shall refer to this composite saint as San Francisco.[3]

This particular statue of San Francisco Xavier's incorrupt body as it lies in state in Goa, India, is itself the subject of a large cycle of legends. The statue, according to local belief, was brought into the region by Father Kino himself, and was originally intended, not for Magdalena, but for the mission community of San Xavier del Bac, just south of the present-day city of Tucson. However, when the statue reached Magdalena, it indicated its desire to stay there by becoming unmovable. This theme of a statue taking its fate into its own hands is a common one in the Hispanic Catholic world. Other legends cluster around the statue's relationships to the reclining San Francisco statue at San Xavier del Bac outside of Tucson, as well as its possible fate during the Revolutionary era in twentieth-century Mexico.

San Francisco is thought to be a very powerful and miraculous personage, and thousands of pilgrims visit in Magdalena each year, especially during the fiesta period, which lasts roughly from September 20 until October 4. These pilgrims come from all over Sonora and Arizona, and include Mexicans and Mexican Americans, as well as Tohono O'odham, Yaqui, and Mayo Indians.

Not only is San Francisco considered *un santo muy milagroso* (a very miraculous saint), but also *un santo muy cobrador, y lo que debes, pagas* (a saint who exacts his price, and what you owe, you must pay). A common vow to San Francisco in exchange for services rendered involves walking to Magdalena at fiesta time from the international border or some other point. Once a debt of this sort is incurred by a devotee of San Francisco, the feeling is that if the debt is not repaid within a reasonable time, San Francisco will himself collect what is owed him, possibly by maiming or killing the debtor or some member of his or her family, frequently by means of fire.

The fiesta de San Francisco is as surely owned by the common people as are the legends concerning him and his statue. While the Magdalena civic authorities lease land in the town's main plazas for booth sites, they and the official church exert little control over the activities of the fiesta itself. These simply happen, as thousands of people throng into town in the week before October 4. San Francisco has touched the lives of a wide variety of people in the Pimería Alta, and many of them pay their respects to him on October 4. Tohono O'odham and Yaquis from Arizona and Sonora, Mayos from southern Sonora, Mexicans and Mexican Americans from both states—all come to Magdalena, visit the statue in its chapel, and then set out to enjoy themselves. For this occasion, the area near the church is packed with temporary booths selling food, drink, and a wide variety of manufactured goods. Musicians stroll through the bars and restaurants, seeking temporary patrons. A full-scale carnival is set up between the church and the nearby Río Magdalena.

Although much of the resulting activity may seem to have little to do with religion, the religious focus is apparent to the more than casual visitor. Pilgrims arrive in town footsore from their long walk and head straight for the chapel containing San Francisco's statue. The line outside this chapel can number in the hundreds, and can take several hours to pass through.[4]

In addition, many of the stores and temporary booths around the main plaza focus on healing in one way or another. There are stands at which herbs and other medicinal substances are sold, frequently with instructions for their use. One can also purchase much of the material culture of regional folk Catholicism, including *hábitos* (religious habits worn for a period of time in repayment of a vow), *milagros* (small images in metal symbolizing the needs of the petitioner), and printed prayers and holy pictures. The holy pictures most commonly represent San Francisco, but they also depict a wide variety of saints and members of the Holy Family. Some holy pictures are sold in the elaborately painted glass and tin frames which are the subject of this essay.

The Frames and Their Makers

What I shall call the Magdalena holy picture consists of a commercially printed religious card placed under a sheet of glass. The card is usually of postcard size; the glass sheets average around 20 x 25 cm., or 8 x 10 inches. Before the holy card is installed, the back of the glass is painted with floral or geometric designs in a combination of opaque and translucent paints. The card is then placed within framing lines that have been made for it, and the whole is backed with a sheet of crumpled and then straightened aluminum foil. Light hitting the foil through the paint gives a wonderful, shimmering quality to the painting.

Some of the cards are centered within their frames. In this case, the area between the picture and the edge of the glass is painted with nonrepresentational motifs. Sometimes these consist of rows of opposed triangles. Sometimes the picture will be surrounded by an oval line, itself framed with dots and separating zones of different colors.

Sometimes the design will consist of wavy lines of contrasting colors, a technique that some scholars call combing. The vast majority of frames, however, have their cards in an upper corner, or, more rarely, in the center of the upper edge. These frames are painted with clusters of flowers in bright colors. The flowers are occasionally accompanied by birds or butterflies. Often, a scroll with the word *Recuerdo*, "souvenir," is placed diagonally across the frame. (The frames are described in greater detail in the Appendix of this essay.)

The effect of these frames, with their opaque backgrounds setting off brilliant, translucent, shimmering colors, must be experienced to be appreciated. They add wonderful splashes of color to the booths where they are sold, as well as to the walls and altars which are the final destination of most of them.

In 1982, when the first version of this essay was written, there appeared to be five families engaged in making and selling the frames. By 1993 the number was reduced to three. This activity takes place during fiesta time, in temporary booths set up on Magdalena's main plaza and on adjacent streets. Some of the men made and sold crosses and boxes in addition to the frames, and many also repaired religious statues and framed holy pictures that were brought to their stalls by private individuals. The women sold other kinds of materials in addition to the frames. Olga Ruiz, for example, sold medicinal herbs and printed charms and prayers at her space at the northwest corner of the plaza.

The frame makers are not considered to be *artesanos*, "craftspeople," by their fellow citizens, but rather they belong to an underclass called *pajareros*, "birdcatchers." Pajareros tend to live on the outskirts of their towns, and are looked down upon by other townspeople. They pursue a number of traditional occupations as the time of year and circumstances permit. They trap birds and make bird cages. They pick crops in season and gather medicinal herbs and the edible acorns, or *bellotas* (*Quercus emoryi*), which are an important regional snack food. The father of the late Jesús León, for example, was both a tinworker and puppeteer and traveled through Sonora in the 1930s with his puppet show. Some of the men also make the tin and clear glass boxes in which small statues of San Francisco are sold the year round in the shops on the plaza. Pajareros, in fact, seem to occupy much the same marginal social niche within Sonoran society that Gypsies, tinkers, and others do in Europe. They are ill-considered, peripheral individuals whose traditional skills (which often include a persuasive way with words) keep them alive on the edges of the communities which shun them.

Jesús León at his booth at the Magdalena Fiesta, holding a framed picture of San Francisco. Other pictures, along with paint and brush for statue retouching and a statue of the Baby Jesus, stand on the counter behind him. October, 1981, photograph by James Griffith.

The only time the frames appear for public sale in Magdalena is during fiesta time, in temporary booths. For the rest of the year, some craftspeople will make frames for special orders, or to sell in Yaqui country to Yaquis, for example. In the early 1990s, one family was filling orders for boxes placed by a folk art dealer based in Tucson. While several permanent stores on the plaza sell *artículos religiosos* all year round, over the past fifteen years I have seen only two frames for sale in such stores.

Each painter has his or her style within the generalized Magdalena style and layout described above. The designs are drawn in ink on the back of the glass, often using a template, and then filled in with opaque and translucent colors. The use of templates leads to easily identifiable personal styles. In many cases the shapes of the flowers and other motifs done by a painter will remain the same, and only the colors will vary from piece to piece. When members of the same family share a template, family styles are created as well. Álvaro Moreno, at one time the most innovative of the frame painters, commented that the template allows him to get the designs straight. However, he continued, every time he uses the template, it moves slightly, ensuring that each picture will be unique. After the painting is done the glass is backed with tinfoil and with either tin or cardboard. Some craftspeople insert the holy picture and seal the frame, while others leave the choice of picture up to the customer.

In 1982, the commercially made cards which were inserted in the frames were glossy, postcard-sized photographic reproductions of actual statues, paintings, or chromolithographs. They were made in Mexico City, and were hand-tinted with a wash of two or three colors. Since the mid-1980s, however, these cards have become unavailable, and mass-produced colored chromolithographs are now the rule. Nevertheless, the older photographs, and even occasionally a still older popular engraving, do occasionally show up, as some artist or shopkeeper discovers a few put away in a dark corner.

The most popular depiction is of the reclining statue of St. Francis Xavier as it looked before it was removed from the Magdalena church and destroyed on orders of the anti-clerical Sonoran state government in 1934. (The present statue, which replaced it several years later, looks very different from the one depicted in the pictures.) Next in popularity are Our Lady of Guadalupe, the Holy Child of Atocha, the Guardian Angel, St. Joseph, the Sacred Heart of Jesus, and perhaps one or two others. Our Lady of Guadalupe's picture is often dressed with flat pieces of cloth or ribbon, and otherwise embellished by appliqué on the picture itself. Hers is the only picture I have seen treated in this way. Composite scenes such as *la omnipresencia de Dios*

Olga Ruiz outside her house in Barrio Crucero, Ímuris, Sonora. She is painting a rose on a frame using a template under the glass. Several finished frames and a box of Reynolds Wrap are on the table. July, 1983, photograph by James Griffith.

Framed picture of Our Lady of Guadalupe by Anastacio León. Her figure has been dressed in strips of colored ribbon. The *nopal* (prickly pear) cactus is a common accessory for the Virgin of Guadalupe; the saguaro cactus and the three birds are not. Photograph by David Burkhalter.

Composite picture by Anastacio León with San Francisco at the top, Our Lady of Guadalupe appearing to Juan Diego on the left, and a rather uncommon depiction of the Guardian Angel on the right. the Mexican Tricolor is in the upper left; the Mexican eagle, serpent, and nopal are at bottom center. Photograph by David Burkhalter.

(the omnipresence of God) or *la mano poderosa de Dios* (the powerful hand of God) are occasionally found. Occasionally an artist will purchase a set of cards which may include pictures of saints who are quite obscure in terms of local devotion. These, too, will be framed and eventually sold.

The Customers

Although Jesús León always maintained that all sorts of people bought his picture frames at all times of the year, it appears to me that most frames are traditionally sold at fiesta time, and to a certain sort of customer. When asked what kind of people bought his frames, Álvaro Moreno replied, "Papago Indians." When asked why they bought the frames, he said that it was because they liked the bright colors.

Tohono O'odham and other Piman-speakers once occupied much of what is now northwest Sonora. Few of the present-day occupants of northern Sonora retain Indian identity and culture. About 200 Tohono O'odham live in the desert area west and north of Magdalena, while the vast majority are in Arizona. These live on their reservation, which lies to the west of Tucson, contiguous with the Mexican border, or in such cities as Tucson, Casa Grande, or Florence.

Many O'odham follow a tradition of Catholicism which has been evolving within their culture since at least the mid-nineteenth century.[5] O'odham Catholicism is a system of Christianity in which apparently Catholic acts and ceremonies have complex native meanings. The externals of O'odham Catholicism include the celebration of Catholic feast days with eating, dancing, and processions, the accumulation of power-charged holy pictures and statues, and the making of pilgrimages to Magdalena. (Going to Magdalena with one's family is mentioned in a Papago grade school reader published in 1981 as one of the "things that have kept our people strong. . . .")[6]

A trip to Magdalena at fiesta time may be made for the purpose of acquiring or replenishing a saint's image. A Tohono O'odham may acquire such an image (usually spoken of as a saint) when a family member or animal needs help, often in the form of continued or renewed health. A saint, once it has been obtained in Magdalena, will often be placed in contact with the large reclining statue of San Francisco Xavier in the church, so that it may absorb some of that image's power. I have heard an account by a Tohono O'odham healer who left his smaller statue lying next to the larger one for a while. When he returned, he discovered his statue sitting up and talking with the large statue. From then on it assisted him in his work of curing people. O'odham taking saints to Magdalena for renewal will also place them next to the big San Francisco statue. One O'odham

Altar of the Tohono O'odham chapel at San Luis, Papago Indian Reservation, March, 1970. Several of the holy pictures are in Magdalena glass frames. Photograph by James Griffith.

described this to anthropologist Bernard Fontana in terms of recharging a battery.[7]

Once the picture or statue is brought into the Tohono O'odham community, it may be blessed by a priest. Even if a priest is not present, there is often a ceremony similar to baptism by which the saint is welcomed into the community. On such an occasion, the person who looks after the saint (a common O'odham way of expressing the relationship) may ask another O'odham to cosponsor the image with him, thus entering into a *compadrazgo* (co-godparenthood) relationship with that person. Once it is securely attached to the community, the saint may be looked after at home or in a village chapel. Here it stays in company with other privately owned images, on an altar decorated with paper flowers.

A typical O'odham Catholic chapel features a low altar on the west, or head, wall. The altar may be built out from the wall, or it may be a table. It often consists of one or more steps. It is covered with a white cloth which is frequently embroidered. The wall behind the altar as well as those portions of ceiling and side walls near the altar are usually covered with white sheets. These are often decorated with rows of paper or plastic flowers. Statues of saints, including the reclining San Francisco, are placed on the altar, along with a collection box or basket, candles, candle holders, containers for holy water, and other ritual objects. Holy pictures are hung on the wall behind the altar, often in vertical rows, separated by rows of artificial flowers. Most if not all of these holy pictures come from Magdalena; many are in decorated glass frames of the sort described in this essay.[8]

Not all the framed pictures end up on altars in reservation chapels. I have seen a few in public, roadside shrines, and several on home altars in Tucson. Many Yaqui and O'odham families use the cardboard-backed frames for family pictures.

Comparable Traditions

So here we have the Magdalena holy picture, produced in northern Sonora by a handful of craftspeople and used to a great extent by Tohono O'odham, members of a culture and citizens of a country quite different from those of the artisans. The tradition may not be very old in Magdalena; I have yet to find a recognizable Magdalena-style frame in a reliably dated pre-World War II photograph of a chapel interior. Furthermore, my earliest slides of Jesús León's booth at a Magdalena Fiesta show him in 1968, working on arrangements of dried flowers behind curved plastic frames. Not a painted frame is in sight. So, although Jesús León insisted in 1982 that he had been making the painted frames all his life, there seems a possibility that this craft has become popular in Magdalena in relatively recent years.

Within the state of Sonora, the frames are apparently unique to the Magdalena area. I have found nothing even remotely similar at Sonora's other major pilgrimage fiesta, that of Our Lady of Balbanera in the old mining community of Aduana, near Alamos in the southern part of the state. Indeed, according to Teresa Pomar, former *directora* of the *Instituto Nacional Indigenista's Museo de Artes e Industrias Populares* in Mexico City, Magdalena is the only place in all Mexico where such frames are currently made and sold.[9]

I have seen older frames from elsewhere in Mexico which combine reverse-painted glass with shiny paper backing. One which appears to come from Oaxaca has different colors of paint over what could be metallic cigarette paper. Another and perhaps closer parallel exists in some of the glass and tin work done in New Mexico in the

Cross in the "combed paint" style, made in the 1980s by Jesús León. The central image is of Our Lady of Guadalupe appearing to Juan Diego; at the bottom is San Francisco. This cross closely resembles, in details of its construction as well as in its painted design, those made around the turn of the century by the so-called Mesilla Combed Paint Artist. Photograph by David Burkhalter.

nineteenth and twentieth centuries. Paint, wallpaper, and textiles were used to back glass panels in tin frames and mirrors, and one artist in southern New Mexico specialized in combed paint patterns and occasional flowers over foil that are surprisingly similar to some of those being produced in Magdalena in the 1980s and 1990s. This anonymous artist, dubbed the Mesilla Combed Paint Tinsmith by art historians, also constructed tin and glass crosses in a way identical to the Magdalena artists. He seems to have worked in the period 1890–1920 and may have travelled westward along the border as far as Douglas/ Agua Prieta or even Ambos Nogales in Arizona and Sonora. In their treatment of this artist's work, Coulter and Dixon speculate that he might have had an influence on the Magdalena tradition.[10] The absence of reliably dated older material from Magdalena casts a shadow of doubt over this theory, however.

Historical antecedents for the reverse painted frames seem to go back in North America at least as far as the mid-nineteenth century, when reverse painting on glass was a popular middle-class craft in the United States. Patterns were published for the paintings, just as they were—and are—for quilts, and American housewives of the Victorian era produced still lifes, landscapes, and idealized portraits of such dignitaries as Abraham Lincoln. These reverse paintings, called tinsel paintings by collectors of Americana, seem to have decreased in popularity before the turn of the century.[11] It is possible that this craft influenced the development of reverse glass painting in New Mexico.

The tradition has a much longer history in Europe. *Hinterglasmalerei*, as reverse glass painting is called in German, was practiced in classical and medieval times and became very fashionable in the eighteenth century. Hinterglasmalerei typically involves human figures and scenes. The European tradition sometimes makes use of metal foil as a backing for the glass. Although the art form lost popularity in most of Europe, it continued as an important folk art in Bavaria and the Tyrol, lasting through the nineteenth century, and indeed up to the present in revival form. It is quite possible that middle-class American tinsel painting and even Mexican glass painting owe their existence, either directly or indirectly, to this European tradition.[12]

Two other parallels should perhaps be mentioned here. In far-off Cajamarca, Peru, a tradition of reverse glass painting flourishes, possibly a survivor from colonial times. And in the late 1980s, the Potrero Trading Post in the northern New Mexico pilgrimage town of Chimayó sold framed, foil-backed reverse glass paintings which had been created by silk-screening or some similar process. In this case, the letters and designs have been screened out of the monochrome opaque background; glittering color is supplied by different colors of foil rather than translucent paint—a totally different technique which achieves much the same effect as the Magdalena system. The one in my possession is a rectangular 28 x 12 cm. frame. It has an inset picture of the Sacred Heart of Jesus on the left, surrounded by a wreath of leaves and flowers in red, gold, and green foil. On the right, red foil neogothic letters spell out the motto "God Bless our Mobile Home." I have also seen beer advertisements employing a similar technique in bars in Sonora in the late 1980s.

The Frames Today—A New Group of Users

Manufacture of the frames in Magdalena in the 1980s and 1990s seems to be very much market-driven. Jesús León told me that he kept trying new ideas to see if they would sell. Olga Ruiz, Álvaro Moreno, and Jesús León's descendants all seem to try a few new ideas each year. The use of painted flowers on the frames may well be a comparatively recent innovation. Their appearance is not surprising. Roses surround the traditional image of Our Lady of Guadalupe, and Tohono O'odham as well as Mexicans and Yaquis use artificial flowers on altars as well as to decorate the graves of family members at All Souls' Day. Although I have not found any specific case in which O'odham customers influenced the making of frames by verbal requests, they certainly do influence their appearance by buying or not buying certain designs. Popular designs may be made another year; ones which are slow to sell will probably not be repeated.

Álvaro Moreno told me that O'odham customers liked bright colors, and that is why he employed them in the frames. This is a common stereotype concerning the taste of "primitive" peoples, and may reveal more about Moreno's beliefs than O'odham preferences. It indicates a certain cultural distance between craftsperson and buyer. Identifying stereotypes is always potentially risky, however; Moreno seems to be perfectly correct in his assessment of O'odham tastes!

Since I wrote the first published version of this essay in 1981, a third group of people has entered into the equation. Beginning in 1982, I have curated several exhibitions (or, rather, several versions of the same exhibition) of the painted frames, boxes, and crosses. The objects were exhibited first in Nogales, Arizona, then in Tucson, and subsequently in several other locations in and beyond the state of Arizona, in a travelling exhibition called "Glittering *Recuerdos*—Glass Painting Traditions from Magdalena, Sonora."[13] Another selection was exhibited in 1988 in Tucson.[14] This has had the effect of popularizing the frames among Anglo Americans who are interested in owning and contemplating folk art. Several of these have travelled to Magdalena at fiesta time specifically to obtain frames, and at least two crafts stores in Tucson stock the glass paintings. In 1991, a Tucson-based crafts wholesaler started ordering painted glass boxes in some quantity from the León family and is marketing them in various parts of the country.

Anastacio León and his cousin Francisco Silvas participated in the July, 1993 edition of the Smithsonian Institution's Festival of American Folklife on the National Mall in Washington, D.C. In addition to giving the artists both exposure and confidence, the process leading up to their trip involved the establishment of a relationship between them and Dr. Felipe de Jesús Valenzuela, a medical doctor living in Magdalena. Dr. Valenzuela photographed both men and their work and helped them get passports and U.S. visas. He has since emerged as a champion of the local pajareros and their traditions. Both León and Silvas later demonstrated at the Tucson Meet Yourself festival in October, 1993. As I write these lines in March, 1994, it seems likely that they will be making other trips to southern Arizona to demonstrate and sell their art.[15]

Anglo Americans who purchase the frames in Magdalena and in Tucson seem to do so with a completely different set of motives than do the Tohono O'odham who make up the traditional market for the objects. Tohono O'odham buyers seem to be buying potentially powerful icons in decorative settings; the frame is incidental to the saint's picture, which must itself go through certain rituals before acquiring its desired beneficent power. For many Anglo buyers, the painted frame with its picture becomes the icon. Rather than an indication of the presence of a powerful supernatural helper, it serves as a reminder of a fascinating place—the old Pimería Alta, and of the colorful traditional cultures which inhabit that portion of the U.S.-Mexico borderlands.

Concluding Thoughts

The painted glass frames, crosses, and boxes, then, are made in one cultural world, that of the Mexican pajareros of Magdalena and Ímuris, Sonora. They are created to the craftspersons' conception of the tastes of Tohono O'odham living in Arizona, who purchase them, import them into the United States, and use them to maintain the health of their families and communities. Increasingly, the items have been purchased by a third group of people, Anglo Americans, who buy frames as examples of that complicated and often hazy category, folk art. Finally, by emphasizing painted frames, boxes, and crosses in illustrated lectures, in published articles, and in museum exhibitions, I have entered them as tokens in a complex system of information sharing and professional advancement—the world of the academically based folklorist.

The objects themselves are far from static, changing constantly over time to meet these various demands and challenges. Through all their transformations and gradual changes, however, the Magdalena glass paintings add color to whatever setting—O'odham chapel, private home, or art exhibition—they may be in. It is pleasant if not particularly profitable to speculate the future for these small works of art. Will mainstream Anglo America reach equal importance as a market with the Tohono O'odham? If this happens, will stores in the plaza start selling frames? It is not inconceivable that, if reverse-painted glass work becomes more important economically, others besides pajareros will start filling the demand, just as Mexican entrepreneurs have responded to the popularity of Seri Indian ironwood carvings by setting up factories in Magdalena and elsewhere. Only time can give us answers to these and other questions.[16] Meanwhile, the frames themselves remain, lustrous reminders of the social and cultural complexity of the Pimería Alta.

Appendix

Description of the Frames

Although most of the frames are made to take a holy card of regular postcard size (9 x 14 cm.), I have seen cards as large as 19½ x 24 cm., and as small as 5 x 7 cm. Most of the decorated glass frames measure about 20½ x 25½ cm., although frames as large as 27½ x 35 cm. have been collected, and as small as 13 x 17½ cm. Undecorated frames are made in tiny sizes, suitable for hanging in one's car or even around one's neck.

The card may be vertically or horizontally oriented. It may be in the center of the frame, or in an upper corner, or, more rarely, in the top center. The most common locations are the center and the upper left-hand corner. The glass is painted on its underside with both opaque and translucent colors in such a way as to fill completely the space not occupied by the card. The designs may be geometric or floral. Occasionally a word such as *recuerdo* (souvenir) appears on the glass, usually surrounded by a painted scroll. Crumpled tinfoil is placed beneath the glass, giving a special, luminous quality to the translucent portions of the painting.

Glass, card, and foil are then backed with either cardboard or sheet tin, depending upon the technological resources of the individual craftsperson. It has been my experience that tinsmithing technology is limited to men; it is women who back their frames with cardboard. The tin is frequently recycled from oil or beer cans. The tin-backed frames are bound along the edges with strips of tin which have been shaped on a metal rod and a grooved anvil and which are then slipped over the edge of the frame and clamped into place. The cardboard frames are simply clamped to the glass by means of two or three pieces of bent tin on each side. The tin frames are provided with a small tin loop at the top, through which is passed a brightly colored ribbon for hanging the frame on the wall. The ribbons are often selected separately by the buyers of the frames.

Not all the frames are displayed for sale with holy cards inserted in them. Some are left blank, so the purchaser may insert a picture of choice. Some pictureless frames have rectangular apertures for regulation holy pictures; others have one or more heart-shaped apertures, and are intended for family portraits rather than religious cards.

The opaque paint used on the frames is purchased locally in small bottles or jars; the translucent colors are bought in powdered form and mixed with alcohol and *goma de laca* (shellac). I have seen black ink and a crow-quill pen used for outlining the designs, and a small paintbrush used for filling in colors. The foil is commercial kitchen foil, most often Reynolds Wrap. Tin for the backing may be recycled from beer cans; however, I get the impression that much of the tin used for binding the edges of the frames and panels is purchased in sheets.

Although the frames constitute the major fiesta-time sales of the craftspeople involved, crosses and boxes are also made, using the same techniques. To my knowledge, crosses are only made by the family of the late Jesús León, who also made crosses. These crosses may be 31 x 13½ cm. or smaller, and consist of several glass panels joined together by their tin frames. The shape is that of a Latin cross standing on a trapezoid. Two holy cards are usually inserted: one at the crossing and one in the trapezoidal base. The glass panels are painted and backed in the same way as are the frames. Floral motifs are used, as are combed paint motifs.

All of the craftspeople who do tin work make boxes. These vary greatly in size and proportion, but may be as large as 22 x 12½ x 9 cm. high. The lid of the box may be decorated with a religious card or with the words *Recuerdo* or *Cariño* (love, or affection). I have also seen a box lid containing a scene of Juan Diego picking roses in front of the apparition of Our Lady of Guadalupe. The Virgin is represented by a printed holy picture; all other figures, including Juan Diego, his burro, and a burro-load of wood, are painted on the glass. The lid and sides may also be decorated with floral motifs, with opposed triangles, or with combing.

The basic layout for the frames is as follows: if the picture is in the upper left-hand corner of the frame, there will be a cluster of flowers occupying the rest of the space, with or without the word recuerdo. The word, when it appears, is contained within a diagonally oriented scroll. In the early 1980s, Álvaro Moreno experimented with the English words "Souvenir" and "Souvenir of Magdalena de Kino, Sonora." This innovation has not been taken up by other painters. If the holy picture is centered in the frame, the surrounding area will be relatively small and filled with opposed triangles or an oval within a rectangle. In both these layouts the lines are often framed by rows of dots. A few centralized frames are bordered with combed or marbleized patterns. All these layouts allow for vertical or horizontal placement of the holy picture.

Occasionally, one finds strikingly original layouts. In 1982, Álvaro Moreno used a church facade as a framing device for a holy picture, as well as a free-form, art deco-like design. In 1991, the same artist was producing small octagonal frames filled with combed patterns. In the late 1980s, Jesús León painted occasional frames depicting the Mexican eagle perched on a cactus with a snake in its beak. These patriotic motifs, usually combined with a picture of Our Lady of Guadalupe, have been carried on since Jesús' death by his sons Anastacio and Martín. In 1992, members of the León family experimented with figures cut from holy cards and placed against a monochrome background. One very dramatic picture of this sort had the solitary figure of Juan Diego, clutching his tilma filled with roses, standing against a stark black background. These and other innovations appear to be experimental designs to test the market.

The flowers painted on the glass frames are susceptible to wide variations. They are shown on both front and side views, as buds and as mature blossoms. A large number seem to be modelled on rose or camellia blossoms, although morning glories, thistles, and poppy-like flowers occasionally appear. Clusters of three flowers, or of two flowers and a bud, are most common, although I have seen as few as one and as many as five flowers on a single frame. Most flowers are colored in shades of red and orange. They are usually shown with green stems and leaves. Stems, leaves, and blossoms are outlined and given interior detail with black or occasionally white pigment. Flowers, stems, leaves, and a thin framing band around the picture are translucent, allowing the tinfoil to show through. The background is opaque. Black is the most common background color, with white next and occasional use of yellow, orange, tan, and shades of blue. In recent years a few painters, mostly women, have experimented with birds and butterflies in addition to the flowers.

Chapter 3

Cascarones

A Florescent Folk Art Form in Southern Arizona[1]

We now move to an examination of one minor form of traditional art—cascarones. These are basically party supplies—they are decorated eggshells that have been filled with confetti, and are intended to be broken over the heads of partygoers, thus increasing the celebratory atmosphere of the occasion. Cascarones have been a part of Mexican culture for at least 150 years, and are made and used all over the borderlands. In the Tucson area, cascarones have become elaborate works of art, colorful confections of paper, paint, glitter, and eggshell. They have also been adopted by some Anglo Americans as decorations symbolizing southern Arizona's regional culture. This interest on the part of members of the dominant society may well be one of the elements that has led to the cascarones' elaboration in form.

Some Background

Cascarón is Spanish for "eggshell." The word is related to *cascara*, a "shell" or "outer covering," and to the verb *cascar*, "to break or shatter." In traditional Mexican culture, cascarón also refers to eggshells which have been emptied of their contents and then refilled with confetti. They are intended to be broken over the heads of fiesta or party goers, adding to the festive *ambiente*, or atmosphere, of the occasion.

Cascarones have been a part of Mexican culture since at least the early nineteenth century. The earliest accounts I am aware of describe them being used at Carnival, that time of feasting and partying just before the austerities of Lent. An account of a Carnival ball in Monterrey, California, in 1829, describes an animated scene where young men and women broke cascarones over each other's heads and splashed each other with vials of red, green, and black paint. The cascarones were filled with tiny bits of gold and silver paper, and each participant brought his or her own. It is unclear whether or not the eggs themselves were decorated in any way.[2]

A much later nineteenth-century Carnival ball, this one in a California mining camp, featured rather more elaborately decorated cascarones. In the words of the author,

> They were egg shells, emptied of their contents by means of a small hole in one end, over which was pasted a patch of bright paper, cut in various forms, a star, a flag, or many pointed sun. The egg was painted in gay colors with spots or stripes, or circled with bands like rings of Saturn. Some of them were colored, one half blue, the other yellow or red. Altogether they were a gorgeous collection. No sober-minded, respectable hen would have claimed them; she would never have dared to set on them for fear of hatching a brood of frivolous chicks, too erratic in their tastes to earn a living by plain scratching.[3]

In these examples, the users of cascarones were young adults, and the cascarones had been made by the various families attending the ball, and brought along as their contribution to the merriment.

U.S. Army Lieutenant John Bourke, author and early ethnographer, described the use of cascarones in Tucson, Arizona Territory, in the early 1870s. The setting was a dance, but the occasion could take place at any time of the year.

> The moment you passed the threshold of the ballroom in Tucson you had broken over your head an egg-shell filled either with cologne of the most dubious reputation or else with finely cut gold and silver paper. This custom, preserved in this out-of-the-way place, dates back to the "Carnestolenda" or Shrove-Tuesday pranks of Spain and Portugal, when the egg was really broken over the head of the unfortunate wight and the pasty mass covered with flour.[4]

Anthropologist Frederick Starr observed and purchased cascarones in central Mexico in 1897 while collecting material culture and folk art for the Folk-Lore Society of London. Women would bring great baskets of eggshells to market in Guadalajara at Carnival time. There they would color the shells using a rag or their fingers dipped in different colored paints, and fill them with bits of colored paper (*amores* or *gasajo*), candies (*colación*), or even perfume or ashes, before selling them to prospective partygoers.

Starr collected other, infinitely more elaborate cascarones that same year in Mexico City and Puebla. The eggshells were mounted on cones or sticks, covered with foil or fringed tissue paper so that they resembled flowers, or surrounded by paper wreaths, or even surmounted by wax faces or figurines.

Starr illustrates two of these elaborate cascarones in his book, *Objects Illustrating the Folklore of Mexico*. One, described in the catalogue as "comic," represents a stout soldier in a white uniform. The egg constitutes the soldier's body; his head, complete with kepi, is modelled of clay. He wears epaulettes and a Sam Browne belt, carries a rifle slung over his left shoulder and a bugle in his right hand. The other, more elaborate, is described by Starr as "fancy," and a "careful and delicate piece of work." The egg is covered with embossed tinfoil. Atop the egg rests a bull's head which in turn supports a foil-covered lyre. A bullfighter, fully dressed in his *traje de luces*, "suit of lights," stands within the horns of the lyre, his right hand raised. Tiny wax flowers adorn both the egg and the lyre. Complex works of art such as these would cost far more than the simple cascarones, and were usually purchased as gifts. They may well not have been intended to be broken.[5]

Cascarones are still made and used all over Mexico and in Mexican communities in the United States. In most localities I know of, the cascarones resemble those seen by Starr in Guadalajara: they are colored eggshells filled with confetti or glitter. The users of the cascarones and the occasions on which they are used appear to have changed over the last several decades, however. Today's cascarones are almost without exception used by children.

One family I know, a family with strong roots in the eastern Arizona mining community of Clifton-Morenci, makes and uses cascarones at Easter time. During the last days of Lent, the entire family decorates the eggshells it has been saving throughout that season. The shells are painted in one or two colors, filled with confetti made from cut-up newspapers, and sealed with a scrap of kleenex glued over the hole in the end. Then on Easter Sunday, after Mass, the fun—characterized by one family member as "egg wars"—begins. There are well-understood rules to the game: the activity takes place out-of-doors, for instance, and older family members must bow their heads at the request of younger and smaller relatives.[6]

The change from a courtship ritual to a children's activity seems to have taken place fairly recently. One Tucson cascarón maker remembers her mother talking about making cascarones in the mid-1930s to be sold at special fiestas at her family's dance hall in Coolidge, Arizona. Each was purchased for a nickel by adults attending the dances. The cascarones consisted of decorated eggshells placed on short stems or cones of rolled paper. Some were filled with perfume-scented confetti, while others (kept in a separate container or marked in a special way) were filled with ashes or flour.[7]

The Form Becomes Complex

In Tucson and southern Arizona in the 1990s, cascarones are a popular commercial craft item. They are no longer associated with Carnival or any other specific time of year, but appear for sale at the outdoor fairs, festivals, religious fiestas, and church bazaars that are important parts of southern Arizona's annual cycle. Cascarones cost little to make and sell for between one and three dollars apiece, depending on their complexity.

Cascarones in the Tucson area have gotten complex indeed. Simple filled and decorated eggshells are still occasionally sold, but most locally made cascarones are mounted on newspaper cones twelve to sixteen inches long. These conical stems are covered with cut and fringed *papel de china*, or colored tissue paper.[8] The paper work on the stems can be simple or complex. Rows of paper fringes may be arranged in bands of brilliantly contrasting color. Paper streamers, ribbons, or even feathers often hang from the end of the cone, or are inserted in one of the fringes of paper partway up from the end. For many artists, the paperwork on the cone is the most elaborate part of the cascarón, while the eggshell is painted with plain colors or relatively simple designs of bands or dots. There are numberless ways in which the colors of the egg and the colors of the tissue paper around the cone can be played off against each other.

Other artists concentrate on the eggshell itself, leaving the paper covering on the cone relatively simple. I have seen cascarón eggshells with representations of cactus, flowers, landscapes, and even the baroque, eighteenth-century facade of nearby Mission San Xavier del Bac painted on them!

Some artists paint faces on the eggshells. Sometimes these are simply generalized people—blondes, Indians, cowboys, clowns, or even monsters. Sometimes they are characters out of Mexican or Anglo American popular culture, like Pancho Villa or Adelita the revolutionary *soldadera*, or Fat Albert or Batman or Dick Tracy or, perhaps inevitably, the Teenage Mutant Ninja Turtles and Bart Simpson.

A few makers create animal cascarones as well as human ones. When creating animal forms, many cascarón artists set the eggshell at right angles to the cone. Animal cascarones I have seen include snakes, rabbits, squirrels, cats, pigs, and skunks. These latter, as created by Ángela Montoya of Tucson, are especially charming. They have blue eyes and a broad white stripe down their backs, while a wispy black-and-white tail made of plastic fiber arches over all.

Cascarones, like piñatas, can be made to conform to seasonal themes. For Hallowe'en, witches, devils, and pumpkins. (In October, 1992, I saw a series of Dracula cascarones, complete with bloody teeth.) For Christmas, Santas and Santa's helpers. For Easter, bunnies and baby chicks. And at graduation time in June of 1989, one enterprising cascarón maker turned out male and female graduates and sold them outside the ceremony at Tucson High School.

Occasionally the cascarones are even more elaborate, becoming actual figurines. The most striking of these figurine cascarones are made by a young Yaqui Indian woman named Feliciana Martinez. She told me she had long thought of creating something different in the way of cascarones and finally did so in 1990, for a raffle to raise funds for a Yaqui arts education program.[9] The cascarón figurines she made for this occasion represented *folclórico* dancers from the Mexican state of Jalisco. Great attention was paid to details of make-up and hairdo, and the full, tissue-paper skirt of each figurine had appliqued embroidery in the form of cut paper of a contrasting color. In place of a cone, the cascarones had legs. The following winter, she made a series of angel cascarones for sale at Christmas time. These were complete with long white dresses and gold haloes. The elaborate figurines sold for around $7 apiece, considerably more than the price of ordinary cascarones at public events.

In October, 1994, a traditional paper artist living in Nogales, Sonora, gave me two equally elaborate figurine cascarones she had made. Each one represented a woman dressed in a long paper gown and holding a basket made of folded scraps of slick paper. The baskets were filled with tiny paper flowers. Each woman's hair was done into an elaborate pompadour, the curls being of colored paper. The base of each cascarón was an inverted newspaper cone.

Cascarones Across Cultural Boundaries

Mexican Americans are not the only folks in Tucson who make cascarones. Yaquis and Tohono O'odham also make and sell the colorful, ephemeral objects. I have yet to isolate a specifically Tohono O'odham style of cascarón. The outstanding O'odham cascarones I have seen seem to be the results of individual creativity, rather than reflections of a specifically O'odham cultural tradition. Thus Frances Manuel of San Pedro Village made cascarones in the shape of blossoms, while members of the Moreno family of San Xavier Village concentrated rather on elaborately wrapped, elongated cones. The only constant feature I have observed in regard to O'odham cascarones is an emphasis on the paperwork rather than on the eggshell—I have yet to see an O'odham-made cascarón with any representational painting on the egg.

Yaqui cascarones are a different matter. One prolific Yaqui cascarón maker, Ernesto Quiroga, may have had a major influence on the southern Arizona cascarón scene. Mr. Quiroga was raised in Summerland, California, and as a boy made stemless cascarones with faces

painted on the eggshells and sold them on the street at the Old Spanish Days Fiesta in nearby Santa Barbara. When he moved to Tucson's
Old Pascua Yaqui community as a young man, he started making cascarones to raise funds for community projects. Learning to make stems
from friends, he combined these with his faces. Later, he started using
specifically Yaqui designs such as sun symbols and pascola dance
masks. He began putting Yaqui phrases on his cascarones so that Yaqui
kids would become familiar with elements of their own culture.[10]

Mr. Quiroga, by the way, has made a strong start towards inte-
grating cascarones into Yaqui culture. For him, the confetti inside the
egg has much the same meaning as the confetti used at the dramatic
climax of the annual Yaqui Easter ceremony.[11] On this occasion, the
confetti represents flowers, which for many Yaquis are the visible manifestation of God's grace. When Christ died on the cross, according to
a common Yaqui belief, His blood changed to flowers as it fell to the
earth. It is with this meaning in mind that Mr. Quiroga always waits
until Good Friday night to take his cascarones to the plaza to sell. In
his words, he doesn't bring the cascarones out until after "Jesus Christ
turned the world into flowers."[12] By the same token, having a cascarón
broken over one's head is to have blessings conferred upon one.

This very Yaqui interpretation of the use and meaning of cascarones is not pushed at purchasers, it simply exists, in Mr. Quiroga's mind.
That the confetti constitutes a blessing of sorts may not in fact be a
uniquely Yaqui notion but one shared by some Mexican Americans and
Anglos who also sometimes refer to the good luck or blessings the eggs
bring.[13] The importance of flowers in Yaqui culture may go far towards
explaining the fact that one frequently finds cascarones in the shape of
flowers being made and sold by Yaquis.

As a male cascarón maker, Mr. Quiroga is definitely in the
minority. Most people I know of who make cascarones are women, and
in many cases, making cascarones for sale is a family affair. Children
and grandchildren help out on many of the stages of manufacture and
often suggest new ideas for cascarones. Incidentally, Anglo Americans
often express surprise at so much work and creativity going into the
creation of an object whose destiny is to be broken. Most of the cascarón makers with whom I have discussed the subject have told me
that, aside from the money they earn, the whole point of their work is
to make kids happy. If that happens, the work is worth it.

It is difficult to judge these things, but it does seem that the
major consumers of cascarones at Tucson's fiestas are children. Bits of

A cluster of Santa Cruz Valley-style cascarones. From left, a representation of a Yaqui ceremonial *pascola* mask (made by Yaqui artist Ernesto Quiroga), Mickey Mouse, a plain eggshell decorated with strips of colored paper, Bart Simpson, and Spider Man. The last two were made by Ángela Montoya. The long stems typical of this style may be clearly seen. Photograph by David Burkhalter.

Three cascarones. On the left, an elaborate figurine made by Gloria Moroyoqui of Nogales, Sonora. The head is an eggshell; all other details, including the elaborate coiffure, are of paper. The basket is plaited of tiny strips of newspaper and filled with tiny paper roses. Center, a flower cascarón, also made by Doña Gloria. It has an egg in its center. On the right, a Yaqui cascarón with a thick stem and a painted egg. Photograph by David Burkhalter.

shattered eggshell, scatters of confetti, and broken paper cones are a common sight on the ground at most of these occasions. As I suggested above, most cascarón makers with whom I have discussed the matter see children as the ultimate consumers of their product. However, a small but growing number of adults—mostly Anglo Americans—are purchasing cascarones as art objects. I often see them in homes, hung on walls or bundled up and thrust into Mexican or Indian pots and baskets. Thus displayed, they add a regional touch to the decor of many kitchens and living rooms in the Tucson area. They are colorful, make excellent conversation pieces, and are supremely inexpensive as well. Regional folk art at $2.00 is hard to resist. Cascarones don't keep their brilliant colors forever, but when they start to fade, one can always give them to some kids and let them fulfill their original destiny.

In fact, at least one cascarón maker has started making a new kind of larger cascarón strictly for decoration. Lou Gastelum saves L'EGGS stocking and pantyhose containers and makes outsize cascarones from them. When I asked her what would happen if I tried to break one over somebody's head, she hastened to explain that these cascarones were for decorations only. Red and blue cascarones (the colors of the University of Arizona, located in Tucson) are especially popular in this decorator size. Some of these even bear the legend "U of A," painted on the plastic egg.

Another innovation has been made by a local Yaqui woman who substitutes cardboard cylinders from paper towel rolls for the paper cone on which the eggshells are mounted. The cylinder is decorated with fringed tissue paper and can then be filled with candies and other favors, thus combining the function of a cascarón with that of a piñata.

Two women in Portland, Oregon—Jan Wheeland and Elizabeth Johnson—have independently carried out a similar adaptation. Far from being brought up with cascarones, they were unaware of the tradition until 1986, when *Sunset* magazine published an article on how to make Tucson-style cascarones.[14] Intrigued by what they saw, they started making cascarones for their own children's parties. They then got the idea of combining the cascarón with the English party cracker tradition, creating what they call "Egg Bonkers."[15] Each bonker consists of a decorated eggshell mounted on a stubby cone of stiff, colored paper. The eggshells are usually painted to represent faces. While obviously derived from Tucson-style cascarones, the bonkers actually look quite different. The cone is stubbier, for one thing—about four inches long, as opposed to the eight-inch or longer Tucson cones—and is made of stiff gift-wrapping paper. The real difference appears when the eggshell is broken, however. In addition to confetti, each bonker contains a toy, a balloon, candy, and a printed joke (or "yoke"). A sample of the latter: "What kind of gum do chickens chew?—Chickletts." Oof.[16]

There is evidence that the Tucson style of cascarón-on-a-cone is spreading into other parts of the Southwest. A Tohono O'odham man whom Ernesto Quiroga taught to make cascarones has recently moved to Santa Fe, New Mexico. There he has introduced the style to his friends, including members of several of New Mexico's Pueblo communities. It remains to be seen whether or not the style catches on there.

But Why in Southern Arizona?

The question remains of why all this creative activity has taken place in Tucson in the 1980s and 1990s. In the first place, the Tucson calendar typically includes a number of out-of-doors festivals and fiestas. Yaqui Easter is celebrated in three communities in or near the city. Many Catholic parish churches have annual fund-raising events, which are typically held out-of-doors. The annual Tucson Festival, an important local celebration from the 1950s to the early 1990s, included The San Xavier Fiesta and La Fiesta del Presidio which featured regional Native American and Mexican American cultural traditions respectively. The Mexican patriotic and cultural holidays of the Cinco de Mayo and the Dieciseis de Septiembre draw large crowds to the city's parks. Other annual open-air events which have a strong Mexican flavor have been started in comparatively recent years: Tucson Meet Yourself, the Norteño Festival, the Mariachi Conference, the Fiesta de San Agustín, and the Tumacacori Fiesta.

Each of these events attracts large numbers of families in a festive, money-spending mood; each provides a setting in which cascarones may be purchased and also broken.

There is a good chance that the fact that Tucson is a university town also enters into the equation. The university attracts graduate students and faculty, many of whom are culturally liberal, interested in regional traditions and celebrations, mildly affluent, and have young families. Just the folks to buy cascarones for their kids.[17]

Just the folks, also, to buy them as decorations, or even as objects of casual collection. Some of the university people I know who buy cascarones do not break them right away, but hang them on their walls at least until the paper fades. These people are often attracted to new and innovative cascarón designs.

These various commercial settings and markets seem to have led to a degree of competition. If one has something new in the way of cascarones, one's work may well sell better. So it is that this may be one of the reasons for the remarkable "cascarón explosion" that has taken place over the past few years in Tucson. Not that I believe this to be the entire explanation. The arrival of certain key individuals such as Ernesto Quiroga, the natural desire of many artists and craftspeople to keep experimenting and produce something different, suggestions from the artists' children and grandchildren—all these seem to be factors as well.

Whatever the explanations, and I am sure they are far more complex than I have outlined here, it remains that the cascarón tradition in Santa Cruz and Pima Counties in southern Arizona is currently in a state of florescence.

Chapter 4

El Tiradito
and Juan Soldado

Two Victim Intercessors
of the Western Borderlands[1]

In this essay we move from portable art forms to shrines and the beliefs that are associated with them. For at least a century, Tucson has been home to a shrine dedicated to a saint-like figure which seems to function within the patterns but outside the sanctions of the Roman Catholic Church. This spirit belongs to a class that I have called "victim intercessors." The essay examines several victim intercessors in the western borderlands and suggests parallels and historical antecedents for these beliefs. The Tucson shrine is examined in detail as well, as are the different ways in which it is used by various segments of local society.

El Tiradito

Next door to a Mexican restaurant, in one of Tucson's oldest surviving *barrios*, an adobe wall stands at the end of a vacant lot. A metal plaque in English and Spanish announces this to be a National Historic Landmark. It is El Tiradito, "The only shrine in the United States dedicated to the soul of a sinner buried in unconsecrated ground." *El tiradito* is Spanish for "The Little Cast-away One," and refers both to the site and to the legendary person or persons said to have been buried there. (In this essay, I shall distinguish between person and place by means of capitalization. The place is El Tiradito; the person, el Tiradito.) El Tiradito is above all a place where something is said to have happened. Exactly what took place is not at all clear. The more than twenty narratives in the archives of the University of Arizona Library's Southwest Folklore Center agree only on one point—someone was suddenly killed and buried where he or she fell, in unconsecrated ground.[2] Many versions involve some sort of love triangle, with a woman, her lover, her husband, her brother (who was mistaken for a lover by the jealous husband), or two of them being killed in a fit of passion and buried on the spot. The general feeling is that the action, whatever its precise nature, took place in the 1870s or 1880s.

Here is the Tiradito narrative which the Tucson City Council declared in 1927 to be the official legend and story: Dr. F. H. Goodwin employed a young sheep herder named Juan Oliveros, who lived on Goodwin's ranch with his wife and his father-in-law. Juan had become infatuated with his mother-in-law who lived in Tucson, and one day he to visited her. Later that day, the father-in-law also came into town, and, completely unsuspecting, surprised Juan with his wife in their adulterous love. The young man was violently evicted from the house, and in the ensuing struggle the father-in-law seized an axe from the woodpile and killed him. The older man fled to Mexico and Juan was buried where he had fallen.[3]

Many other accounts involve love and violence. A 1927 article quotes pioneer Bishop Salpointe as the source of a story concerning a "border ruffian" who betrayed a young woman, who subsequently died. The young woman's brother challenged the ruffian, and they fought with knives. Both men were killed. The young man was buried near his sister, and their mother for years afterwards would come and light candles and pray for their souls.[4]

A contrasting account has it that a half-witted boy who had the reputation for doing "wonderful, miraculous things" was murdered and buried where he had fallen. After death he continued helping his neighbors.[5] Other narrators (including the well-known Mexican American singer and composer, Lalo Guerrero, who grew up in the barrio), say a man walking along the street was struck by a bullet flying out of an open barroom door. He died instantly and was buried where he had fallen.[6] Another recently collected account simply states that "el tiradito fué un pobrecito que le mataron y le tiraron del tren. Y por eso le nombraron el tiradito." (El Tiradito was a poor fellow who was killed and thrown off the train. And that's why they called him *el Tiradito*.) The nearest railroad track is a quarter mile away, downhill from the site.[7]

The legends all agree on one fact concerning el Tiradito. Soon after death and burial, this murdered person started successfully interceding with God on behalf of petitioners. The El Tiradito shrine has become a place where people seek supernatural help. Many older accounts have it that one should keep vigil at the shrine all night (or that one's candle should burn all night) in order for a petition to be granted. A boy who lived in the area once told a folklore student: "There's this wishing shrine down by the community center. This old man was killed, and if you want something real bad, like if you want a new car or if you're in the third grade and want to pass into the fourth, you go there, and you tell the old man that if you get it you'll go and light a candle for him."[8]

This statement, collected in the 1970s, indicates that for some at least, the Wishing Shrine, as El Tiradito is often called in English, was still important as a place of petitions. I can personally state that, although I have never seen anyone praying or keeping vigil at the site, I have never been there when at least one or two candles have not been burning. While Mexican Americans still use the shrine, it has attracted a number of Anglos as well. One woman, for example, leaves a candle at the shrine whenever she intends to show one of her dogs; a man stops by and lights a candle every time he goes hunting for javelina (the wild peccary of the Sonoran desert); another woman lit candles during her daughter's problem pregnancy.

In recent years the shrine has taken on an additional significance for many residents—as a community symbol for ethnic identity and a

El Tiradito from the east, May, 1992. The central object in front of the wall is a wrought iron candle rack; other metal candle holders are visible to either side. The discoloration of the central part of the wall is from candle smoke; the dark stain on the ground is from candle grease. Photograph by James Griffith.

rallying point for local activism. In 1971, the proposed Butterfield Parkway was planned to pass through several barrios on Tucson's southwest side. A sizeable area of historic residential Tucson had already been swallowed up during the construction of the Tucson Convention Center. In what many thought would be a futile effort to oppose the predominantly Anglo American establishment in its notions of progress, several neighborhood organizations formed, composed largely of long-time Mexican American residents of the area, to halt the freeway construction. The freeway plans were eventually abandoned, in large measure, according to local belief, because El Tiradito was placed on the National Register of Historic Landmarks. Debates in the state legislature eventually led to a statewide moratorium on all inner-city freeway projects.[9]

The lessons learned from this struggle have not been lost on subsequent generations of activists. In the late 1980s, a project to widen Mission Road on the west side of the Santa Cruz River threatened to destroy the remaining foundations of the mission structure that served the Indian village that was there long before the European settlement of Tucson. Chicano activists fought the project and deliberately followed the lead of the earlier Butterfield Parkway-El Tiradito strategy. A small nicho or shrine was cast in cement from a bathtub belonging to one of the activists. A large cross was erected in the path of the road project. The shrine was placed in front of the cross, with a statue of the Virgin of Guadalupe inside it. The site was blessed by a Jesuit priest and a Tohono O'odham medicine person. Then the activists, with the ball securely in the developers' court, sat back and waited. It is the spring of 1994 as I write, and the road project seems to have been postponed indefinitely.

The El Tiradito site had not been unknown to the greater community of Tucson prior to the Butterfield battle. Newspaper and magazine articles from the 1920s on have described the vigils at the shrine and have recounted one or more of the legends associated with it. The present shrine, surrounded on three sides by an adobe wall with a scalloped outline and a niche at the west end, was constructed in 1940 under the auspices of the Neighborhood Youth Administration.[10] This, by the way, is not El Tiradito's original site; the present site was donated to the City of Tucson in 1927 when road construction destroyed the earlier shrine. At that time, a great deal of public attention was paid to El Tiradito; it was then that the official version of the legend was adopted.

By the late 1920s, in the eyes of at least some of Tucson's decision-makers, El Tiradito was becoming something other than a place where lower-class Mexicans prayed for miracles. Tucson was beginning to discover that its regional Mexican heritage made good copy. The baroque revival Saint Augustine's Cathedral and Pima County Courthouse were built in 1920 and 1929, respectively. Yaqui culture had been discovered by adventurous members of the Anglo majority a few years earlier, and Phoebe Bogan's booklet on the Yaqui Easter Ceremonies at Pascua Village had been published in 1925.[11] Once Arizona was admitted to statehood in 1914, Mexicans and Indians started becoming elements of local color and tradition, rather than being seen as impediments to progress. And so El Tiradito became the subject of magazine articles and came under the protection of the City Fathers.

That protection still holds good, by the way—the site is regularly cared for by employees of the Tucson Department of Parks and Recreation.

Not all Catholic Mexican Americans use—or have used—the shrine. One friend told me that his family never prayed at El Tiradito; they prayed in church as they were taught. Because the unsanctioned devotion to el Tiradito was never popular with the clergy, it is interesting to see the site accepted by some priests in its new role as a symbol of ethnic unity and identity.

For El Tiradito seems to be changing. Candles are still burned at the shrine, and other religious objects appear from time to time, but there seems to be a general feeling that el Tiradito's powers are not quite as strong as they once were. In fact, el Tiradito the person may well be losing out to El Tiradito the place as the source of supernatural power.

The uses of the site are expanding as well. The first written mentions of El Tiradito are in a 1893 newspaper article and a 1909 diary.[12] Apparently, the shrine was visited by Mexican Americans at that time and was known to some extent by the rest of the downtown community. By at least 1927, however, El Tiradito had a value to the larger community of Tucson as a part of the city's local color. Articles on the shrine were written for such magazines as *Progressive Arizona*.[13] The city accepted the land on which the new shrine was located and even adopted an official version of the origin legend.

The shrine remains a multiple-use area to this day. People light candles there, and the site is a frequent stop on formal and informal tours of Tucson. The daily papers average an article on El Tiradito once every three or four years. Local writers, myself included, make sure the site and its story show up occasionally in magazines, on radio, and on TV. The site is a shrine, a place where one takes visitors from out of town, and a reminder of the power of a group of men and women who succeeded in stopping City Hall. Meanwhile, El Tiradito still attracts those who need help or power but may have no other place to find it. It is still important in the neighborhood and in the culture that have long supported it.

Juan Soldado

I was driving along Mexico's Highway 15, south of Magdalena, Sonora, on December 10, 1982, when a sign over the door of a roadside chapel caught my eye. It read "El Ánima de Juan Soldado" (The spirit of Juan Soldado). Neither my travelling companion Richard Morales nor I had ever heard of Juan Soldado, so we stopped and walked into the *ranchito* at the end of the road behind the chapel. There we learned the following narrative about Juan Soldado from the woman of the house:

> Juan Soldado is an *alma* (a soul), not a *santo*. He was a *soldado razo*, an "army recruit," in Tijuana, Baja California. His *capitán* raped and killed an eight-year-old girl who had come to the garrison with food or laundry or something. The captain accused Juan and then applied *la ley fuga* on him. (*la ley fuga*, "the law of flight," is a Mexican euphemism for shooting a prisoner and then explaining that he was killed while trying to escape.) Juan began appearing to the captain and to the captain's *novia*, or "sweetheart." A chapel to Juan has been constructed in a cemetery in Tijuana.

The woman heard of Juan in Hermosillo (capitol of the state of Sonora), asked his help in healing her sick daughter, and built the chapel south of Magdalena after the daughter was cured. According to her, most priests who know of Juan (whom she calls "my Juanito") approve of his devotion. One priest did not; he said it was all the devil's work. That priest, she told us, is now in Tucson, dying of diabetes with both legs amputated. (There was indeed a Mexican priest in that condition in Tucson at that time, but I could not bring myself to interview him about Juan Soldado.)[14]

The chapel on the highway contained a three-foot-high statue of Juan Soldado, as well as smaller statues of the Sacred Heart of Jesus, the head of the Suffering Christ, and Saint Martin of Porres (*San Martín de Porres*).[15] All these are locally popular devotions. Curiously enough, in the years from 1982 and the present, I have never seen in the chapel a statue of San Francisco—the reclining St. Francis Xavier whose devotion brings thousands of pilgrims annually to Magdalena, only about five miles to the north of the chapel.[16] In addition to the statues, masses of flowers and several candles adorned the chapel, as well as slabs of composition marble bearing written testimonials to Juan Soldado's efficacy in granting miracles.

Needless to say, this encounter with Juan Soldado piqued my curiosity. I was in San Diego several months later with a few hours to spare and drove across the border to Tijuana. My wife and I located the cemetery—*Panteón Jardin No. 1*—where Juan Soldado was buried and not only found his grave and chapel but the reputed site of his execution. We also heard more versions of his legend from several people we encountered at his grave. These versions basically stayed within the pattern that had been established by the woman in Sonora—Juan was executed for a horrible crime actually committed by his commanding officer, who gave the orders for his execution. Some details were given concerning the eventual repentance of the officer after Juan appeared to him and to others. Juan started his apparitions quite soon after his death, it appears, while his mother and other women were keeping vigil at his execution site. There was also a statement concerning a rock pile at his execution site; it miraculously retained its original size, no matter how many rocks were added or removed. (It has long been customary in Mexico to raise a rock pile surmounted by a cross at the death site of a traveller. Passersby are supposed to add a rock and offer a prayer for the repose of the soul of the departed.)[17]

It was also explained to us that Juan Soldado derived his powers from God. Like Jesus, he had been falsely accused and killed. He has now been judged by God and proven innocent. Here, as in Sonora, there were tales of opposition from the Catholic Church. The improvised chapel by Juan's grave, I was told, would be a beautiful church except that the priests will not permit such a building to be built or even allow a caretaker to be hired.

The chapel was filled with candles, flowers, and testimonial plaques. Most of the plaques did not give details of the petitions answered but merely thanked Juan Soldado for having granted an unspecified miracle. They were usually signed and dated. As was the case in Sonora, Juan Soldado (represented by busts from two different molds) shared the chapel with other holy figures. There were several representations of the Sacred Heart of Jesus, a Virgin, and a Holy Family. I observed only one *milagro*, or metal representation of the part of the body involved in the petition. There were none in the chapel near Magdalena, Sonora. This is in contrast to the statues of San Francisco at San Xavier del Bac, Arizona, and Magdalena de Kino, Sonora, which are usually plentifully supplied with milagros.[18] Testimonial plaques also line the exterior of the chapel and appear on Juan's grave nearby.

At the south end of the cemetery against a cliff is Juan Soldado's supposed death site. It is protected by a brick wall and is furnished with several crosses, more plaques, and a pile of rocks. Outside the cemetery gates were two pushcarts with vendors selling devotional objects, including two printed prayers to Juan Soldado, candles with a prayer and a photo of Juan, and photographs of Juan. The picture is of a teenage boy in army uniform, leaning against a table on which stands a crucifix. This sort of picture was commonly taken of young men upon joining the army and does not presuppose any special religiosity or piety on the part of the subject. The pictures are supplied with Juan's full name—Juan Castillo Morales—and the traditional date of his death, February 17, 1938.

Unlike el Tiradito, Juan Castillo Morales (in Mexican custom, the patronymic comes first and the matronymic second) appears in the historical record. An eight-year-old girl named Olga Camacho disappeared on February 13, 1938; her raped and murdered body was discovered the next day. That same day, Juan Castillo Morales, a 24-year-old soldier, was arrested for the crime. Tijuana was at the time a volatile place—the end of prohibition in the United States, along with a presidential decree in Mexico prohibiting games of chance, had affected the recreation patterns of many adult Californians and led to the closing of bars and casinos in Tijuana. With widespread unemployment, the situation in Tijuana was ripe for some sort of public outburst. Olga Camacho's murder provided the spark.

The next day, labor agitators are said to have incited an angry mob to demand Juan Castillo be released to them for lynching. The demand was not granted. In its anger, the mob burned the municipal police headquarters and the municipal palace on the early morning hours of February 15. As the civil authorities were by this time apparently powerless, a military tribunal took over the responsibility of trying Juan. He was pronounced guilty and publicly shot at 8 A.M. on February 18. His mother put a stone on the place where he fell and erected a sign requesting all passers-by to place stones on the pile and pray an Our Father. As the stone pile grew, Juan Castillo Morales—Juan Soldado—left the realm of history and entered that of legend.[19]

Parallel Figures

So here we have two traditional figures of religious belief and legend along the western Mexican-American border. Although the stories are dissimilar in many ways, they have one basic point in common.

Chapel by the grave of Juan Soldado, Panteón No. 1, Tijuana, Baja California. A bust of Juan Soldado sits atop the roof; testimonial plaques line the visible side wall. Photograph by James Griffith.

Postcard with multiple, hand-tinted images of Juan Soldado's photograph. Such a postcard, probably manufactured in Mexico City, would normally be cut into four smaller pictures, which could then be framed. Photograph by David Burkhalter.

They deal with a subject who was murdered and buried, at least for a while, on the spot where he or she fell. I have since discovered three more such legends. Two concern individuals in Nogales, Sonora. A soldier named Pedro Blanco was killed one night, possibly in the 1920s, while he crossed an arroyo on his way home from a gambling game with considerable winnings. And a woman named Tita Gomez was gathering wild onions on a hill south of Nogales when her boyfriend struck and killed her with a tire iron. These individuals were buried for a while where they fell. Each was believed to grant petitions, and in both cases, the bodies were later removed to public cemeteries in Nogales. Today, Pedro Blanco rests in the Panteón Rosario while Tita Gomez lies in the Panteón Nacional. I have found no evidence at either grave of a living devotion—no milagros, no plaques, and few decorations—even on November 2, the Day of the Dead in Mexico.

Three Mexican men are said to have been arrested for a serious crime immediately after they got off a train in Benson, Arizona, possibly around the turn of the century. Although innocent, they were swiftly hanged without a trial and buried just outside of the Benson cemetery. For years, offerings of candles and ribbons would be left at a mesquite tree near their graves. Now tree, graves, and devotion have all vanished.

Similar figures exist outside of the western borderlands. A bandit named Jesús Malverde is said to have lived in the state of Sinaloa in northwest Mexico. According to popular belief, he preyed upon the wealthy and helped the poor with his spoils. He was hanged in 1909 at Culiacán, Sinaloa, and has been described as a "patron saint to contemporary thieves and smugglers."[20] Other evidence suggests that his devotion is not confined to those outside the law. Shrimp boat captains leave portions of their catch at his shrine in Culiacán, and people appeal to him for the same miracles of healing, business success, and escape from legal problems that are asked of Juan Soldado.[21]

I have seen printed prayers to Jesús Malverde. The cover illustrations depict a young man dressed in a light-colored shirt with flap pockets and a kerchief around his neck. His hands are apparently tied behind him and a noose hangs behind his head. The other end of the rope has been thrown over a tree branch above his head. A bunch of cattails stands to his left; the trunk of his hanging tree is to his right.[22]

A woman in Magdalena who makes plaster statues of Juan Soldado once told me that Malverde was another *inocente*, like Juan. She knew no stories about him, but said that she would make statues of him, too, if she knew what he looked like. Jesús Malverde seems to be another successful victim intercessor, performing much the same services for his west-coast region that Juan Soldado and el Tiradito do for the borderlands.

Moving farther from home, Antonio Gil of northwest Argentina seems to be another such figure. Gil deserted from the Argentine army in the late nineteenth century, refusing to shed the blood of his fellow Argentines, and was shot. Miracles are still sought and obtained at his grave and death site, which have become elaborate shrines with heavy pilgrim visitation.[23] I am beginning to realize that there are many such figures throughout Latin America. Most exist outside of, or in spite of, the official church.

I call these legendary characters who exist outside of the structure of the Roman Catholic Church but behave like Catholic saints "victim intercessors." Perhaps the only characteristic they share is the fact that they were victims. Somehow this is felt to enable them to intercede with God. The owner of the Juan Soldado chapel in Sonora was emphatic that Juan was not a saint, but an *alma*, or "soul." In fact, the theme of official Church opposition is often found in the narratives concerning these legendary figures.

What is a saint, and how is sainthood achieved in the Catholic Church? According to the *Catholic Encyclopedia*, a saint is a person "recognized by the church, either traditionally or by formal canonization, as being in heaven and thus worthy of honor." This applies only to those saints who make their presence known to the living; there may be, of course, many others. A saint's whole life must be "as nearly as possible governed by the complexus of virtues centered about religion."[24] This qualification is remotely approached only by that narrative which describes el Tiradito as a strange, mentally defective boy—a narrative which I suspect to be of rather recent origin. For the rest, little or nothing about any aspect of their lives is told, other than the essential fact of their being victims. The statue maker in Magdalena used the word *inocente* while talking about Juan Soldado, with the implication of guilelessness as well as technical innocence.

The Catholic saint whose case presents the closest parallel to these victim intercessors is St. Maria Goretti, a young Italian girl who was stabbed while resisting rape in 1902 and was subsequently canonized. But she was recalled as a very virtuous child, who died in defense of the Christian virtue of chastity. Butler, in his account of St. Maria Goretti, makes it clear that "a violent and unjust death alone is not enough to constitute martyrdom."[25] But precisely that sort of death seems to be the only distinguishing feature of the victim intercessors.

Why are they so important? I suspect one reason is that, like so many of the people who ask them for help, they were, through no fault of their own, on the receiving end of injustice and violence. They were victims, no more and no less. Juan Soldado was persecuted and killed but later judged by God and found innocent. His identity as an innocent victim may mean more to his devotees than it would have had his life been filled with Christian virtues and resistance to temptations. The official church needs evidence of a life lived on Christian religious principles in order to presume an individual's existence in the presence of God. For many poor folks, it seems enough to hear of suffering and victimization that leads to death, that great mysterious leveller. Acceptance by the Catholic Church bureaucracy might seem unimportant and even irrelevant to people whose experiences with bureaucracies may not have been positive. So it is, perhaps, that victim intercessors have gained their power over the minds of people accustomed to Catholic forms and concepts, even if not dwelling completely within the conceptual framework of the official church.[26]

These figures appear to be very old in the Catholic folk world. A biography of St. Martin of Tours, written about 400 A.D. by Sulpicius Severus, tells how the saint became curious concerning an altar said by the common people to be placed over the grave of a Christian martyr. Going to the site and standing over the grave, he prayed that God would reveal to him who was buried there. A "loathsome and fierce shadow" appeared at his left side. When St. Martin questioned the shadow, it replied that the dead person was a brigand who was executed for his misdeeds. The common folk had been duped into believing the man was a saint in glory, rather than a sinner dwelling in punishment.[27] This narrative certainly gives our borderlands intercessors a long pedigree, if not a respectable one in the eyes of the church.

I should add two parenthetical observations at this point. One is a reminder that while the subjects of this discussion are all said to behave like saints and intercede with God on behalf of petitioners, northern Sonora's most important saint, San Francisco, the great composite saint whose devotion centers at Magdalena de Kino, apparently does nothing of the kind. He is described as not only effecting cures himself but as exacting vengeance on those who fail to return with the promised payment.

The other point that must be raised is that miraculous appearances and occurrences are still important in the western borderlands. In 1980, for instance, images of Christ, the Virgin, and Saint Theresa have appeared in the soot of a fireplace in a home in Sahuarita, just south of Tucson.[28] Our Lady of Guadalupe appeared on a school window in Sonora in 1982,[29] and in 1985 the face of Christ was discovered on a photograph taken of clouds near Tucson.[30] As I write this, the owner of a local shrine has just called to tell me that she sees an image of the Blessed Virgin on a blank wall in a recently-taken photo of the shrine. The photo was taken and printed by myself.

Getting back to our two victim intercessors, the problem remains as to why el Tiradito seems to be changing rapidly, if not secularizing, while Juan Soldado seems more or less stable as his influence expands from Baja California to Sonora.[31] I suspect it is to a great degree a matter of unified legend. Nobody is quite sure who el Tiradito was. Knowledge of that shadowy figure seems confined to the facts of a murder, a burial, and subsequent miracles. This may be one reason why the place is becoming more important than the person.

In the case of Juan Soldado, on the other hand, we know his name—Juan Castillo Morales—and the date of his death. To some extent, his story is corroborated by historical documentation. We have only one basic narrative concerning his death and a photograph exists purporting to be his portrait. This combination of precise information and graphic representation may be an important factor in Juan Soldado's continuing popularity.

Conclusions

El Tiradito and Juan Soldado can now be seen not to stand alone but to fall well within a pattern of victim intercessors that reaches back locally at least into the late nineteenth century and in Europe to the early days of Christianity. Although these folk saints have no standing within the Catholic Church, the devotions to them follow well-established Catholic patterns of prayer to saints for intercession. These saints, however, have not been selected by the church hierarchy. They function as sources of power for those who, while belonging to a Catholic culture, seem to be—and feel themselves to be—somewhat separated from mainstream Catholicism. In need of intermediaries between themselves and God, poor people—the underdogs, or *"los de abajo"*—

have chosen individuals who are victims like themselves to speak to God in their behalf. The list of victim intercessors is by no means stable; several have appeared, served their purpose for a number of years, and slipped back into oblivion. Others, like el Tiradito, have changed in meaning as a wider community embraced them. Only Juan Soldado on the border, like Jesús Malverde in Sinaloa or Antonio Gil in Argentina, appears to have remained relatively unchanged over the years. Collectively, however, victim intercessors seem to be an important and stable part of this region's spiritual life.

Appendix

Printed Prayers to Juan Soldado and Jesús Malverde[32]

Juan Soldado

There are two different editions of printed prayers to Juan Soldado in the archives of the Southwest Folklore Center. Although the pictures on the front pages differ, the same text appears on both. It is as follows:

ORACIÓN
A LA ÁNIMA SOLA DE
JUAN SOLDADO

Alabado sea el Santísimo Nombre del Padre, el hijo y el Espíritu Santo; tres divinas personas y un solo Dios verdadero. Quienes con el infinito y Misericordioso Poder, han colmado de gracia y milagrosas indulgencias a mí querido hermano y protector Juan Castillo Morales.

En el Nombre de Dios Todo Poderoso, Espíritu y Anima de Juan Soldado, por motivos muy ciertos y con el corazón rebozante de Fé en tu inmediata ayuda, vengo a confiarte todas mis penas que me atormentan moral y materialmente, no dudando ni un instante que por medio de tu

VISITA Y ORACION A LA
ANIMA SOLA DE

JUAN SOLDADO

Venerado en el Panteón I
Tijuana, B. C.

Obverse of printed prayer card to Juan Soldado. The prayer on the other side of the card appears in the appendix. The text on this side reads "Visit and Prayer to the Solitary Soul of Juan Soldado, Venerated in Cemetery No. 1, Tijuana, Baja California." Photograph by David Burkhalter.

Infalible Intercesión ante el Todopoderoso vea colmados mis buenos deseos, se estos convienen a mayor Gloria de Dios Nuestro Señor y Tuya en Particular.

SE HACE LA PETICIÓN DESEADA

Como te darás cuento JUANITO, mis anhelos están desprovistos de capciosas maldades y todo lo que deseo es encontrar un apoyo eficaz de tu parte para acallar la indigencia moral y material en que me encuentro sumido.

HERMANO JUAN SOLDADO: Yo te suplico encarecidamente que no me abandones con tu protección en esta dificil prueba.

Confío en la Omnipotencia Misericordiosa de Dios y en tu Infalible Ayuda, prometiendote desde este momento, ser uno más, de tus innumerables devotos. AMÉN.

Como final se rezan tres padres Nuestros.

NOTA: Ofrézcase la presente Oración en cualquier momento, pero de preferencia a las 12:00 y 15:00 horas.

PRAYER
TO THE SOLITARY SOUL OF
JUAN SOLDADO

Praised be the Most Holy Name of the Father, the Son and the Holy Spirit; three divine persons and only one true God. Who with their infinite and Merciful Power, have filled my beloved brother and protector Juan Castillo Morales with grace and miraculous indulgences.

In the Name of Almighty God, (Oh) Spirit and Soul of Juan Soldado, for very evident reasons and with my heart overflowing with faith in your prompt assistance, I come to confide in you all the moral and material sorrows that torment me, not doubting for one instant that through your Infallible Intercession with the Almighty I will see my worthy desires amply filled, if those agree with the Greater Glory of the Lord our God, and with Yours in Particular.

ONE MAKES THE DESIRED PETITION

As you are well aware, JUANITO, my desires are
obstructed by insidious evils and all I wish is to find an
effective support from you to quell the moral and material
poverty in which I am plunged.

BROTHER JUAN SOLDADO, I earnestly entreat you not
to remove your protection from me in this difficult trial.

I trust in the Merciful Omnipotence of God and in
your Infallible Assistance, promising you from this moment,
to be one more of your innumerable devotees. AMEN.

In closing, one prays three Our Fathers.

NOTE: Offer this Prayer at any time, but preferably at
12:00 and at 3:00 P.M.

This prayer, except for the first paragraph, was also printed on a
sheet of paper glued to a votive candle that was purchased near Juan
Soldado's gravesite in Tijuana, Baja California in May, 1983.

Jesús Malverde

There are in the archives at the Southwest Folklore Center two
printed prayers dedicated to Jesús Malverde. Each bears a picture of
Malverde as described in the main body of the text. Although the pictures are alike in almost all details, they are in fact different renderings
of the same idealized portrait. In each case the portrait is labelled
"JESÚS MALVERDE," and bears the legend "DI TU VOLUNTAD Ayudar a
mi gente en el nombre de Dios." ("SPEAK YOUR WILL Help my people
in the name of God.") Each sheet bears the following prayer on the
back:

La Verdadera Oración del
Ánima de Malverde

HOY ANTE TU CRUZ POSTRADO
OH MALVERDE MI SEÑOR
TE PIDO MISERICORDIA
Y QUE ALIVIES MI DOLOR.

TU QUE MORAS EN LA GLORIA
Y ESTÁS MUY CERCA DE DIOS
ESCUCHA LOS SUFRIMIENTOS
DE ESTE HUMILDE PECADOR.

OH MALVERDE MILAGROSO
OH MALVERDE MI SEÑOR
CONCEDEME ESTE FAVOR
Y LLENA MI ALMA DE GOZO.

DAME SALUD SEÑOR
DAME REPOSO
DAME BIENESTAR
Y SERÉ DICHOSO.

Se hace enseguida la petición personal y se reza 3 Padres Nuestros y 3 Aves Marias.
Se Finaliza encendiendo dos veladoras.
SE DEBE CARGAR UN AMULETO O LA PIEDRA IMAN, PRINCIPALMENTE ROJA.

The True Prayer of the Soul of Malverde

TODAY PROSTRATE BEFORE YOUR CROSS
OH MALVERDE MY LORD
I BEG OF YOU MERCY
AND THAT YOU RELIEVE MY PAIN.

YOU WHO DWELL IN HEAVEN
AND ARE VERY CLOSE TO GOD
HEAR THE SUFFERINGS
OF THIS HUMBLE SINNER.

OH MIRACULOUS MALVERDE
OH MALVERDE MY LORD
GRANT ME THIS FAVOR
AND FILL MY SOUL WITH JOY.

GIVE ME HEALTH LORD
GIVE ME REST
GIVE ME WELL-BEING
AND I WILL BE JOYFUL.

One immediately makes the personal petition and prays 3 Our Fathers and 3 Hail Marys.

One ends by lighting two candles.

ONE SHOULD CARRY AN AMULET OR THE LODESTONE, MOSTLY RED.

The only difference between the two printed prayers that I have examined is that one omits the mention of the amulet and the lodestone.

Chapter 5

The Black Christ of Ímuris

A Study in Cultural Fit[1]

As far as I can discover, Juan Soldado is relatively unknown in Arizona. I have seen no depictions of him on altars or in shrines, and have met none of his devotees outside of Mexico. El Tiradito, on the other hand, is not only located in the United States, it has "crossed the border" into Anglo American culture. El Tiradito has become a multiple-use location, and perhaps as many Anglos as Mexicanos tell the stories of el Tiradito the person. Although the stories and the understanding of the place appear to be pretty much the same in both cultures, new uses and meanings have been added by the mainstream culture.

The statues and the shrine discussed in this essay, however, appear to have different explanatory narratives among different groups of people. The process of cultural adaptation in this multicultural region has here gone a bit farther, become a bit more complex, than it has with El Tiradito.

Ímuris, Sonora, lies about forty miles south of the border city of Nogales, on Mexican Highway 15. It is a junction town. Mexican Highway 2 splits off at Ímuris and heads east to the mining town of Cananea, the border community of Agua Prieta, and beyond, into the state of Chihuahua. Highway 15 continues south to Magdalena de Kino, Santa Ana, the state capitol of Hermosillo, and eventually all the way to Mexico City. Ímuris is an agricultural town as well, with rich fields along the valley of the Río Magdalena, and cattle grazing in the hills and valleys round about. Among its natural resources, Ímuris even counts a hot spring.

Finally, Ímuris is a historic community. It was a village of O'odham speakers when Father Eusebio Francisco Kino, S.J., visited it on March 15, 1687, in the company of Father José Aguilar. Kino described the village a "good post, with plenty of docile and domesti-cated people," and assigned it to the protection of San José—St. Joseph. The first of five successive churches and chapels was built shortly thereafter; the most recent in the series probably dates from the present century.[2]

The church of San José is a small building with two short tran-septs. Its left transept consists of a small chapel containing a life-sized crucifix which probably dates from the late eighteenth or early nine-teenth century. The figure of Christ on the cross is a dark brown color, and the statue is frequently referred to as *el Cristo negro de Ímuris*—"the black Christ of Ímuris." It is this statue and the various narratives that explain its presence and appearance that provide the impetus for this essay.

While churches and chapels succeeded each other at Ímuris, Sonoran history moved on its course. The Pimería Alta became dot-ted with Jesuit missions; the Jesuits were expelled in 1767 and replaced a few years later by Franciscans. In 1821, Ímuris ceased being a part of New Spain and became a village in the new nation of Mex-ico. In December, 1853, Mexico sold a large tract of land—the Gads-den Purchase—to the United States, leaving Ímuris forty miles south of a new international border. In January of 1856, Adjutant Inspector Ignacio Pesqueira left what had been the Mexican frontier *presidio* (military outpost) of Tucson with the greater part of that frontier post's Mexican garrison. The troops moved to Ímuris, where they were to stay for the next few years. They took with them a life-sized crucifix with a black or dark brown corpus, later to be known as the black Christ of Ímuris.[3]

That there was a black crucifix in Tucson prior to this we know; a report of May, 1843, mentions a "majestic representation of the miraculous image of Our Savior of Esquipulas" as being in one of the rooms of the old mission church of San José on the west bank of the Santa Cruz, across the river from the presidio of Tucson. (This church, popularly called *el convento*, "the convent," no longer stands. The ground on which it stood was converted into a landfill.)[4] An 1855 inventory reiterates the fact that the church contained a statue of Our Lord of Esquipulas. The reference to "Our Savior of Esquipulas" is enough to identify the representation as a black crucifix, or a black Christ.

Esquipulas is an important pilgrimage center in eastern Guatemala. It was famous since before the Conquest for its healing earth and hot springs. It is the home of el Señor de Esquipulas, a statue of the crucified Christ which was carved on commission from the local Bishop by master craftsman Quirio Cataño in 1594. Tradition has it that Cataño was requested to make the corpus of dark brown balsam and orange wood, as the Indians were justly suspicious of white people after their experience with their Spanish conquerors. Further blackening by the smoke of candles and incense is said to have contributed to the statue's present smoky black coloration.[5] As the statue increased in importance as a pilgrimage focus, the identification grew between the black Christ and healing earth and water.

The devotion to Our Lord of Esquipulas arrived at the frontier village of Chimayó in northern New Mexico sometime before 1805.[6] Permission to build a chapel dedicated to this manifestation of Christ was granted in 1814 to the residents of El Potrero, near Chimayó. The result, completed in 1816, was *el Santuario de Chimayó*, one of the most famous and best-loved traditional churches of northern New Mexico. The chapel was built on a site that had long been noted for its healing mud. The healing power of the earth remains, although the task of divine agency which blesses this healing process was transferred in the later nineteenth century from Esquipulas to the Santo Niño de Atocha, another specifically New World manifestation of Christ.[7]

So apparently there was in Tucson in the 1840s a statue of the black Christ of Esquipulas, a manifestation which is traditionally connected with healing earth or hot springs. There may have been, until blocked by the earthquake of 1887, hot springs near the area where the mission stood.[8] When the soldiers departed from the presidio (accompanied by several Mexican citizens who were concerned about rumors that the incoming United States soldiers would treat them badly), they took with them the town's archives and the religious paintings and statues from the convento de San José and the presidial chapel. Among these, according to an eyewitness, was "el crucifijo de Nuestro Señor de Esquipulas" (the crucifix of Our Lord of Esquipulas).[9]

The eyewitness in question was a six-year-old girl named Atanacia Santa Cruz, who later married pioneer settler Sam Hughes and lived well into the twentieth century as a respected link with Tucson's past. Her recollections were given orally in 1929 to Donald W. Page who wrote them down and deposited them in manuscript form at the Arizona Pioneers' Historical Society, now the Arizona State Historical Society. Interestingly enough, Doña Atanacia remembered the statue had been taken, not to Ímuris, but to Magdalena. Her memory could be accurate. Two statues known to have been in Magdalena during the eighteenth century are now in the nearby village church of San Ignacio. The period of religious persecution in the 1930s, when at least one sacred image (the reclining statue of San Francisco Xavier) was removed from the Magdalena church and burned on order of the Sonoran state authorities, would provide a perfectly logical setting for the removal of the black Christ statue to Ímuris.[10]

The preceding paragraphs serve as an explanation for the presence of an unusual statue—a black crucifix—in the modern church of San José de Ímuris. I have drawn upon the disciplines of history and anthropology to assemble this explanatory narrative, and the end product seems convincing. A few loose ends, perhaps, but on the whole it ties together quite nicely. That last sentence provides a hint that my explanatory narrative is assembled according to a set of cultural rules—an aesthetic—for such narratives. In my cultural tradition, which is that of a university-trained scholar, such a narrative must first of all *explain*. It must provide a convincing set of reasons why the object of discussion is the way it is. The reasons must be believable to secularly oriented participants in the contemporary Anglo American academic world. That the narrative is also complex, taking us from nineteenth-century Tucson to sixteenth-century Guatemala and back by way of northern New Mexico, that it allows all sorts of seemingly unrelated facts—the movement of a garrison, the presence of hot springs in two locations, the mention of a statue in a church inventory—to be brought together into an apparently seamless whole—adds virtue to the explanation. However, this is only one of several available narratives, or constructions, that explain the black Christ in the church at Ímuris.

San Ignacio, Sonora, is another mission community on the Rio Magdalena, some fifteen miles south of Ímuris. Unlike Ímuris, San Ignacio retains its eighteenth-century church. The *sacristana* of San Ignacio, Josefina Gallegos, learned the following explanatory narrative several years ago from an old woman in Ímuris.

> Once a very pious farmer lived in Ímuris. His custom was to pray every day in the Ímuris church before going into his fields. At the end of his prayers, he would kiss the feet of the crucified Christ and go about his business. An evil man wanted to kill the pious man. To this end, he smeared poison on the feet of Christ in the church. When the good man finished his prayers, he tried to kiss Christ's feet but was prevented by a mysterious force. Looking up, he saw the toes, then the feet, then the entire statue turning black. Due to this warning, his life was saved.[11]

According to this explanatory narrative, then, the crucifix was originally the color of normal flesh but turned black as a result of divine intervention to prevent a terrible crime from being perpetrated upon an innocent and virtuous person. Christ, expressing Himself through the statue, took action to save the life of one who had shown devotion to Him. Virtue is rewarded (but evil is not punished) and God's power to protect those who love and serve him is made evident once more. I personally find it significant that both the person who told me the story and her informant are older women. Older women are usually the active carriers of traditional religious lore in Mexican families.

A similar story is told concerning another black crucifix in far-off Mexico City. The side chapel closest to the door on the right hand side of the Mexico City Cathedral is dedicated to San Ysidro, patron saint of farmers. On the altar of this chapel there stood in the 1960s a black crucifix some two feet tall, known locally as *el Señor de veneno*, "The Lord of Poison." A 1969 bilingual guidebook to the cathedral includes the following explanation of this statue:

Christ of Poison

The best legend relating to the color of this venerated image is as follows: "This image used to hang in the Bishop's private chapel. The Bishop was accustomed each morning to kiss the feet of the image. An unbeliever (*un impio*) wanted to kill the Bishop. He thought of a plan. So, one night he got into the chapel and smeared poison on the statue's feet. Next morning, when the Bishop leaned over to kiss the statue, he was surprised to see the entire statue turning black and withdrawing its legs, keeping him from being poisoned. Later, the assassin confessed his crime, and naturally, people considered the occurrence to be like a miracle." The news spread rapidly among the common people, who from then on called the statue The Lord of Poison.[12]

This is obviously the same story that Sra. Gallegos learned from her friend in Ímuris, except the pious farmer has become the bishop of Mexico City. It, too, explains the presence of an unusually pigmented crucifix to the satisfaction of the people who tell it. For the outsider, the story neatly connects the frontier community of Ímuris with the capital city of Mexico. Incidentally, I have not met anyone in Ímuris who is aware of the Mexico City statue and its devotion. Neither have I heard the statue referred to by Sonorans as el Señor de Esquipulas, although the statue was apparently thus known a century ago. (I did, however, speak with a young woman in Aconchi, Sonora, which also has a black Christ. She was unaware of the Ímuris statue, but told me that there was said to be a black Christ in Guatemala.)

An increasing number of guided tours take groups of tourists from the United States through the mission towns of northern Sonora. As Ímuris is on the main highway leading from the border to the important mission towns of San Ignacio and Magdalena de Kino, and because it is locally famous for its *quesadillas*,[13] it is a regular stop for many tour guides. One such guide is Cathy Giesy of Fiesta Tours International, of Amado, Arizona. Ms. Giesy tells the following story which she remembers learning around 1990 from one of the ladies cleaning the church, who said that the padre who was there, prior to the padre who is there now, told her the story.

Every day there was a man that went to the church and piously prayed and kissed the feet of the Christ, that crucifix that was hanging on the wall, and there was a bad man in town. He wanted this good guy, this pious man, to do a business deal with him. Of course there was some *transa* in there that was not quite legal, not quite good, and our pious man did not want to do this bad act. So he refused. The bad man, knowing he had confronted the good guy with this and that he could create a backlash, wanted to kill the good guy. So he put poison on the feet of the Christ, and the next morning when the good guy was going to go to the church and kiss the feet of the Christ, there was a fire in the town. So he went, being a good man, went to help the people with the fire, and saved all of their goods and hauled stuff out of the burning house, went back to kiss the feet of the Christ the following day, and the Christ had turned black with the smoke of the fire."[14]

When Ms. Giesy first told me this story in a small cafe in Ímuris, she was with a group of tourists. In the story as she told it that day, the burning house was located next door to the church, and it was left uncertain whether the statue had been blackened by the smoke or the poison. In her formally taped interview, however, the house is not located and she states unequivocally that it was the fire that had turned the statue black.

Francine Pierce, who used to live and farm in Santa Ana, Sonora, about thirty miles south of Ímuris, guides tours through the area under the auspices of Pima Community College. She sometimes tells the following narrative, which she learned from a mimeographed sheet of paper she saw many years ago, with details added from conversations with friends and neighbors in the Santa Ana area.

There was a fight to the death between the Pimas and the Apaches: 9 men against 9 men. Eight had died and the last two fighters were the Pima chief and the Apache chief. The Pima chief had the Apache chief down and was about to do him in, when the Apache chief cried "Mi Señor de Esquipula [*sic*]." (This was the name of the Christ figure in the church at Cocóspera.) The Pima says, "You worship the same Señor as I," and he gives the Apache his life. About a year later when the Apache chief burned the church at Cocóspera the rest of the church burned and the Christ figure was merely charred. It was a miracle, and hence this is an especially revered figure.[15]

The mission church of Santiago y Nuestra Señora del Pilar de Cocóspera lies in a fertile valley some thirty miles east of Ímuris. The village of Cocóspera was abandoned in the 1840s due to continued Apache raiding. The church was destroyed and rebuilt six times since its original construction in the 1690s, but stands in ruins today, not from the depredations of the Apaches, but rather from the ravages of time and would-be treasure hunters, who have dug into the walls of the building looking for buried gold and silver that was likely never there.[16]

These are the explanatory narratives I have collected so far concerning the black Christ of Ímuris. It is my contention that each exhibits a high degree of fit with the world view and aesthetic of the group owning it. As I remarked before, the historical/anthropological explanation doesn't just stick with the documentable facts—it presents an interesting, somewhat complex narrative, with loose ends ignored. It brings in data from many kinds of sources, with the result, intentional or not, of presenting a rather dazzling bit of research to the lay person. "How in the world did you find all that out?" would be an appropriate lay response to being told such a story.

In a like manner, the narrative of the pious man and the poison attempt satisfies the needs and aesthetic of the traditional Catholic believer. Evil is thwarted, God protects His own through a display of power, and the unusual color of the statue is explained.

At a slight remove is the narrative collected from tour guide Cathy Giesy. To be sure, her version is validated by having come from an old woman who was cleaning the church, but at the same time it perfectly suits its current recipients—groups of older Anglo Americans, quite possibly possessing both a secular skepticism towards miracles and a romantic acceptance of other cultures' belief in them. I find the ambiguity to be very significant—one is given alternate explanations for the statue's color (although the statue doesn't really look as though it was smudged in a fire) and therefore can enjoy a good story without having one's credulity stretched or challenged.

The final narrative, also used in a tourist context, departs from all the others in most details, although it keeps the motif of smudging in a fire. It is typical of many stories told by people of European descent concerning Indians in that it deals with dramatic confrontations between leaders, or "chiefs."

It is interesting to note that Ms. Pierce, the source of this narrative, does not use it every time she takes a tour group to Ímuris. In her words, if "after six hours in the van, the trippers are still tending to see Mexican people as poor, lazy, unintelligent, superstitious aliens (as some still do), I will give them no fuel for their opinions and I will not even touch a religion issue. I will point out similarities between Tucson and Mexico and I will only tell them the black Christ story which centers on Guatemala, Tucson, etc." (This refers to what I have been calling the historical/anthropological narrative.)[17]

Ms. Pierce told me that the version she tells, which is given above, is "essentially a synopsis of the other versions" she had heard of the story. "I do not remember if I dropped portions of the originals which did not fit in with my overall goal in telling stories in Mexico. In general, however, I do believe there are some things best left unsaid." She also told me that "a person (no matter what his profession) would be a pretty crummy story teller, if he or she did not refine the story based on audience reaction. . . . To assume all story changes are unconscious makes story tellers out to be an unreflective lot. . . . Depending on the teller and the goal, the story is bound to change."[18]

Another Black Christ

There is at least one additional black Christ in Sonora, in the colonial church in the town of Aconchi, on the Río Sonora, some 150 miles south and east of Ímuris as the crow flies. Aconchi was a village of Opata-speaking Indians, being well to the east of the Pimería Alta. Mission activity at this village started in 1638 and was continued by Franciscans after the expulsion of the Jesuits until at least 1815.[19] The church of San Pedro de Aconchi is a rather plain eighteenth-century church with the Franciscan coat-of-arms carved above the door. Over the altar hangs a life-sized crucifix whose black corpus seems to be very similar to the one at Ímuris. Both avoid the dramatic intensity of the baroque style (an intensity which, when expressed in angularly flexed knees, gave rise to the legend in the Mexico City Cathedral of the statue bending its legs so as to keep its poisoned toes out of reach of the Bishop). On May 10, 1992, I was in the church at Aconchi and collected three explanatory narratives concerning this statue. A young woman told me she had been told that when the state and federal governments took the statues out of the church to burn them (acts which took place in many parts of Sonora in the 1930s), all the statues were burned except the Christ, which merely was smudged black in the smoke of the conflagration. She also said that others had told her that the statue turned black "because of sins" (presumably on the part of the villagers).

An older woman who was also in the church, preparing a statue of the Virgin for a Rosary to be held later, told me the following more detailed narrative, which she referred to as a "beautiful history."

Some women in the village didn't like their *padrecito* or priest (the diminutive frequently expresses affection in Mexican Spanish), and decided to kill him by feeding him a poisoned meal. The priest had the excellent custom of kissing the feet of the crucified Christ after his prayers. The poisoners decided that the non-ringing of the scheduled church bell after the meal would be the sign that they had been successful, so they waited until the appropriate time, listening. But the bell rang. When the padrecito kissed Christ's feet after eating his poisoned meal, the statue sucked the poison out of him, turning black in the process. God didn't want the padrecito to die just then. "And after hearing that story," she asked me, "Who could disbelieve in the power of God?"

On a recent trip to Mexico City, I visited the statue of el Señor de Veneno. It has been moved from the San Ysidro chapel where I first saw it to a more centralized altar—the *Altar de Perdón*—right inside the main doors. Several printed prayers and devotional texts devoted to el Señor de Veneno were for sale in and beside the cathedral. In an undated guidebook, apparently published in the 1950s or 1960s, I found an explanatory legend for the statue that directly paralleled the one I had collected in Aconchi. My translation is preceded by the original text in Spanish.[20]

Altar del Señor de Veneno

Este Santo Cristo de color negro se veneró primitivamente en la iglesia de Portacoeli y sobre él se cuenta ésta sugestiva leyenda. Un pastelero, devoto suyo, iba a ser envenenado por un compañero de oficio que le envió un apetitoso pastel. El buen pastelero, después de comerlo con toda buena fe, fuese a hacer su diaria visita al Santo Cristo, entonces blanco, y al levantarse y besar sus pies el Santo Cristo tornóse negro, absorbiendo el veneno, según dice la conseja, y quedando el devoto pastelero sano y salvo.

The Altar of the Lord of Poison

This black-colored Holy Christ was venerated earlier in the church of Portacoeli and this interesting legend is told about it. A pastrycook, one of its devotees, was going to be poisoned by a fellow worker who sent him a luscious pastry. The good pastrycook, after eating it in all good faith, went to make his daily visit to the Holy Christ, which was then white, and upon his getting up and kissing its feet, the Holy Christ turned black, absorbing the poison, according to the story, and the pastrycook remained whole and healthy.

I have searched in vain for a pre-World War II reference to el Señor de Veneno in the guide literature. My edition of *Terry's Guide to Mexico*, dated 1943 but possibly only slightly revised from the 1909 edition, gives a chapel-by-chapel description of the cathedral. Had the Black Christ, with its colorful legends, been there at the time the guide was written, it would surely have been mentioned.[21] One possible explanation was suggested to me by the art historian Arquitecto Jorge Olvera of Mexico City: the statue had been moved to the cathedral from another nearby church (the Portacoeli mentioned above) during the 1920s or 1930s.

In his study of black Christ statues and healing earth, Stephen de Borhegyi does not mention any such devotion in Mexico City.[22] By the same token, I have not yet encountered any instance in which the statue in the cathedral is called "Esquipulas."

We have come a long way in this part of the story—from Tucson to Guatemala; back to New Mexico and Tucson; down south into Sonora; all the way to Mexico City. I suspect that were we to follow the story farther it would take us to peninsular Spain and the Mediterranean world, as well as into the beliefs and traditions of those who lived in Mexico before the Spaniards arrived.

Christianity was, of course, a Mediterrenean import into Mexico. There seems to be only one major black crucifix in Europe that might antedate the carving of Our Lord of Esquipulas: the Volto Santo of Lucca, west of Florence in Italy.[23] But folk as well as formal devotions may travel to the colonies, and there is some evidence that a devotion to a black Christ has long been in place in sheep-raising regions of Spain and in the old Spanish possessions in southern Italy.[24]

Black is one of the sacred colors, associated with a specific direction and specific values for many native peoples of North and Middle America. According to Stephen de Borhegyi, the color black seems to have been associated by at least some Mayas with night and darkness, black rain clouds, and unlucky days. At the same time, the deity Ek-Chu-Ah, "The Black Lord," was the protector of travellers, merchants, and pilgrims. And Esquipulas was not only noted in pre-conquest days for its healing earth and hot water, but it was located on a well-known prehispanic pilgrimage route. As Borhegyi also remarks, "If the Indians had wanted a black Christ, there must have been an underlying significance to it."[25] The notion that the Christ statue should be a color contrasting to that of the feared conquerors may well have been a red herring to disguise the real ritual significance of the statue's color.

A Parallel Case—The Children's Shrine

When I first started hearing these several stories concerning the Black Christ of Ímuris, I was interested in the efficient ways in which each one served the population who used it. I was also reminded of a parallel situation far to the north and west of Ímuris, but still within the Pimería Alta.

In the midst of the great Santa Rosa Valley in the central portion of the Papago Indian Reservation stands a circular shrine made of peeled ocotillo stalks set into the dirt. There are gaps in the circle for each of the four cardinal directions. The center of the circle is taken up with a pile of rocks. Offerings of pennies, shells, candy, or small toys are often found on the pile of rocks. Flanking the circle on the east and west are two huge piles of discarded ocotillo stalks. This is the Children's Shrine, the most sacred place in Tohono O'odham country.

The story associated with the shrine is as follows: In that portion of time which is only accessible through oral tradition, an angry farmer dug into a badger hole near the village of Gu Achi (now called Santa

Rosa on many maps). The animal had been eating his crops for some time, and he intended to kill it. As badgers are protected in Tohono O'odham belief, this deed was liable to have unforseen consequences. The consequences became apparent when water started gushing out from the hole, accompanied by a roaring wind.

Frightened, the farmer went to the village for help. The villagers, as scared by the volume of water as he was, turned to the local medicine men, who said that if something were not done to stop the flood, the whole country would be drowned. After sending various kinds of living creatures down the hole to stop the flooding, the medicine men realized what must be done. Four children, a boy and a girl from each of the major divisions of the Tohono O'odham, must be placed down the hole.

The children were selected and prepared. Then, as the people sang, the children danced in the hole and slowly sank out of sight, while the flood waters receded. The Flood Children, as they are sometimes called, are believed not to have died, but to be in the Underworld, from which they come every four years to dance with the people when the shrine is renewed and its materials are replaced in a four-day ritual.[26]

This is the essence of the story as told by Tohono O'odham. There are variations, to be sure—I have been told that I'itoi, the Elder Brother and creator of the Tohono O'odham, became so angry at the behavior of his People that he stamped his foot, causing the flood to start. But in O'odham narrative the threat is always a flood, and four children are always sacrificed to avert that threat. The narrative is an important one in Tohono O'odham tradition; besides explaining one particular shrine, it is referred to in other O'odham traditions, including the well-known *chelkona*, or "skipping and scraping dance."

There has been another version of the story of the Children's Shrine current among nearby Anglo Americans for at least fifty years. In 1943, Joyce Rockwood Muench published an article about the shrine in *Desert Magazine*. Her explanatory narrative, which she later said she had collected from a state senator in Casa Grande and a trading post owner (neither of whom could have possibly been Indian) differed in two significant details from the narrative I have just outlined. In the first place, it was a drought that was threatening the People rather than a flood. In the second place, three, rather than four children were sacrificed.[27]

One explanation for these discrepancies might be as follows: Anglo farmers in the Casa Grande area (and Casa Grande is only a about thirty miles from Santa Rosa and the shrine), hearing about the shrine and its legend, have created a version which fits their cultural norms and aesthetic better than does the original O'odham story. For one thing, drought may not be the threat for Tohono O'odham that it is for European-descended farmers.

Normal conditions for the O'odham are close to what most other farming peoples would call a drought; their culture, after all, has evolved in a desert. Their traditional farming depends upon runoff and sheet flooding from the heavy summer rains. If the summer rains did not come or their crops failed for some other reason, a common strategy was for the Desert People to visit their O'odham cousins who lived in permanent villages along one of the area's year-round rivers until things got better. (Under the Tohono O'odham system, a person lived in two villages over the course of the year: a winter village near a dripping spring or some other permanent water source, and a summer village down in the flats, to utilize runoff from the summer floods.) For Anglo American farmers, however, with a larger material culture inventory and permanent dwellings, a drought could—and often did—spell disaster.

By the same token, while four is the ritual number for Tohono O'odham, as it is for many Native American groups, the European, Christian number of significance is three. A Holy Trinity and Three Kings appear in Christian tradition. Well-known sayings tell us that troubles come in threes, and that the third time is the charm. In baseball, you are out after three strikes. Countless jokes start off, there was a ———, a ———, and a ———, and any child raised in mainstream culture knows that one gets three wishes and three guesses.[28]

It seems likely that some Anglo tellers of the Flood Children story, consciously or otherwise, changed the narrative concerning the important, sacred shrine to make it make sense to Anglo people. And indeed, one of the letters to the editor in *Desert Magazine* seems to bear this out.

Anthropologists and others had written the magazine saying that the story as told by Muench was not the way they had heard it from O'odham sources. Muench replied, listing her informants. Another letter was received from Ruth C. Woodman, author of the *Death Valley Days* radio program, saying that she had in fact heard the version with a flood on an earlier visit to Papago Country. She concluded, "I must say, though, that Mrs. Muench's version appeals to me more after visiting that country."[29] In other words, it fit Anglo American culture and perceptions of life in the desert better than did the O'odham version.

This drought narrative of the Children's Shrine still has currency among Anglos in the Casa Grande region. A version of it was published as recently as 1990 in the local newspaper.[30]

It is easy to dismiss these versions of the Flood Children story as Anglos co-opting and diluting native beliefs, but to my mind such a dismissal misses the point. It seems just as likely that the Anglo versions of the story result from an Anglo need to account for the importance of the shrine and the seriousness of the sacrifice of the children in terms that are relevant to Anglo values.

This kind of cross-cultural borrowing and remodelling of narratives has gone on for a long time in our region, and not just from natives to Europeans. A European narrative which has been reworked by the Tohono O'odham to fit their their cultural aesthetic is the recently published "Gold Placer of Quijotoa, Ariz.," originally collected in 1897.[31] In it, a young man named Johnny is sent by his father to take some gold from the placer mine to Guaymas, a Sonoran seaport. On his way, he uses the gold to purchase a young woman from a band of thieves who had stolen her. She turns out to be a king's daughter, and after undergoing a series of trials, Johny marries her. Johny's uncle, Buzzard, also features in the story—a purely O'odham touch in what appears to be a transplanted tale of the European *märchen*, or "Wonder Tale," variety.[32]

Some Final Thoughts

It appears, at least in the small sample presented here, that cultural fit is an important factor of legend transmission. The academic explanation of the black Christ perfectly suits the needs and aesthetic of mainstream Euro-American academic society. The version of the good man being saved from death by poison is adapted to the needs of traditional Mexican Catholics, just as Giesy's narrative, with its ambiguities, suits the needs of Anglo tourists in Sonora.

All this is, of course, saying the obvious. I am certainly not the first to conclude that a culture's folklore expresses the culture's values. But I strongly suggest that these values include aesthetic ones. I also suggest this process goes on continuously, not just with "old stories," but with any narrative we pick up from others and retell, be it a legend, a joke, or a piece of what we call "news." The story—*any* story—needs to feel right—to fit—or it will be changed around until it does, just as

Anglo settlers in the Casa Grande Valley appear to have changed the details of the O'odham story of the Flood Children, crafting an explanation of the sacred site that made sense to them in the same deeply satisfying way the original narrative made sense within the context of its own culture.

Appendix A

Additional Texts of the Señor de Veneno Narrative

Both these texts are taken from printed prayers addressed to el Señor de Veneno, and purchased at the Mexico City Cathedral on November 26, 1993. The texts are in the Archives of the University of Arizona Library's Southwest Folklore Center. The first text also appears on a prayer card in the same archive, collected at Santa Cruz Parish Church in Tucson in December, 1992.[33]

Text A

Oración

Poderosísima y milagrosa imagen de Nuestro Señor Jesucristo, que bajo la advocación del Señor del Veneno eres venerada. Yo te ruego, que así como le salvaste la vida a su Señoria ilustrísima cuando por media de su sacratísimo cuerpo trataron de envenenarlo al ir a besar tus divinos pies, así te suplico, oh mi adorado Señor, que el ponzoñoso veneno del pecado no penetre más en mi corazón, haz que se purifique ejercitando todas las obras que sean de tu agrado. Es lo que te pido en honor de tu admirable transfiguración con lo que manifiestas lo grande de tu infinito poder. Amen.

PRAYER

Most powerful and miraculous image of Our Lord Jesus Christ, (you) who are venerated under the name of The Lord of Poison. I beg you, that just as you saved the life of his most illustrious lordship when they tried to poison by means of your most holy body when he went to kiss your hands and feet, that the venemous poison of sin does not penetrate further into my heart. Make it purify itself, doing all the works that please you. This is what I beg in honor of your admirable transfiguration through which you manifest the greatness of your infinite power. Amen.

Text B

PIADOSO TRIDUO AL SEÑOR DEL VENENO
ORIGEN DE ÉSTA ORACIÓN

Narra un pía y antigua tradición que, en tiempos remotos, el Arzobispado de México se hallaba situado en la calle de Moneda. Allí, en el descanso de una escalera se hallabe colocada una escultura, tamaño natural, de un hermoso Crucifijo. El Arzobispo que por aquel entonces gobernaba al Arquidiócesis de México, muy devoto de ésta Santa Imagen, cuantas veces pasaba enfrente de Ella le besaba los pies, con profunda veneración y edificación de quienes lo observaban.

Su Señoría ilustrísima, como suele suceder a los ministros del Señor, tenía enemigos gratuitos. Uno de ellos concibío la sacrílega idea de envenenarlo. Con este fin esparcío en los pies de la Sagrada Imagen un activísimo veneno con la intención de causar la muerte del Prelado. Más quedó frustrada la maligna intención del criminal, pues cuando el devoto Prelado aplicó los labios en los pies de la Imagen, ya el veneno se había difundido milagrosamente por todo el Cuerpo el Señor Crucificado. Desde ese momento la Santa Imagen quedó ennegrecida. Este acontecimiento fue la causa de que la piedad de la gente lo llamara "EL SEÑOR DEL VENENO."

EXTREMELY PIOUS THREE-DAY PRAYER
TO THE LORD OF POISON
ORIGIN OF THIS PRAYER

A pious and ancient tradition tells that, in remote times, the Archbishipric of Mexico was situated in la calle de Moneda. There, in the landing of a staircase, hung a life-sized statue of a beautiful Crucifix. The Archbishop who in those times governed the Archdiocese of Mexico, very devoted to this holy image, whenever he passed in front of it would kiss its feet, with deep veneration and to the edification of those who observed him.

His illustrious lordship, as usually happens to the ministers of the Lord, had gratuitous enemies. One of these conceived the sacriligeous idea of poisoning him. To this end he spread an extremely active poison on the feet of the holy image, with the intention of causing the death of the prelate. But the malign intention of the criminal was frustrated because when the devout prelate put his lips on the feet of the image, the poison had already spread miraculously through all the body of the Crucified Lord. From that moment the holy image remained blackened. This event was the reason that the piety of the common people would call it (the image) "THE LORD OF POISON."

Appendix B

A Printed Prayer to el Señor de Veneno

This printed text, accompanied by a poorly reproduced photograph of the el Señor de Veneno statue in the Mexico City Cathedral, was purchased in one of the religious articles stores that cater to pilgrims on the main plaza of Magdalena de Kino. Magdalena is in the same river valley as Imuris, about twenty miles downstream. I first saw and purchased this prayer in April, 1992. It had not been in the store on my previous visit in October, 1991. Curiously enough, the prayer contains no references to the specifics of the Señor de Veneno legend; it is a generic prayer to God. It is also interesting to note that the prayer uses the same formal, almost obsequiously humble language as does the prayer to Juan Soldado presented in Appendix A to Chapter 4.

ORACIÓN
A LA MILAGROSA IMAGEN DEL
SEÑOR DE VENENO

QUE SE VENERA EN LA
CATEDRAL METROPOLITANA
MEXICO, D.F.

ABRE SEÑOR, MIS LABIOS QUE SEPAN EXPRESAR LAS QUEJAS QUE ME ABRUMAN, TENGO MUCHO QUE PEDIRTE Y AUNQUE NADA MEREZCO, POR MIS CULPAS, ES INMENSA LA FE QUE TENGO EN TI YO SÉ QUE TU DESEAS SOCORRERME Y QUE QUIZÁ ME PERMITAS MIS PESARES, PARA QUE VENGA A TI, VENGA Y TE ADORE LLORANDO EN TUS ALTARES, POR ESO ME ACERCO A TU TERNURA, CON LA QUE PUEDES REMEDIAR MIS MALES Y EMBARGADA LE VOZ POR MIS GEMIDOS HE DE DECIRTE LO QUE SUFRE MI ALMA, QUE DUDAS Y DOLORES AMARGOS DESENGAÑOS, LA HAN PLAGADO DE LLAGAS Y DOLENCIAS. BIEN CONOZCO QUE ES JUSTO TU CASTIGO Y QUE MÁS MERECIÁN MIS PECADOS; PERO YA ES BASTANTE PARA MÍ QUE SOY DE CARNE, QUE DE DIOS SOLO TENGO SEME-JANZA Y NUNCA COMO TÚ, LA RESISTENCIA.

NO PUEDO MÁS, CESE TU ENOJO Y DEJAME QUE TE AME COMO A PADRE PROTECTOR DE LAS NECESIDADES. QUIERO SENTIR LA GRATITUD DE VER MIS MISERIAS SOCORRIDAS, MIS DEMANDAS JUSTAS, SATISFECHAS; SENTIR EL BIENESTAR Y LA PAZ EN MI ALMA. EN MI PATRIA Y EN MI HOGAR Y LA FELICIDAD DE MIS PARIENTES Y BIENHECHORES. QUIERO, EN VEZ DE TENER LAGRIMAS MIS OJOS ALZAR LA VISTA A TI Y CON MIS CANTOS RENDIRTE ADORACIÓN Y VENERARTE Y ADORNAR CON LINDAS FLORES, ESE TU SOLIO, DONDE TE PRESENTAS CON LOS BRAZOS EXTENDIDOS, COMO EL QUE ESPERA CON CARINO PARA ESTRECHARNOS EN ELLOS; COMO ÉL QUE MANDA QUE SE APLAQUEN LAS TERRIBLES TEME SE APLAQUEN LAEDIENTES SU SUJETAN A SUS DACTADOS. ASÍ

QUIERO LLEGAR A OFRENDARTE DE MI GRATITUD CELESTES
FLORES; QUIERO QUE SEAN MIS LAGRIMAS DE AMORES LAS
QUE ENLACEN A LOS SERES TODOS. PARA QUE TODOS TE
EMEN Y REVERENCIEN Y CON ELLOS AL ALMA MIS TE GLORI-
FIQUE POR UNA ETERNIDAD. AMEN.
EL ILMO. SR. DR. NICOLAS PEREZ GAVILAN, CONCEDE
50 DÍAS DE INDULGENCIA A LOS QUE RECEN DEVOTAMENTE
ÉSTA ORACIÓN.

PRAYER
TO THE MIRACULOUS IMAGE OF THE
LORD OF POISON

WHICH IS VENERATED IN THE
METROPOLITAN CATHEDRAL
MEXICO, D.F.

OPEN, LORD, MY LIPS THAT THEY MIGHT KNOW HOW
TO EXPRESS THE COMPLAINTS THAT OVERWHELM ME, I
HAVE MUCH TO ASK OF YOU AND ALTHOUGH I DO NOT
DESERVE ANYTHING, THROUGH MY FAULT, THE FAITH I
HAVE IN YOU IS IMMENSE AND I KNOW THAT YOU DESIRE TO
HELP ME AND THAT PERHAPS YOU WILL GRANT ME MY
REGRETS, IN ORDER THAT I MIGHT COME TO YOU, COME
AND ADORE YOU CRYING AT YOUR ALTARS, FOR THIS REASON
I APPROACH YOUR TENDERNESS, WITH WHICH YOU CAN
CURE MY ILLS AND MY VOICE OVERCOME BY MY WAILING I
MUST TELL YOU WHAT I SUFFER IN MY SOUL, WHAT DOUBTS
AND BITTER SORROWS AND DISAPPOINTMENTS, HAVE
PLAGUED IT WITH WOUNDS AND ACHES. I WELL KNOW THAT
YOUR PUNISHMENT IS JUST AND THAT MY SINS DESERVE
MORE; BUT IT IS NOW ENOUGH FOR ME THAT I AM OF
FLESH, THAT OF GOD I HAVE ONLY THE SEMBLANCE AND
NEVER LIKE YOU, THE RESISTANCE.
I CAN DO NO MORE, CEASE YOUR ANGER AND ALLOW
ME TO LOVE YOU LIKE A FATHER PROTECTOR OF NECESSI-
TIES. I WISH TO FEEL THE GRATITUDE OF SEEING MY MISER-
IES HELPED, MY JUST DEMANDS SATISFIED, TO FEEL THE
WELL-BEING OF PEACE IN MY SOUL, IN MY COUNTRY AND IN

MY HOME AND THE HAPPINESS OF MY FAMILY AND BENE-
FACTORS. I DESIRE MY EYES, INSTEAD OF BEING FILLED
WITH TEARS, TO BE LIFTED UP TO THE VISION OF YOU, AND
WITH MY SONGS RENDER YOU ADORATION AND VENERATE
YOU AND DECORATE WITH BEAUTIFUL FLOWERS YOUR CAN-
OPIED THRONE, WHERE YOU PRESENT YOURSELF WITH OPEN
ARMS, LIKE HE WHO WAITS TENDERLY TO HUG US IN THEM;
LIKE HE WHO COMMANDS THAT THE TERRIBLE STORMS
OBEDIENTLY SUBJECT THEMSELVES TO YOUR WILL AND
CALM THEMSELVES. I THUS WISH TO COME TO OFFER YOU
OUT OF MY GRATITUDE CELESTIAL FLOWERS, I WISH THAT
IT BE MY TEARS OF LOVE THAT ENFOLD ALL BEINGS. SO
THAT ALL MAY LOVE AND REVERE THEE AND WITH THEM
MY SOUL MAY GLORIFY YOU FOR AN ETERNITY. AMEN.

THE MOST ILLUSTRIOUS DR. NICOLAS PEREZ
GAVILAN, GRANTS 50 DAYS OF INDULGENCE TO THOSE WHO
DEVOUTLY PRAY THIS PRAYER.

This is the only printed devotional literature concerning a black
crucifix that I have found in northern Sonora. Apparently the statues at
Ímuris and Aconchi do not attract enough devotees to have made
printing special devotional literature dedicated to them a worthwhile
activity. When I asked the salespeople in the store whether the el Señor
de Veneno of the printed prayer was in any way connected with the
black Christ of nearby Ímuris, they showed no evidence of having even
noticed that the prayer was in their shelves. Whether or not there is
any perceived connection between the two black Christs, the language
of the prayer itself is interesting as being typical of the extreme humility and even self-debasement that is to be found in much of the devotional literature of Mexican popular Catholicism.

The Mormon Cowboy

1st stanza (Couplets 1 & 2)

I— am a Mor-mon cow-boy, and U - tah is my home.

Tuc - son, Ar - i - zon - a is the first place I did roam.

From there in- to— El Cap - i- tan,— a place you all know well

To des - cribe that brush- y count- ry, no mor- tal tongue can tell.

3rd stanza (Couplets 5 & 6)

We all went to the dance that night at the school-house by the road

Man- y folks— came from Drip- ping Springs, and man- y came from Globe.

The mus- ic they— brought with them I nev- er shall for - get

'Twas a col- ored man with his gui- tar,— I can hear him sing- ing— yet.

Musical copywork: Charles Leinberger

Chapter 6

"The Mormon Cowboy"

An Arizona Cowboy Song
and its Community[1]

With this essay we move north from the Pimería Alta into the mountains of Gila County and the mining and cattle country south of Globe, Arizona. The song that is the subject of this case study has never achieved importance within the canon of cowboy songs, although a few revival singers have seen fit to add it to their repertoires. As the essay makes clear, however, borders of a kind exist beyond an international context, and materials which are shared by more than one subculture within our dominant society may well serve different functions and have different meanings in their various cultural contexts.

Texts on Record and in Tradition

On 13 October, 1929, a Texas cowboy singer named Carl T. Sprague stepped up to a microphone in a Victor recording studio in Dallas and performed a song which he called "The Mormon Cowboy."[2] Sprague was no stranger to the recording process. Inspired by the success of Vernon Dalhart's 1924 recording of "The Prisoner's Song," he had appeared at the Victor offices in Camden, New Jersey, in August 1925 with his guitar and a collection of Texas songs, including some fine cowboy ballads. This was his fourth, and, though he did not know it, his last Victor recording session.[3] Here are the tune and the text of the song "The Mormon Cowboy" that he recorded that day and which was issued as Victor V-40246. (I have divided the text into numbered couplets for easy reference, although the song is actually divided into seven verses of four lines each.)[4]

The Mormon Cowboy

1) I am a Mormon cowboy, and Utah is my home,
   Tucson, Arizona, was the first place I did roam.
2) From there into El Capitan, a place you all know well,
   To describe that brushy country, no mortal tongue can tell.
3) While at the old post office, a maid came riding down
   Upon a bronco pony, and was soon upon the ground.
4) She gave to each and every one an invitation grand,
   Inviting us to a grand ball at the old El Capitan.
5) We all went to the dance that night in the schoolhouse by the road;
   Many folks came from Dripping Springs and many came from Globe.
6) The music they brought with them, I never shall forget,
   'Twas a colored man with his guitar, I can hear him singing yet.
7) There were lots of married women there, and single girls, too;
   I soon became acquainted with all except a few.
8) The cowboys in their high-heeled boots were leading the grand march,
   While the city dudes soon followed, in collars stiff with starch.
9) After dancing two or three sets I stepped outside to cool,
   Every bush that I passed by was loaded with white mule.
10) Then after serving supper, it was a quarter past one,
   I heard a fight had started, each cowboy grabbed his gun.

11) Up stepped a little cowpuncher, his eyes were flashing fire,
    He said he was the ramrod of the ranch called Bar F Bar.
12) I started for my pony, the guns were flashing fast,
    I could hear the cowboys shouting "We broke it up at last."
13) So I bid farewell to my new-made friends and the place called El Capitan;
    The fairest face I ever saw was in that wild and happy band.
14) I jumped into my saddle and started back toward home,
    Made up my mind right then and there that I never more would roam.

Although the basic action of the song is easy to follow, certain usages should perhaps be explained. A "bronco pony" is one that is only partly broken. That the maid should ride such a horse is an indication that she is a good horsewoman and probably part of the local ranching community. "White mule" in this instance is bootleg or moonshine liquor. Stills were plentiful in Arizona as they were elsewhere during Prohibition, and illicit whiskey-making provides a popular topic of local cowboy reminiscences. (In the area around Globe and El Capitan, it was whiskey that was made; in the Santa Rita Mountains south of Tucson it was mescal, a distilled product of the agave plant.) The "ramrod" of an outfit is the foreman or person in charge. Bar F Bar is the brand of the local ranch, and would be written —F—.

Nearly fifty years later, Sprague recalled that the song "was sent to me by a party whom I did not know but who had some of my early recordings and who had asked me to record this 'Mormon Cowboy.' She sent me both the words and the music. I worked it over to suit my guitar playing and recorded it. It seemed to go over real well. I know nothing of the history of the song because the lady told me nothing about it. She just liked my recordings and wanted me to record 'The Mormon Cowboy' the way I had made all the other records."[5]

Although Sprague was pleased with its reception, the song seems to have not been picked up by other early commercial cowboy singers. Nineteen twenty-nine was late for genuine cowboy songs to take hold, and singing western movies were just around the corner, bringing with them the western song and its highly romanticized view of cowboy life. Furthermore, the localized, low-key events of "The Mormon Cowboy" do not seem to have had the appeal of, say, "The Sierry Petes (or Tying Knots in the Devil's Tail)" (Laws B17).[6] Composed as verse by Arizonan Gail I. Gardner in 1917 and set to music by Gardner's fellow Prescott cowboy, Bill Simon, in the late 1920s, "Tying Knots in the Devil's Tail" was disseminated by radio, record, and dude ranch performances at about the same time "The Mormon

Cowboy" was recorded. Gardner's song rapidly gained considerable currency in tradition.[7]

The story line of "The Mormon Cowboy"—a young man experiencing wild and exciting times while on a trip and then returning to the security of home—according to my colleague Hal Cannon, appears at least occasionally in the narratives of older Mormon men.[8] This presents a strong contrast not only with such widely distributed cowboy songs as "The Trail to Mexico" (Laws B13)[9] but also with many songs in the western genre that was to become so popular in the 1930s and 1940s. These latter often remark on the narrator's eagerness to return to the adventure and freedom of the open range.[10] In some of the older cowboy songs, all does not go well for the protagonist. He dies in "The Streets of Laredo" (Laws B1), learns that his sweetheart back home died with his name on her lips ("Cowboy Jack," Laws B24), or decides that cowpunching is pretty unpleasant work ("The D-2 Horse Wrangler," Laws B27). These and similar songs appear to involve the theme of an individual being visited with the results of his own actions. This fits in well with the cow country aesthetic of individual responsibility, but it represents a far different outcome, in my opinion, from a hasty and relatively unscathed return to the fold after a fling at the wild life.

Although "The Mormon Cowboy" was not recorded again until the 1980s, it has been recovered in oral tradition. Al Bittick of Winkelman, Arizona, sang it on two recordings, now preserved in the Fife Collection at Utah State University.[11] Neither of Bittick's texts contain any couplet that does not appear in Sprague's recording. Couplets 7 and 14 are omitted, however, and there are minor word changes throughout the song, although the general sense and the sequence of activity remain as Sprague presented them. Winkelman is a mining and ranching community a few miles south of Dripping Springs. It is close enough to Dripping Springs that Bittick might have been a member of the community described in the song.[12]

Yet another version of the song is in the performance repertoire of folklorist Barre Toelken. Toelken first heard the song from ex-cowboy Buck Fisk on the Navajo Reservation about 1954. In Toelken's words, ". . . he didn't know all of it, so I didn't learn it or begin singing it until I heard Joannie O'Bryant of Wichita sing it. She had learned it from a guy in Colorado, when she spent summers there (around Durango)."[13] The late Joan O'Bryant was an English professor who collected and

sang folksongs; two albums of her singing were issued by Folkways.[14]
Toelken went on to state that O'Bryant was aware that the song was
also available on record, but felt that her version "had a clearer statement of story line or whatever." He describes her tune as being similar
to that used by Buck Fisk. The text of the O'Bryant/Toelken version
appears below.[15] (For ease in reading, I have chosen to present the text
in four line stanzas rather than in numbered couplets.)

I am a Mormon Cowboy and Utah is my home.
From here to old Phoenix was the first place I did roam;
From there down to El Capitan, a place you all know well,
To describe this brushy country no human tongue can tell.

I was standin' by the post office when a maid come a-ridin' down,
She stopped her pinto pony and soon was on the ground;
She gave to all us boys out there an invitation grand,
To attend a cowboy ball at the old El Capitan.

Well, Saturday night we all met there at the school-house by the road,
Some came in from Drippin' Springs, some came in from Globe;
Well, the music that they brought with them I never will forget,
'Twas a colored man with his guitar, and I can hear him singin' yet.

Now the cowboys in their high-heeled boots, they led us in the march,
The town dudes they all followed with their collars stiff with starch;
After dancin' around it once or twice I went outside to cool,
But every bush that I passed by was loaded with white mule.

Before I could reach my pony, the guns was flashin' past,
And the cowboys started yellin', 'It's breakin' up at last;'
So I bid farewell to the whole affair and to the old El Capitan,
But the prettiest girls that I ever met was in that wild and wooly land.

The Sprague recording was reissued in 1965 on the LP, *Authentic
Cowboys and Their Western Folklsongs*.[16] Since then, it has been "covered" by Sprague himself and by the Deseret String Band.[17] I first
heard the song on the Sprague reissue and was intrigued by the fact
that it appeared to describe incidents that took place in Gila County,
Arizona. I determined to attempt to trace the song's history and place
it within its context. The remainder of this essay presents the results of
that effort.

"The Mormon Cowboy" in Central Arizona

The ruins of the El Capitan schoolhouse stand along Arizona State Highway 77, between the tiny settlement of Dripping Springs and Globe, the county seat. It was built by the residents of the El Capitan area on land donated by a local rancher, probably before 1920. School had previously been held in a tent, until the local people donated money and labor to build the schoolhouse. It had one room and was made of cement. In the early 1920s (the period described by our song) it accommodated about twenty students, between first and ninth grades. The teacher lived in a tent nearby. I have been unable to locate a photograph of the building.

Approximately once a month, the community would get together for a Saturday night dance. The young people would raise the money to pay the musicians by selling watermelons and box suppers, and a fine time was had by all. Local musicians would play, and the dances included squares, two-steps, and one-steps. The evenings would always end with "Home Sweet Home." The dances were attended not only by the families living in the area, but also by many of the cowboys who worked on nearby ranches. That part of Gila County was still rugged, open range, and roads were few. The Saturday night dances at the schoolhouse became important local events for the El Capitan area residents.[18]

The well-known Arizona writer and cowboy artist Ross Santee devoted a chapter of his book *Lost Pony Tracks* to the El Capitan dances and to some of the shenanigans that he remembers happening there.[19] His was a cowboy's view of the proceedings. The dances were apparently well-chaperoned, and whatever homemade liquor there was remained well outside of the schoolhouse. However, some rather spectacular fights do figure in the memories of even the most respectable of my informants.[20]

Santee prints a version of the ballad which differs in three places from that sung by Sprague. This is of some interest, because Santee's version appears to be the source of the only other printed version I am aware of, which is in a mimeographed songbook distributed in the early 1970s by Coyote Wolfe, a local Globe character and author. Wolfe calls the song "The Mormon Cowboy, or El Capitan."[21]

As a result of a letter to the editors of the *Globe Silver Belt*, I was sent ten texts of the ballad. Two are identical with the Santee/Wolfe version and were probably taken directly from a printed text. Six others are similar to Sprague's text in that they have either the same or fewer couplets, with only the sort of variations one might expect from material in oral transmission. Among these variations are "Some cars came from Dripping Springs" in couplet 5, "wild and wooly band" in couplet 13, and "A Colorado man with his guitar" in couplet 6. There are also paraphrases such as:

She invited each and every one a grand ball to attend
to be held that Saturday night at the old El Capitan school.

None of these variations suggests to me that it might not derive from the same basic source as Sprague's text.

Two texts, though similar in many respects to Sprague's, contain an additional couplet after Sprague's last couplet. It reads:

And as she rode away, on her face a smile did gleam
And every time I thought of her, it seemed a happy dream.

This seems to introduce a new element—romantic attachment between the maid and the cowboy—into the song. This is elaborated in one of the two texts, which concludes with the following three "alternate stanzas:"

I went back to Utah, which is my native state,
I never was contented, no longer could I wait:
I received a lot of letters, mailed at El Capitan,
I knew that they were written by my lover's hand.

I saddled up my pony and headed out her way,
I know that she'll be waiting for that happy day;
Miles are getting shorter, I hope to be there soon,
In Safford we'll be married when the manzanitas bloom.

We'll give a dance and supper in the school house by the road,
Our friends will be invited from Dripping Springs and Globe;
The past will be forgotten, our troubles will be o'er,
We'll bring back ol' friendship and be happy evermore.[22]

These variations, in addition to many not detailed, should be suf-
ficient evidence that the song was in oral tradition in Gila County and
had a certain degree of independence from the recording. Another bit
of evidence pointing in this direction is the attribution of authorship of
the poem. Two correspondents believe that Sprague wrote the song;
another attributed it to a local rancher named George Graham. Two
more claim Hugh Wills as the author, while still another two opt for
one Brigham Young. (Young did exist; he was a well-known local
musician and band leader.) Yet another correspondent (who identifies
herself with one of the characters in the song) mentions both Young
and a Clarence Wills. Santee mentions being handed a manuscript of
the poem by one "Bill Young," while Coyote Wolfe attributes the song
to Santee and Shorty Carroway.[23] I take all this apparently conflicting
information as evidence that the song was around for a good while.

One informant, a man in his mid-eighties, felt that the song
under consideration, which he called "El Capitan," is a 1920s rewrite
by Hugh Wills of an earlier song, "The Mormon Cowboy." This he
said was popular around the turn of the century. The only couplet of
the earlier song he could recall is:

We all met at the old rock house, two men was shot that day,
But the lady who rode the buckskin horse was the one that got away.

This intriguing couplet stands alone so far, and I have found
nobody else who remembers an earlier song.[24]

Perhaps the most interesting aspect of the information I elicited
concerning the song involves the glosses. Several people (including
Santee in his book) identified both the black musician in couplet 6 and
the feisty little cowboy in couplet 11. The former was a well-known
local character named "Old Kentuck" or "Nigger Tuck." Stories concerning his behavior are still remembered and told. One Gila County
text even mentions him by name:

The music they brought with them I never shall forget
Ol' Kentuck with his guitar, I can still hear him singing yet.

The "little cowpuncher" was Lyn Mayes, well known both as a
cowboy and as a fighter. One informant volunteered that a fiddler
named Jack Vineyard often appeared at the dances, while others identified Brigham Young's band as being regular musicians. Another caller

identified the maid who came riding down in couplet 3 as Blanche Brittain, who later married the Mormon Cowboy, a man named "Teet" Hill. This was later corroborated by Blanche Brittain Hill, who provided many of the details used in this essay. For her, this song is a reminder of courtship and marriage.[25]

Other glosses are of equal interest. One woman called long distance from Missouri to sing a partial text for me and to tell me that the "brushy country" of couplet 2 consisted of manzanita thickets. (Anyone who has tried to ride or walk through a manzanita thicket will understand the comment in the couplet; manzanitas are thick-growing, tough and tangled, and a thicket of them is almost impenetrable.) This same woman told me she had lived as a child with her grandmother in the El Capitan area during the 1920s. Those were wonderful times in her eyes. They had picked manzanita berries to make jelly. They would cut their own Christmas trees, which stood from floor to ceiling, and had wonderful Easter-egg hunts. Mention of the song brought these and other memories back to her.[26]

A man wrote: "I was raised in that country and my father, grandfather, and many friends had ranches there. In those days there were a lot of cowboys and a lot of wild cattle. I don't know which was the wildest. . . . The event described wasn't as bad as it sounds. It was just a sort of cowboy harassment of a stranger for dancing with all the pretty girls and the fact that he was a Mormon didn't help him any." This interpretation of the song seems quite different from that given by Mrs. Hill.

Yet another correspondent put Sprague's record in perspective: "I came to Globe in April of 1918 and was a cowboy in Gila County for many years. The song which we called "The Mormon Cowboy" came out in the 1920s and was patterned after an actual incident that happened at a dance at the school. . . . There was a phonograph record cut of it, and all the 'houses of joy' in Globe played it constantly for a while."[27]

I started my investigation of "The Mormon Cowboy" with one isolated text, that of a commercial record cut in 1929. I now have several additional texts and evidence that "The Mormon Cowboy" is in fact a folk song, using a fairly conservative definition of that term. That is to say, it is of uncertain authorship and has existed over time in more than one version. It certainly is not widely known or performed in Arizona or the West today. The late Van Holyoak, who lived about sixty miles north of Globe, had a copy of Coyote Wolfe's text, but didn't like the song enough to add it to his extensive repertoire of songs and recitations. My informants, on the other hand, had thought well enough of it to write it down, to learn, in some cases to remember and sing the words, and to send me their texts and reminiscences.

The reason seems at least partly clear. The song is a record of a series of incidents that were important to a specific community at a certain time. To those who had lived in the El Capitan area in the 1920s and were acquainted with those Saturday night dances and the people who attended them, the song was important. To others it held little interest. For some members of that western community, however, it brought back memories—of wild cattle, men, and times; of courtship and marriage; of making manzanita jelly with Grandma. How a person looked at the song depended to a great extent on who he or she was, but it is clear that the song was—and still is—the property of a community. A diverse community, to be sure, including cowboys and ranchers, town and country dwellers, Mormons and Gentiles—but a community nevertheless. "The Mormon Cowboy" in its variants and interpretations is in a real sense their song.

Moving Beyond Gila County

Sprague's recordings, the O'Bryant/Toelken text, and the Deseret String Band recording provide our only real recorded evidence that the song has moved beyond the Gila County community that gave it birth. I have already stated that Sprague's recording was not covered by any other commercial artist prior to the Deseret String Band, an aggregation that includes among its members the folklorist Hal Cannon. Only the O'Bryant/Toelken version (and, to a lesser extent, the related Bittick version) represents a real departure from the Sprague recording. Although the O'Bryant/Toelken melody is related to that used by Sprague, it has a certain point of variation. While Sprague's melody is basically AABA, with the "coarse" and "fine" parts of the widespread Anglo American, two-part "fiddle tune" pattern, the O'Bryant/Toelken melody, which has an ABBA organization (typical of Irish ballads), seems to derive from a different tradition. It is possible to speculate that this difference in melodies may reflect the changes that Sprague described as making the melody ". . . suit my guitar playing."

The O'Bryant/Toelken text also differs from the others in significant ways. In the first place, while the text contains no action or couplets that are not in the Sprague version, couplets 7, 10, 11, and 14 have been deleted. The omission of couplet 11 removed Lyn Mayes, "the little cowpuncher," from the song. His presence was not important to the development of the plot, but he was a part of the community present at the dances and, as such, is recognizable to many Gila County residents. The deletion of couplet 14 makes the song more readily acceptable to a community unfamiliar with (and indifferent to) more conservative narrative models that may involve returning to the safety of home after adventures in the outside world.

With couplets 7, 10 and 14 omitted, the narrator becomes less of an actor and more of an observer. Michael Korn has suggested that the narrator's involvement may be an important characteristic of western folk narrative, in contrast to the detached observer stance so prevalent in older Anglo-Celtic balladry.[28] Finally, by changing "the fairest face" to the "prettiest girls" in couplet 13, the O'Bryant/Toelken version substantially changes the nature of the narrator's reminiscences. All this becomes more interesting in light of the fact that O'Bryant deliberately learned this version because she preferred the story line to that in Sprague's recording.

It should be noted here that both versions sung by Al Bittick, currently in the Fife Collection, were collected by O'Bryant. Both Bittick texts omit couplets 7 and 14, while including couplets 10 and 11. Both also use the phrase, "prettiest girls," in couplet 13. O'Bryant recorded Bittick twice, once in Arizona and once in Arkansas. I do not know whether or not he was the informant in Colorado who taught her the version she sang. If he was, either she or Toelken seem to have made additional changes in the text. The O'Bryant/Toelken melody seems quite close to Al Bittick's melody as it is transcribed in the Fife Archives.

There are other changes as well. While the Gila County texts do not as a rule express the present participle ending as "in'" (as in "singin'" or "Drippin' Springs"), the O'Bryant/Toelken text does. By the same token, the Gila County texts tend more towards standard English usage in verb pluralization than does the O'Bryant/Toelken text. In other words, there seems to be a deliberate attempt in the O'Bryant/Toelken text to use dialect of a sort that does not appear in the Gila County texts or in other recorded performances. This may well be connected with the fact that both O'Bryant and Toelken may be described as "revivalist" singers. That is, they perform songs not directly within their tradition for an audience which may contain participants in a wide range of cultures. A typical audience for Toelken may well include people who are totally unfamiliar, not only with the Gila County community of the 1920s, but with any aspect of cowboy life or song. For such audiences, non-standard grammatical usages may provide an important stamp of authenticity, signalling the presence of a "real" cowboy song.

This seems to indicate that, with the Bittick and O'Bryant/ Toelken renditions of "The Mormon Cowboy," we have some evidence of the song beginning to move away from its local constituency towards a wider audience. A local character is omitted, and narrative, language, and style seem to have been changed to conform to interests other than those of the community. Whether or not this process will continue is yet to be seen. Perhaps a new wave of interest in western song will carry "The Mormon Cowboy" further on his journey. But even if this does not happen, the song remains to remind us not only of events that took place some sixty years ago in central Arizona but also of some of the still important differences between communities in the western United States.

Finally, it seems appropriate to attempt to place "The Mormon Cowboy" within a larger body of folksong. Is it, for example, a "Mormon Song?" I think not. The songs I would be comfortable referring to by that label deal with some communal concern of the Mormon world: Mormon theology, for instance, as in "None can Preach the Gospel as the Mormons Do," or some event, large or small, of Mormon history, as in "The Handcart Song," or "Echo Canyon."[29] These songs deal with issues and experiences specific to the social and religious concerns of the Mormon community: the virtues of Mormon religion and order; pushing handcarts across the plains; the experiences of communal labor. (This pattern is perceived by many non-Mormons living in Mormon country; I have more than once heard statements to the effect that "every time those Mormons dig an irrigation ditch, they write a song about it.") Our ballad certainly does not fit into this pattern of communal concern.

Yet, as I mentioned above, its theme reflects a conservative approach to adventures outside the home community—an approach that at least one folklorist found in conversations with older Mormon men who had cowboyed for a while and then been glad to get home.[30] So while ours is not a Mormon song in the same sense as much of the material in the Hubbard and Cheney collections, it is apparently informed by attitudes that are compatible with Mormon tradition and world view.

However, it remains sufficiently ambiguous in its cultural approach that it has been sung and valued by Mormons and Gentiles alike.

It is certainly a song of the American West. This is apparent in several ways. In the first place, it comes out of a uniquely western community composed of Mormons, Gentiles, cowboys, miners, and ranchers. It uses a vocabulary specific to that community. The melody is relatively sparse and unornamented, a quality which is shared by many older cowboy and western songs. As performed by Sprague, the song fits neatly into the rhythm of a walking horse, an important consideration for those who believe, as I do, that some of the older cowboy songs were adapted to a horse's various gaits. Cowboys sang to each other, of course, but many cowboy singers and reciters of my acquaintance do most of their singing and reciting while travelling from one place to another. Nowadays this can be in a pickup; in the old days it was on horseback.[31]

Whether the action be interpreted as a Mormon outsider being harassed because he danced with all the girls or as a young man half-regretfully returning to the security of the fold after a fling in the outside world or, given the alternative reading of one informant, as a tale of a courtship ending in marriage, the concerns of the song involve the maintenance of a community. In my opinion, this is not as surprising a theme to find in a cowboy song as one might think.

In an essay on western music, Thomas Johnson states that the thematic focus of older western songs is upon "man's relation to nature, and away from society and women."[32] While final confirmation or denial of this hypothesis will have to await careful statistical analysis of a body of song that is commonly agreed upon as being "western" or "cowboy," I would like to comment briefly at this point.

The basic theme of cowboy songs as I know them strikes me as involving the individual, certainly, but often within the setting of the working community. Little Joe joins the trail drive, makes himself useful, and then dies while doing his part ("Little Joe the Wrangler," Laws B5). Charlie, who won't see his mother when the work's all done this fall, suffers a similar fate and is mourned by his fellows after he distributes his worldly goods among them ("When the Work's All Done this Fall," Laws B3). Sam Bass and Jesse James went up not against nature but against organized society and met their fates ("Sam Bass," Laws E1; "Jesse James," Laws E4). In each case, their betrayer is reviled in the song—certainly an application of social values important for the functioning of a community.

The "Educated Feller" comes into camp and breaks social taboos by talking too much. "The boys" (read "local working community") attempt to punish him by giving him the Zebra Dun, a notorious outlaw horse, to ride. He redeems himself by proving himself a competent rider and therefore a worthy member of a working community ("The Zebra Dun," Laws B16). To me, it is this combination of individual will, action, and responsibility with community concerns that gives much of the older body of cowboy song its special flavor. The individual is certainly important and often must prove himself, but frequently this proof takes place in a community context, rather than in a solitary struggle against nature.

"The Mormon Cowboy" exhibits some of this concern with society, no matter what interpretation one places upon the action. Our narrator, however, does not prove himself in the classic manner, but vows to hightail it for home, adhering to values other than those of his working community. A far cry from High Chin Bob, who roped a mountain lion around the middle and, as a ghost, bragged that

"I took a ragin' dream in tow
And if I never laid him low
I never turned him loose" ("The Glory Trail" by Charles Badger Clark)[33]

This brings us once more to the ambiguity of the song. Not really a Mormon song or a cowboy song to the fullest extent, it rather seems to reflect the specific community from which it comes. In the culturally mixed community of the Globe-El Capitan area, several sets of values and cultural traditions coexisted, albeit uneasily at times. And it is my strong contention that this coexistence—between Blacks and Whites, Mormons and Gentiles, cowboys and miners, ranch and town folk, is reflective of the ethnic, religious, and occupational diversity that has always been a very real part of the American West.

Chapter 7

Leonardo Yañez
and "El Moro de Cumpas"

A Borderlands Horse-Race
Ballad and its Composer

The ballad (or rather, corrido) which is the subject of this essay differs from "The Mormon Cowboy" in several ways. In the first place, it is in Spanish. In addition, while "The Mormon Cowboy" never really entered tradition to any great extent beyond its home community, "El Moro de Cumpas" is one of Sonora's two best-known corridos. The community that danced at the El Capitan schoolhouse and sang the song was a complex one, composed of several religious and occupational groups; the community that sings about el Moro appears to be more unified, especially in a border context where it contrasts with Anglo American society. Finally, "El Moro de Cumpas" is by a known author and celebrates a famous event: a particular horse race in Agua Prieta, Sonora.

The corrido, like the ballad, provides a window into a specific group of people at a certain time and place. In this case, it is the rural and recently urbanized Sonoran community—a community with a its own history, cultural heritage, and sense of values, all of which are reflected in one song—"El Moro de Cumpas."

Horses, Match Races, and *Corridos*[1]

Horses are potent symbols in Mexican culture. Their importance began early in the sixteenth century, when the presence of horses often tipped the military scales in encounters between small numbers of Spanish soldiers and huge native armies. In his eyewitness account of the conquest of Mexico, the old soldier Bernal Díaz del Castillo interrupts his narrative early on to list by gender, color, qualities, and owner every one of the 16 horses that the expedition took with them, remarking that they would have taken more, except that horses were worth their weight in gold at that time in Cuba, the expedition's point of departure.[2]

After the conquest, horses permitted the opening of the northern Mexican uplands to cattle raising. Horses continued to be used militarily against native peoples and, after a while, by the native peoples against Europeans. Coming down the years into the present century, horses were used extensively in the Mexican Revolution, the last major conflict in which mounted cavalry was an important factor in combat. One *corrido* singer from Janos, Chihuahua, went so far as to remark that "the horses were the real heroes of the Revolution."[3]

This importance of the horse—and of the horseman—is expressed over and over in Mexican popular culture. The figure of the *charro*, the gentleman horseman of central Mexico, has become a national symbol. Present-day charros engage in their sport of *charrería*, which is similar to American rodeo in that the competitions are derived from the work of mounted men in the cattle industry. These charros consider themselves to symbolize much that is noble in Mexican character and history.[4]

Photographers' stands at fiestas frequently feature statues of horses as props. Men's restrooms are signed *caballeros*—literally, "horsemen." And horses provide a popular subject for *corridos*. The word *corrido* is usually translated into English as ballad. It is safer to say that the category of corridos includes what in English would be called ballads—narrative poems often put to music and sung in a popular context. The category also includes non-narrative poems glorifying the author's home town or state. Corridos have long been an important form of folk and popular Mexican verse. Old corridos are still being sung, and new ones are constantly being composed. Corrido topics include towns and regions, immigration to the United States, love relationships gone sour, conflict with law enforcement officials, violent deaths and assassinations, folk heroes, natural disasters, accidents, and, of course, horses and horse races.[5] These latter topics are sufficiently popular that several commercially produced cassettes and LP records over the past twenty years have been devoted to corridos about *caballos famosos*, "famous horses." A number of these horse corridos deal with the role of horses in the Revolution.[6] Even more concern the popular rural Mexican sport of match racing.

Especially in the northern cattle raising states of Sonora and Chihuahua, horse racing is a popular weekend and fiesta sport. The races are always *parejeras*, "match races"—one-on-one affairs, often featuring horses from different ranches and communities, each one, in the view of many Mexicans, defending the honor of its particular community. Corrido composer Leonardo Yañez eloquently stated the reasoning behind this preference for match races when he told a reporter: "Mexicans wouldn't run a dozen horses all owned by big syndicates nobody cares about, like the Americans do. The Mexican way is for two men to prove who has the finest."[7]

Match races occur when the owners of one horse challenge the owners of another. Before the race, details such as the length of the course, how the race will be started, and the like, are settled through negotiation between the owners. These negotiations can continue up to the very start of the race; I once waited with over a hundred other people outside Phoenix for a race that never took place because the owners could not agree on its details. Large sums of money are bet on these match races; stories of entire ranches being won and lost as a result of race betting are not uncommon in southern Arizona and northern Sonora.

This economic factor leads to a certain amount of one-upmanship being practiced by both the owners and the riders of the competing horses. During the negotiations and, indeed, up to the start of the race, it is expected that these individuals will attempt to create a situation favorable to their own horses. The canceled race outside Phoenix was apparently a case in point. I have witnessed the rider of one horse getting his mount to refuse the starting gate so that the excitable mare he was running against would get even more frantic than she already was. In the event, she injured herself at the gate and lost the race. Such skullduggery is expected behavior, as I said, and it is not uncommon for owners of the losing horse to complain of cheating on the part of the winners. In fact, most of the prose narratives I have heard about match races either involve cheating of some sort or concentrate on the sums of money that were won or lost at the race.

In the eyes of the corrido composers, however, these aspects of the match races seem to be of little or no importance. The match-race corridos, and there are many, deal with the theme of two strong horses set up against each other, with the strongest or bravest one winning. Such a theme parallels the important corrido theme of the human *valiente* who accomplishes his deeds, faces his enemy, makes a statement of his identity, and meets his fate unmoved.[8] In fact, the horse-race corridos simply substitute horses for humans in the perennially important Mexican theme of two strong individuals, each one brave, each one alone, facing off against each other. This theme is best exemplified in the famous couplet from "Arnulfo":

Que bonito ver dos hombres	How beautiful to see two men
Que se matan, pecho a pecho,	Who kill each other, breast to breast
Cada con pistola en mano	Each with a pistol in his hand
Defendiendo a su derecho.[9]	Defending his right.

The list of popular horse-race corridos in the Arizona/Sonora border area is long and constantly increasing as new ballads are composed. The earliest such corrido I am aware of is "El Merino Mentado," commemorating a race held in the late nineteenth century at Los Reales, a few miles south of Tucson.[10] Although the corrido is no longer sung, I know at least one musician in Tucson who used to sing it in his youth, and several versions of it are on file in the Arizona Folklore Archive at the University of Arizona's Southwest Folklore Center.[11] I compiled a list in 1989 of the Arizona and Sonora horse-race corridos for which I had texts; the list numbered fifteen, with several more that I had heard of but had not yet collected.

Horse-race corridos may be of two kinds. The majority seem to commemorate actual races and often include the place and date of the race, along with the names of the horses and their owners. Some corridos, however, especially those of recent composition, appear to be dramatic works of fiction rather than reports of events that actually took place.

The purposes of this essay are two-fold: to recount the story behind one of the most famous horse-race corridos of all time, "El Moro de Cumpas," and to give a short account of the life and works of the composer of that and several other corridos, the late Leonardo Yañez. First, the race.

The Race Between Relámpago and el Moro

In 1957, Rafael Romero was a successful nightclub owner in the Sonoran town of Agua Prieta, just across the border from Douglas, Arizona. His club, the Copacabana, featured many of the most popular artists of the day, and Romero made frequent trips to Mexico City to hear and book new acts. During the course of these trips, he had become friends with Pedro Infante, the great interpreter of *canciones rancheras*.[12] On one occasion, Infante presented Romero with one of his many *trajes de charro*, the ornate, silver-spangled charro costumes which were—and are—obligatory garb for singers of ranchera songs. It would come in useful, Infante suggested, when Romero wished to take part in the parade on *el Dieciseis de Septiembre* (September 16, Mexican Independence Day) or *el Cinco de Mayo* (May 5, anniversary of a victorious nineteenth-century battle against the French). But one doesn't walk in a parade in charro dress; one rides, and Romero didn't own a horse.

Fortunately he had a friend, Pablo Aguirre, who owned a dairy farm. Aguirre, who was an enthusiastic but unlucky match race fan, had recently purchased a fast but gentle horse named Dr. Joe. So Aguirre loaned Dr. Joe to Romero, and everything was fine, until Aguirre died. Aguirre's widow eventually approached Romero, asking him to buy the horse from her. Her husband had left her cows, she told him, and they gave milk which she could sell. The horse simply consumed feed and showed no profit. Romero agreed, paying for the horse out of jukebox receipts.[13]

This left Rafael Romero owner of a horse with a reputation for speed. Eventually word of this got around and he was challenged by Pedro Frisby of Cumpas, Sonora, a town some 100 miles south of Agua Prieta. Frisby's father, Florencio Frisby, had acquired a fast grey, el Moro, in 1955, in trade for some mules.[14] El Moro (the name means "dapple grey")[15] had acquired a local reputation as a fast runner, and Frisby saw an opportunity to race him in Agua Prieta.

Romero agreed, and the date was set for March 17, 1957. The track was to be Calle 4, at that time an unpaved street in Agua Prieta. The finish line would be by the Club Copacabana. The course was 500

meters long, as were all the races Relámpago was to run. Romero then
sought a rider for his horse (which by then he had renamed
Relámpago, or "Lightning"). He found Trini Ramírez, a well-known
local jockey and horse trainer. According to Ramírez, he requested
Romero to show him the horse before he agreed to ride. When they
got to where Relámpago was, Ramírez got out of the car, walked
around the horse examining it, and got back into the car, saying "Let's
go. This horse will win."[16]

The day of the race arrived, and the level of excitement and betting got intense. Many people had come from Cumpas and elsewhere
for the race, and according to some, a total of almost two million pesos
were bet on the outcome (in a day when eight pesos made a dollar). Just
before the race, the two jockeys walked up and down, *paseando* their
horses in order to let the crowd see them and also to get the horses
excited and ready for the race. While Chindo Valenzuela, jockey of el
Moro, was dressed in street clothes with a bandanna around his head
and rode bareback in the old style, with his knees tucked under a *faja*,
"surcingle," Ramírez wore regular jockey silks and was one of the first
men to race in Agua Prieta on a flat racing saddle.

The word was given to start, and el Moro took the lead. But
about halfway through, Ramírez hit Relámpago with his quirt, and the
Agua Prieta horse finished first with a good lead. Many of the crowd,
especially those who had bet on el Moro, were outraged. According to
Ramírez, when he finally got Relámpago stopped and slid off, he was
surrounded by the usual crowd of supporters and well-wishers, slapping
him on the back and offering him drinks. But he felt someone slipping
something into the waistband of his trousers. He looked down and discovered it to be a large pistol. "What's this?" he asked. The response
came: "*Te andan buscando.*" ("They're looking for you.") Ramírez spent
the next day or so in hiding from angry Moro supporters.

It apparently was not unusual for jockeys to ride armed. Trini
Ramírez and Leonardo Yañez told me of another jockey whose horse
reared and fell on him while in the starting gate. He was accidentally
stabbed in the side with the barrel of his pistol, which he was carrying
under his belt. In addition, his horse stepped on his face in its struggle
to get to its feet. The jockey died.

Given the fact that el Moro was the odds-on favorite, and that
many families and individuals lost huge sums of money betting on him,
and given the tradition of match-race skullduggery that I mentioned
earlier, it is not surprising that supporters of el Moro accused Valenzuela of throwing the race and demanded a rematch. This was duly run,

Two famous horses: El Moro, *right*, and Relámpago, *left*, ridden by Rafael Romero in charro regalia. The "A.P." refers to Agua Prieta. Normally, these photos hang, along with one of the finish of the race, over the cash register in the Café Central. April, 1984, photograph by James Griffith.

The finish line of the great race, Agua Prieta, March 17, 1957. Relámpago is on the right; el Moro on the left. This wild crowd scene was reproduced for the movie *el Moro de Cumpas*. Copied from a photograph in the Romero family's collection.

with different riders for both horses, and el Moro won. According to Ralph Romero Jr., this was because a drunken backer of el Moro walked onto the track while the race was in progress and hit Relámpago with a liquor bottle. Another rematch was run, with Relámpago the winner.[17] Trini Ramírez explained that el Moro, being the smaller horse, simply couldn't keep up over the 500 meter course, although he started off very well indeed.

Both horses went on to distinguished careers. El Moro became a great celebrity, being taken around the region to fund-raising events for worthy causes, where his owners would allow the public to be photographed with him for a sum of money. Such a photograph, taken in the mining town of Cananea, Sonora, on November 20, 1966, is in the collection of the Arizona Folklore Archives. In the center stands el Moro. To his left, with his hand resting on the horse's back, is the *presidente municipal*, or mayor of Cananea. To the horse's right stands his trainer, Gilberto Martinez. Flanking the group are two local ranchers. The presidente appears to be gaining merit by having his photograph taken with the horse, the ranchers through association with the presidente. The trainer looks perfectly assured of his status; el Moro appears to be asleep.

When el Moro finally died in Cumpas, according to one woman who was there, the entire town turned out. His body was carried in procession around town in a flat-bed truck, accompanied by a band. She remembers crying when she saw his beautiful white tail hanging over the end of the truck and dragging in the dirt of the road.

Relámpago ran several other races, one of which has achieved a certain amount of fame in its own right. In 1959, Emilio Pinedo, a resident of Pirtleville, Arizona, and owner of a fast horse named Chiltepín, after the fiery local wild chile, challenged Relámpago. Romero accepted the challenge, but a problem arose when U.S. authorities would not permit Relámpago to cross the border because of hoof-and-mouth disease regulations. Pinedo was reluctant to race in Mexico, for fear that Chiltepín would not be permitted to return across the border for the same reason. According to Rafael Romero Jr., the final solution was suggested by the head of U.S. Customs in Douglas. The race was held along the border fence, with each horse running in its own country. This race, like all of Relámpago's races, was held as a benefit. In this case, the Lions Clubs of Douglas and Agua Prieta charged admission and sold food and drinks at the event.[18] Relámpago was the winner.

Following that, the aging Relámpago was put out to pasture. Rafael Romero Jr., a teenager at the time, was allowed to keep him in Agua Prieta and care for him. A Catholic priest who had already built one church on the proceeds of Relámpago's previous races was transferred to a tiny chapel which he wanted to expand into a church building. In order to raise the needed funds, he suggested that the two old horses be run once more in a *carrera de recuerdo* (literally, a "race of memory"). Both parties agreed, and Ralph Jr. started training the elderly Relámpago. El Moro's backers managed to get Mr. Romero, Senior, to agree to having a three-year-old substituted for their horse. Ralph Jr. gave up all hope but continued to train Relámpago anyway. When the race started (apparently after some successful maneuvering for advantage on the part of the Cumpas contingent), Ralph simply walked away from certain defeat and loss of family honor, only to hear the crowd going wild as the 32-year-old Relámpago won the race! This took place on April 10, 1966.

This was the last race either horse ran. When Relámpago died, Rafael Romero had his head stuffed and mounted. When I visited Sr. Romero at his home in Agua Prieta in 1984, the horse's head hung in the main room, over the TV set and next to the gun rack.

Leonardo Yañez, "el Nano," Compositor del Corrido

Leonardo Yañez Romo was born in Barrio la Campana, in the copper mining town of Cananea, Sonora, on April 2, 1907. His family soon moved to Nacozari de García, another mining town, where he grew up. He cut short his schooling to work for a living. He worked as a woodcutter and in the mines but his eyesight started failing, so he turned to music. He had the good fortune to study under Don Silvestre Rodríguez of Nacozari, one of Sonora's foremost twentieth-century songwriters and composers, and with an excellent teacher and violin player named Ángel Urquijo. Yañez became a professional musician and moved with his wife and family to Agua Prieta in 1943. He played with a number of musical groups, including mariachis, tropical-style bands, and orchestras. By the mid-1950s he was playing in the house mariachi at the Club Copacabana. He had already composed corridos, including one—"El Guante"—about a horse race, and when the first race between Relámpago and el Moro was scheduled, Yañez asked permission of his employer, Rafael Romero, to commemorate the race

Leonardo Yañez, "el Nano," photographed outside his house in Douglas, Arizona, April 4, 1984. Photograph by James Griffith.

with a corrido. Permission being granted, he first composed the preliminary, descriptinve verses before the race took place and then posted observers at the start and midway down the course, while he himself stood by the finish line.[19] This is the corrido as he wrote it:

El diecisiete de Marzo
a la ciudad de Agua Prieta
llegó gente de dondequiera,
vinieron a la carrera
de Relámpago y el Moro
dos caballos de primera.

On March 17th
To the city of Agua Prieta
People came from all over,
They came to the race
Of Relámpago and el Moro
Two first-class horses.

El Moro de Pedro Frisby
era del pueblo de Cumpas
muy bonito y muy ligero,
el Relámpago era un zaino
y era caballo de estima
de su amo, Rafael Romero.

Pedro Frisby's Moro
Was from the town of Cumpas
Very good-looking and very fast,
Relámpago was a chestnut
And he was the favorite horse
Of his owner, Rafael Romero.

Cuando paseaban al Moro
se miraba tan bonito
y empesaron a postar,
toda la gente decia
que aquel caballo venía
especialmente a ganar.

When they exercised the Moro
He looked so handsome
That people started to bet.
Everyone said that
That horse had come
Especially to win.

Cheques, billetes, y pesos
le sobraron al de Cumpas
el domingo en la mañana,
por la tarde las apuestas
pasaron de cienmil pesos
en esa Copacabana.

Checks, bills and coins
Were placed on the horse from Cumpas
On Sunday morning,
By afternoon the bets
Exceeded 100,000 pesos
In that Copacabana.

Frank y Jesús Valenzuela
casaron quince mil pesos
con el zaino de Romero,
decía el Puyo Morales
se me hace que con el Moro
nos ganan todo el dinero.

Frank and Jesus Valenzuela
Placed 15,000 pesos
On Romero's chestnut,
Puyo Morales said
"It seems to me that with the Moro
"They're going to win all our money."

Andaba Trini Ramírez
también Chindo Valenzuela

Trini Ramírez and also
Chindo Valenzuela walked along

paseando ya sus caballos,	Exercising their horses,
dos corredores de faja	Two surcingle-style jockeys
dos buscadores de triunfo	Two seekers after triumph
los dos eran buenos gallos.	The two were real sluggers.
por fin dieron el Santiago	At last they started the race
y el Moro salió delante	And el Moro took off ahead
con la intención de ganar,	Intending to win,
Ramírez le tupo al zaino	Ramírez quirted the chestnut
y arriba de media taste	And halfway down the track
dejaba el Moro pa'atras.	He left the Moro behind.
Leonardo Yáñez el Nano	Leonardo Yáñez "el Nano"
compositor del corrido	Composer of the ballad
a todos pide disculpas,	Begs pardon of everyone,
aquí se acabaron dudas	There is no doubt that
ganó el zaino de Agua Prieta	The chestnut from Agua Prieta won
y perdió el Moro de Cumpas.	And the Moro from Cumpas lost.

This is "El Moro de Cumpas" as it is usually sung and as its composer wrote it down for the Southwest Folklore Center.[20] There is another verse, however, composed as part of the original corrido, which is usually left out of performances. Yáñez explained that this was because only eight verses fit comfortably on a 45 RPM single—the usual recording of the 1950s. The verse was intended to go after the fourth verse, which describes the betting that preceded the race. The words are given here, courtesy of Leonardo Yáñez.[21]

Aprovecharon la apuesta	The betting was taken advantage of
rancheros y ganaderos,	By ranchers and cattlemen,
obreros y campesinos,	Workers and peasants,
cantineros y meseros,	Bartenders and waiters,
amigos y visitantes	Friends and visitors
de pueblos circunvecinos.	From neighboring towns.

Although the verse is not necessary to the action, it seems to accurately mirror the excitement of the race day, when people from all over the region came into Agua Prieta for the great event.

"El Moro de Cumpas" became—and remains—incredibly popular. Apparently the excitement of the event, along with the quality of the song itself, combined to make "El Moro" the corrido that everyone simply *had* to learn. In fact, one corrido singer living at the time in Janos, Chihuahua, over a hundred miles east of Agua Prieta, told me that he *hadn't* learned the song simply because "it was too popular— everyone was singing it."[22] On a national level, it was recorded by most famous *norteño* groups, several mariachis, and was even made into a movie.[23] Today, over 35 years after the race, I don't know a single traditional Mexican singer in Arizona or Sonora who can't come up with a version of the corrido on request.

It is through the medium of records that this and other modern corridos are disseminated. Singers of my acquaintance tend to learn their songs from multiple playings of recordings, thus lessening the possibilities for the variations that have been for long such an important mark of folk material.[24] Those variations that do exist in different performances of "El Moro de Cumpas" seem to be learned from the recordings and seem to have resulted from misunderstandings or misrememberings on the part of the recording artists of names or obscure expressions used by the composer.

Thus "Pedro Frisby" of the second verse becomes "Pedro Fimbres" (surely more Mexican sounding for those not acquainted with the Frisby family), or even "Pedro Piter." "Dos corredores de faja" in verse 6 becomes "dos corredores de fama," (two famous jockeys). The other standard variations in the text are of the same sort—"Cuyo Morales" for "Puyo Morales," and "dieron la salida" for "dieron el Santiago." As was the case with "The Mormon Cowboy," "El Moro de Cumpas" seems to have lost some of its localism and idiosyncratic language when it moved beyond its immediate community.

A few details in the text need comment. According to Leonardo Yañez, the total bets placed were more like 1.8 million than 100,000 pesos. (Remember the peso at this time was eight to the dollar.) However, Agua Prietans were concerned that if Yañez publicized the full amount of the wagers, federal tax collectors would descend upon the city, with possibly disastrous results. So Yañez mentioned a far lower sum of money in his corrido.

Betting on the race has become legendary in Agua Prieta. Bets started at a few hundred pesos and then escalated. I have been told of one man who lost 200 head of cattle and a fairly large ranch. Others lost smaller ranches. Many people are described as having lost their cars or trucks and having had to get rides home.[25]

In describing the two jockeys, Yañez calls them both "corredores de faja," even though only Valenzuela used the faja, or "surcingle," in that particular race. The epithet seems to suggest both bravery and traditionality. The phrase "buenos gallos" literally means "good fighting cocks," and implies both aggressiveness and persistence. I have used the language of the boxing ring to give the same flavor in English.

Yañez uses the phrase "dieron el Santiago"—"they gave the Santiago"—to describe the beginning of the race. According to Yañez, this phrase is occasionally used for this purpose. It has deep roots in Spanish and Mexican culture, however. Santiago de Compostela—St. James the Greater—is the patron saint of Spain. His miraculous appearance riding on a white horse during battles between the Moors and the Christians in the Middle Ages led to his being adopted as the patron of the militant expansion of Spanish Christianity. That is probably why the scallop shell, his symbol, appears so often in the mission architecture of northern New Spain.[26] "Santiago" was also the battle cry of imperial Spain. In his eyewitness account of the conquest of Mexico, Bernal Díaz often indicates the beginning of a battle by saying "Our leader gave the Santiago." The use of this battle cry to describe the start of a horse race seems to imply a certain value and importance attached to the race in Mexican culture.

Yañez names himself in the final verse of the corrido. This was because he had previously composed a horse-race corrido, "El Guante," which was claimed by others. This time, he told me, he wished to take no chances. Finally, when asked why he begged pardon in the last verse, Yañez responded that he had told all his friends to bet on the favorite—el Moro—the losing horse!

Years later, after both horses died, Yañez composed another corrido:

El Final de Dos Caballos	*The Last of Two Horses*
Siento un grande tristeza	I feel a great sorrow
al cantar la despedida	Upon singing the farewell
que me tortura la mente,	Which tortures my mind,
al morir los dos caballos	Upon the death of the two horses
de aquella grande carrera	Of that great race
que emocionó a tanta gente	Which stirred so many people.
Esa carrera lucida	That brilliant race
yo la tengo bien presente	I have very much with me
parece que estoy oyendo,	It's as though I am hearing

los gritos de aquel gente	The cries of those people
y el tropel de los caballos	And the hoofbeats of the horses
cuando venían corriendo.	As they ran past.
Relámpago de Agua Prieta	Relámpago of Agua Prieta
famoso Moro de Cumpas	Famous Moro de Cumpas
cuantos recuerdos dejaron,	How many memories they left,
el diecisiete de Marzo	The seventeenth of March
del año Cincuenta y Siete	Of the year 'fifty seven.
que el campeonato jugaron.	When they played the championship.
Los dos caballos corrieron	The two horses ran
en muchas festividades	In many celebrations
sacrificando energias	Sacrificing energies
prestando nobles servicios	Lending noble services
en mejoras de sus pueblos	For the betterment of their towns
y en ayudas colectivas.	And in collective assistance.
Ya todo el mundo sabía	Everyone already knew
que el final de esos caballos	That the end of these horses
ya no se hayaba muy lejos,	Was not far off,
si uno fue mejor que el otro	If one had been better than the other
al llegar a sus destinos	Upon reaching their destinies
allí quedaban parejos.	There they were equal.
Por fin el Moro de Cumpas	At last the Moro de Cumpas
murió en su pueblo bendito	Died in his blessed town
un ventidos de Febrero,	On one February 22nd,
y en la ciudad de Agua Prieta	And in the city of Agua Prieta
bajo atención de doctores	Under the care of doctors
murió el zaino de Romero.	Romero's chestnut died.
Como si fueran humanos	As if they were human
están en sus sepulturas	They are in their tombs
ya despedidos del mundo,	Parted now from the world,
sus perchas están vacias	Their stalls are empty
y en sus pueblos los recuerdan	And in their towns they are remembered
con sentimiento profundo.	With deep sentiment.
Adiós caballos famosos	Farewell famous horses
adiós alegres palenques	Farewell joyful cockpits
adiós carrera lucida,	Farewell brilliant race,
aquí terminan los versos	Here end the verses

| que quedan como recuerdos | Which remain as remembrances |
| de esa triste despedida. | Of that sad parting. |

In this corrido Yañez emphasizes both horses equally, recalling the excitement of that day in 1957. I have often heard people who were at the race say that there will never be another such event. There was something magical about the day. El Moro was a true favorite of the area around Cumpas, and many of his supporters had come to Agua Prieta to see him win. Feelings ran high, and several fights were remembered as having taken place, although both Yañez and Ramírez assured me that nobody got killed. Yañez acknowledges these still-smoldering feelings of rivalry by emphasizing that, even though one horse may have outrun the other in life, they both arrived at the same final destination—death, where they were equals.

He emphasizes his view of the horses as heroic figures, defending the honor of their communities. In my first interview with him, he compared el Moro to a general who dies in defense of his cause. Such a hero is just as worthy of honor as is the winning general, he said. Yañez also uses once again the figure of the cockfight to symbolize the race. In his original corrido, he compares the jockeys to fighting cocks; in the present one he refers to the race track itself as a *palenque*, or "cockpit."

His descriptions are accurate. Just as he stationed friends at different spots along the race course in 1957, he is careful to note that Relámpago died "under the attention of doctors." (In fact, the horse was put down as it was suffering from cancer.)

These were not the only horse-race corridos Yañez composed. Before writing "El Moro de Cumpas" he had written "El Guante," about a race that had taken place in Esqueda, Sonora, south of Agua Prieta. Later corridos commemorated other races: he celebrated the victory of Tío Juan, an Agua Prieta horse, over el Indio from Mexicali, Baja California. He also wrote the "Corrido de Bacerac," describing a race in that Sonoran town. In the late 1980s, he was commissioned to write a corrido about yet another race; I have not been able to obtain a copy of this song.[27]

El Nano's horse-race corridos seem to follow a consistent pattern. The two horses are named, often with something nice to say about the town each one came from. The scene is set, introducing at least some of the owners and riders by name, along with perhaps a major bettor or two. Attention is consistently paid to the matter of betting; it is shown that people are getting excited about the race. The race starts; it is interesting that the word "Santiago" is used in "El Corrido de Bacerac" as well as in "El Moro de Cumpas." A line or two describes the race; and then there is usually a verse ending the song and affirming the winner. This is essentially the pattern established by "El Guante" and "El Moro de Cumpas;" it apparently was sufficiently successful that Yañez was content to follow it in his other horse-race corridos.

One other thing should be said about this body of horse-race corridos: they are eminently singable. The word usage is elegant but not stilted, the lines flow well, and the melodies are exciting. It is no accident that four out of five of them have been recorded and at least three are still alive in local singing tradition.

In addition to the horse-race songs, Yañez composed corridos on several other subjects. "El Corrido de Fronteras" was commissioned by the family of a man who was killed in a fight in Fronteras, Sonora. "El Mojado Mafioso" tells of a man forced by circumstances to support his family by crime. "La Kaguama [*sic*] Topillera" tells of a sea turtle (a *caguama* in Spanish) who wandered through Sonora before returning to the ocean. "La Cárcel de Agua Prieta" tells of a bloody incident in the Agua Prieta jail, and "El Asesinato de Villa" presents Yañez' views on the death of the Mexican revolutionary figure Pancho Villa, some sixty years after the fact. "El Túnel de Agua Prieta" tells of the discovery of the tunnel connecting Douglas and Agua Prieta that was mentioned in the introduction to this book. In this corrido, Yañez alludes to the suspected drug-related purpose of the tunnel by saying that it was designed to carry merchandise. When asked why he had not been more specific, he indicated that he had to live in the same town with the men who had built the tunnel and felt it was safer to be discreet.

Yañez also wrote political corridos. The "Corrido Panista" celebrates Mexico's conservative opposition party, *el Partido de Acción Nacional*, or PAN. Yañez' son, Leonardo Yañez Vargas, a member of PAN, served as *presidente municipal* of Agua Prieta in the 1980s. Finally, his "Arriba Lopez Portillo" describes what Yañez perceived as being wrong with Mexico when it was written in 1976. It was recorded on a 45 RPM disc by Gilberto Valenzuela, the famous Sonoran *ranchera* singer. When President Lopez Portillo visited Agua Prieta, Yañez sang the song to him and presented him with a copy of the record.

Several of Yañez' corridos have been recorded.[28] "El Moro de Cumpas" is by far the most popular of these, having been recorded by such top names as Los Alegres de Teran, Los Donneños, Gilberto

Valenzuela, and many others. "El Final de dos Caballos," "El Guante," and "El Tío Juan" have also appeared on record, as has, more recently, "El Mojado Mafioso."

More important than their existence on records is the songs' existence in the repertoires of regional musicians. I can say from experience that almost everyone in Arizona and Sonora who sings any corridos at all knows "El Moro de Cumpas." "El Tío Juan" is also popular, and I have found "El Guante" in a few repertoires.

Leonardo Yañez remained a well-known figure in the musical world of the Arizona-Sonora border. A Douglas, Arizona, resident since at least 1982, he taught music classes in Agua Prieta's Secondary School #8 from 1978 until his retirement around 1990. A few honors came his way: he was awarded a plaque in 1984 at a ceremony at Coronado National Memorial for his contributions to the regional culture and received a "Copper Letter" from the City of Tucson in the same year. In 1990 he won the annual corrido contest at the Tucson Meet Yourself festival with his "Corrido del Túnel." Occasional features were written about him in Sonoran newspapers. He died in Douglas on March 6, 1993. The 1993 annual corridos contest at the Tucson Meet Yourself festival was dedicated to him, and several of his relatives participated in his memory. In March 1995, a bust of Sr. Yañez was erected in Agua Prieta near the finish line of the famous race.

In Conclusion

The two horses, their owners, and their poet are all dead. In a few years there will be nobody left who remembers that exciting day in 1957 when people from all over northern Sonora came to Agua Prieta to see el Moro race against Relámpago. What remains is a very popular corrido which will probably be sung by amateur and professional musicians in Sonora and Arizona for decades to come. A larger body of songs by "el Nano" have been recorded and therefore stand a chance of being sung for a while at least.

The other thing remaining, of course, is the culture that allowed both race and song to take the form that they have taken. It should be clear by now that the whole match race-and-corrido complex permits the expression of some strongly held values in Mexican culture. These include the importance of the horse, the importance of the individual, and the importance of bravery and stamina. It should also be evident from the texts I have quoted that there are two bodies of verbal expression concerning match races, at least in this region. One is formal, expressed in verses, and concentrates on the heroic aspects of the contest. The other is informal, in prose, and frequently concentrates on the economic aspects of the race and on how the owners and riders of the different horses attempted to turn an even contest into a sure thing. A larger study of these divergent oral traditions is in the planning stages. For the moment, it is enough to have concentrated on one race, two horses, and the poet who celebrated them.

Appendix A

Leonardo Yañez's Other Horse-Race Corridos

El Corrido del Guante	*The Corrido of El Guante*
Prepárense compañeros y afinen bien su guitarra para cantar un corrido a hora que andamos de farra.	Get ready, companions And tune your guitar well To sing a corrido While we go on a spree.
Un venticuatro de junio bonito pueblo de Esqueda dónde dos caballos finos jugaron una carrera.	One June 24th In the pretty village of Esqueda Where two fine horses Ran a race.
Al del rancho del vigía le decían "el Membrillo" como era bueno y ligero a todos los tenía engridos.	The one from the Vigia ranch They called "el Membrillo;" Because he was good and swift Everyone was fond of him.
El otro era de Cuchuta y le decían el Guante que tambien entre los buenos le gustaba andar delante.	The other was from Cuchuta And they called him "el Guante" Who also among the good ones He liked to take the lead.
Toda la gente decía que el guante estaba perdido	All the people said That el Guante would lose

por que sobraba dinero
a las patas del Membrillo.

Les gritaba Ramón Reyes
como buen conocedor
si la carrera se pierde
va a ser por el corredor.

Ranulfo y Juárez jugaron
vacas y mucho dinero
Donaldo y Lolo García
jugaron hasta el sombrero.

Dijo Jesús Valenzuela
cuando se llegó la hora
si mi caballo no gana
lo mando a la empacadora.

Se vinieron los caballos
los dos corriendo bastante
pero al llegar al cabresto
le salió delante el guante

El corredor Jesús Lara
en todo fue superado
dejó perder al Membrillo
y ganó el Guante mentado.

Adios Guante ya ganaste
y no te quieras volar
por que si das la revancha
te puedes quedar atrás.

Este corrido es compuesto
basado en la carrera
y lo dedico con gusto
al pueblo alegre de Esqueda.

El Tío Juan

Voy a cantar un corrido
de dos caballos ligeros

Because so much more money
Was bet on Membrillo's feet.

Ramon Reyes shouted to them
As he was a connoisseur
"If the race is lost
It will be the jockey's fault."

Ranulfo and Juarez bet
Cows and a lot of money
Donald and Lolo García
Even bet their hats.

Jesús Valenzuela said
When the hour had arrived
"If my horse doesn't win,
I"ll send him to the meat packers."

The horses shot out
Both running hard
But on arriving at the cabresto
El Guante took the lead.

The jockey Jesus Lara
Was surpassed in everything
He allowed Membrillo to lose
And the noted Guante beat him.

Farewell Guante, now you have won
And don't get too proud
Because if you grant a return match,
You may be the loser.

This corrido is composed
Based on the race
And I dedicate it with pleasure
To the happy town of Esqueda.

El Tío Juan

I'm going to sing a corrido
About two swift horses

de fama internacional;
un prieto de Mejicali
que le decían el Indio
y un alazán de Agua Prieta
que le llamaban Tío Juan.

Of international fame;
A black from Mexicali
That they called "el Indio"
And a sorrel from Agua Prieta
That they called Tío Juan.

Desde Baja California
vino el Indio hasta Sonora
a correr con el Tío Juan.
y al presentarse le dijo
seguro estoy de ganarte
y el polvo que yo levante
te lo tendrás que tragar.

All the way from Baja California
El Indio came to Sonora
To run against Tío Juan.
And on introducing himself said to him
"I'm sure of beating you
And the dust I raise
You will have to swallow."

Elmer Escarcega andaba
de interventor del contrato
de la apuesta principal;
que nadie quiso taparlo
por que le tuvieron miedo
al Indio esa es la verdad.

Elmer Escarcega acted
creator of the contract
Of the principal bet;
Nobody wanted to cover it
Because they were scared of
El Indio; that's the truth.

Por fin llegó aquel momento
y las puertas de los chutis
se abrieron de par en par;
se vinieron los caballos
casi vienen volando
y el Indio corrió tragando
el polvo que hizo el Tío Juan.

At last that moment arrived
And the gates of the chutes
Opened widely;
The horses started out
They almost came flying
And el Indio ran swallowing
The dust raised by Tío Juan.

Hipódromo Club de Leones
de ti estoy despidiendo
por que el Indio ya se va;
y se despide muy triste
al ver que se ha equivocado
siendo el Tío Juan tan chaparro
y no le pudo ganar.

Lions' Club racetrack,
I'm bidding you farewell
Because el Indio is already leaving;
And he bids farewell very sadly
Upon seeing that he has made a mistake
Tío Juan being so small
And he couldn't beat him.

Vuela vuela palomita
con rumbo hacía Mexicali
y cuentales la verdad;
dile a Indalecio Martínez
que el Tío Juan le da el desquite
a la costumbre de ganar.

Fly, fly, little dove
Over towards Mexicali
And tell them the truth;
Tell Indalecio Martinez
That Tío Juan will give him a return match
In the tradition of winning.

El Corrido de Bacerac

En esas fiestas de Agosto
de Bacerac tan lucidas
año por año la gente
festeja con alegría
y por patrona el pueblo
tienen la virgen María.

A Bacerac yo le canto
con realidad verdadera
ahí se goza deveras
por que la gente es sincera
dónde se hizo este corrido
basado en una carrera.

Andaba Higinio Olivares
buscando sayo y no hallaba,
quería ganar la carrera
por eso se preocupaba
por que traía un caballo
de Casas Grandes Chihuahua.

Le decían el Traguito
y era un potrillo ejemplar,
trecientos cincuenta metros
fue la carrera en total
y corrió con el Talache
que era campeón regional.

José Rascón hizo el trato
firmando Higinio Olivares
pusieron las condiciones
para jugar mas legales
y entraron en las apuestas
Chichi Loreto y Gonzales.

Valencia les dió Santiago
y resumbaron las varas,
salió delante el Talache

The Corrido of Bacerac

In these fiestas of August
So brilliant in Bacerac
Every year the people
Celebrate with joy,
And for the patroness of the town
They have the Virgin Mary.

To Bacerac I sing
With true reality.
There one really enjoys oneself
Because the people are sincere,
Where this corrido was made
Based on a horse race.

Hijinio Olivares went along
Looking for a rival and not finding one,
He wanted to win the race
That's why he was worried
Because he had brought a horse
From Casas Grandes, Chihuahua.

They called him "el Traguito"
And he was a fine young horse,
Three hundred fifty meters
Was the race course in all
And he ran against "el Talache"
Who was the regional champion.

José Rascón made the contract
Signing it, Higinio Olivares
They placed the conditions
In order to gamble more fairly
And Chichi Loreto and Gonzales
Started betting.

Valencia gave them the "Santiago"
And the whips resounded,
El Talache started off ahead

pero luego se quedaba	But he lagged later on
y le ganó con dos cuerpos	And el Traguito of Chihuahua
el Traguito de Chihuahua.	Won by two lengths.

Appendix B

*List of Compositions by Leonardo
Yañez in the Arizona Folklore Archives*

"Arriba Lopez Portillo"
"Corrido Panista"
"El Asesinato de Villa"
"El Corrido de Bacerac"
"El Corrido de Fronteras"
"El Corrido del Guante"
"El Final de Dos Caballos"
"El Mojado Mafioso"
"El Moro de Cumpas"
"El Tío Juan"
"El Túnel de Agua Prieta"
"Gracias Mil Veces Gracias"
"La Cárcel de Agua Prieta"
"La Kaguama Topillera"
"Morena de Ojos Traidores"
"Navidad Mensajera"
"No Me Hagas Menos"
"Para Hacerme Sufrir"
"Puebla de Esqueda"
"Una Canción a Mi Madre"
"Yo le Canto Gustoso a Cananea"

These twenty-one songs and corridos represent only a small part of Yañez' output, which his obituary estimated at over one hundred compositions.

Mission San Xavier del Bac from the south. The scallop shell of Santiago over the window, the *estípites*, and the details of the upper level can clearly be seen. The snow on the trees and bushes is an occasionally added touch. February, 1987, photograph by James Griffith.

Chapter 8

Baroque Principles of Organization in Contemporary Mexican American Arizona[1]

This final essay also deals with one of the cultural components of the region—Mexican American culture. Unlike the preceding chapter, however, it focuses on a much broader issue: the aesthetic ideas that seem to underlie and inform much of what is produced by that culture. I have often been struck by what I perceive as strong cultural continuities over time in the Pimería Alta.

Three centuries after Father Eusebio Francisco Kino introduced wheat and beef into the region, those foods remain the staples of our traditional diet. Over 200 years after Tucson was founded as a Spanish cavalry presidio, or fort, Tucsonans are concerned lest the federal government lessen its commitment to Davis-Monthan Air Force Base. Mining and over-promotion of natural resources have likewise been important economic activities in southern Arizona for more than two centuries. And, as I shall try to show in this essay, the ideas of how elements are assembled into a whole which were dramatically expressed in the architectural decoration of the eighteenth-century mission church of San Xavier del Bac still live as active principles within the local Mexican American community.

San Xavier del Bac

The eighteenth-century mission church of San Xavier del Bac stands some twelve miles south of Tucson, Arizona, on the San Xavier District of the Tohono O'odham Reservation.[2] Finished in 1797, it is the most nearly complete Spanish colonial baroque architectural ensemble in the continental United States.

Begun around 1778 under the direction of Father Juan Bautista Velderrain, O.F.M., the church was completed by his successor, Father Juan Bautista Llorenz, O.F.M., after Velderrain's death.[3] The church is remarkable for its state of preservation: almost every statue and mural painting that it contained at the time of its dedication is still in place, albeit in slightly deteriorated condition. Since February, 1992, an international team of expert conservators from Italy and Turkey have been working to stabilize and clean the murals and statues. It is hoped that the project will be finished by 1997, the 200th anniversary of the church's completion.[4]

Like so many Mexican churches of its period, San Xavier del Bac is a cruciform building with a dome over the crossing and two bell towers flanking the facade. In the case of San Xavier, one of the bell towers remains unfinished, as do other details inside and out. The exterior of the church is covered with lime plaster; this whitish color is interrupted by the light brown of the elaborately carved plaster portal. This portal is organized in three stories, each level consisting of one or more sets of columns flanking a central opening or sculptural arrangement. There are two columns on each side of the lower two stories and one column on each side of the upper level. The columns themselves are of the type called *estípites*, popular in most of colonial New Spain during the eighteenth century. These estípites are elaborate combinations of shapes and appear intended not so much to hold up the next level of architecture but to add structure, complexity, and motion to the facade.

Between the pairs of estípites on either side of the two lower levels of the facade are niches containing saints' statues. The third level is taken up with low-relief sculpture including an emblem of the Franciscan order, the monograms of Jesus and the Virgin Mary, wheat stalks and grape vines, and the two lions which normally support the Spanish coat of arms.

The whole portal was at one time painted in brilliant colors. It is rich in texture, detail, and imagery. Looking at it, one gets the impression of a fascination with complexity, almost for its own sake. Here nothing is simple. Lintels move in and out as they progress from side to side. Complex lines and low relief sculpture serve to catch constantly changing shadows as the sun moves across the sky. Sharp angles cause the eye of the observer to shoot off into space. The whole ensemble clamors for attention, now as a whole, now as a mass of independent details.

The interior of the church is filled with even more intense color and motion. Angels flutter over the main altar and on the three brick and plaster *retablos* (altarpieces) that soar to roof level. These retablos are organized in much the same way as the portal, with multiple levels supported by estípite columns, and saints images between the estípites. The retablo over the main altar is covered with gold and silver leaf, while all the retablos are painted in rich, brilliant colors.

The rest of the church interior is given over to murals. Scenes from the life of Christ and the Virgin are painted in both side chapels and along the nave. Many of the murals have painted frames around them; a few appear to be suspended by painted ribbons from painted scrollwork. Some of the plaster is painted to resemble ceramic tiles, other parts to resemble veined marble. Doors are painted on blank walls to balance actual doors opposite them. The entire interior exudes richness, drama, motion, and a certain ambiguity or sense of illusion. These characteristics tie San Xavier del Bac solidly into the baroque style of eighteenth-century colonial Mexico, relating it to hundreds of its contemporary churches miles to the south.

Baroque Architecture in New Spain

Because it was built on the extreme northwestern frontier of New Spain, San Xavier is relatively small in size and conservative in some of its details. However, it is just as solidly within the eighteenth-century Mexican baroque style as are such larger, richer, better-known examples as Santa Prisca y San Sebastián in Taxco, Guerrero,[5] or San Francisco Xavier (now the Museo Nacional del Virreinato) in Tepotzotlán, Mexico.[6] The best way to understand San Xavier is as an example of its style—the eighteenth-century baroque architecture of New Spain.

The retablo mayor of mission San Xavier del Bac in 1994. God the Father is at the top center, with Our Lady of the Immaculate Conception immediately below, and then St. Francis Xavier. In the spring of 1995, the upper half of the retablo was cleaned by an international conservation team, revealing that the background surfaces, which have been black for over a century, are actually silver leaf, adding greatly to the richness of the entire ensemble. Completion of the entire retablo is planned for spring, 1996. Photograph by Helga Teiwes, courtesy of the Paronato San Xavier.

The outstanding characteristic of the Mexican baroque style of architecture is that it is basically a style of applied decoration. While the manipulation of space is an important, if not vital, aspect of much European baroque architecture, most Mexican baroque buildings are simple blocks with a greater or lesser degree of plastic, decorative detail added to them. In the case of churches, the decoration (and it is often overwhelming in its impact) is usually added on to a building much like San Xavier: cruciform, with a dome at the crossing or over the main altar and one or two towers flanking the portal.

Much excellent research and writing has been done on Mexican baroque architectural decoration. Typologies and even chronologies have been suggested, the most effective of which are based on the shape of the columns that play such an important role in the portals and in the retablos that provide the focus of so much of the baroque decorative impulse. A convincing sequence moves from the tubular column shaft through the twisted *salamónica* that was dear to the seventeenth century to the broken form of the estípite (as seen on the facade of San Xavier) and beyond to no columns at all but merely a series of vertical decorative zones separating rows of images in niches. This last is referred to by some Mexican art historians as the *anastilético*, or "style-less" style.

However, as Wiesmann has pointed out in *Art and Time in Mexico*,[7] all these styles persisted together in various parts of Mexico right on through to the end of the eighteenth century. For this reason, the sequence, useful though it is as an ordering device, does not really help date the building one is looking at, outside of Mexico City and a few other centers of fashion.

Another way to look at the entire movement of the Mexican baroque in the eighteenth century is to try to isolate the aesthetic rules and preferences that underlie the style—the general principles on which it seems to be assembled. While such a general approach is not likely to be helpful in establishing a chronology, it should serve as a useful descriptive tool for comparative purposes.

One characteristic of the Mexican baroque seems to be a sense of dramatic contrast. This contrast may be between plain and decorated surfaces, as is the case on San Xavier's facade, where the plain bases of the towers flank the elaborately textured portal, or in its interior walls, where large stretches of white walls relieve the intensity of the murals and retablos. It may involve colors, as again at San Xavier where the white of the plain plaster is played off against the brown of the portal.

It may be between light and dark, as has been eloquently described by Kubler in his treatment of New Mexico's colonial churches, with their transverse clerestory windows which allow a shaft of light to illuminate the altar at the end of a relatively dark nave.[8] A more common light/ dark contrast is between brightly lit and deeply shadowed exterior surfaces and involves the use of deeply cut relief to catch the shadows.

Motion seems to be another characteristic related to the baroque style. Paintings often depict action—sometimes violent action. Statues gesticulate and frequently seem to be on the verge of movement. Architectural lines, like the vestigial broken pediment on San Xavier's portal, do not form closed, restful patterns but rather propel the eye of the observer off into space. Indeed, when a framing line such as a lintel is carried from one point to another, it usually moves along a complex path consisting of both vertical and horizontal zigzags and undulations.

The most important aesthetic principle behind the organization of the Mexican baroque decoration is the importance of richness—richness of materials, so that retablos glow with gold leaf. Richness of colors, as in the use of dark red and dark green along with the gold on San Xavier's retablos. Richness of texture, as in San Xavier's facade, which is covered with vines and other devices (which also create a sense of motion and provide shadow-catching projections). And a final kind of richness: a richness of content and meaning. What I mean by this is that baroque ensembles such as the one at San Xavier are themselves composed of a vast number of small, complete, independent details, each one of which possesses meaning of its own and each one of which brings that meaning to the total assemblage.

Sometimes the meanings may be complex and the motives for the inclusion of details may be difficult to isolate. For instance, over the central window of San Xavier's facade is carved a scallop shell. This motif is echoed inside the church, over the main retablo, as well as in niches in the nave and transepts and elsewhere in the church. In his analysis of San Xavier's *retablo mayor*, or "main retablo," Goss states that the scallop shell is associated with the pilgrimage cult of St. James the Greater, Santiago de Compostela.[9] As Santiago Matamoros (St. James the Moor-killer), St. James was the patron of the militant expansion of Spanish Catholicism, and the establishment of San Xavier del Bac as a mission to the O'odham was certainly a part of that expansion. However, Goss also notes that for the peoples of the Mediterranean in classical times, the scallop was associated with the goddess Venus and symbolized the female reproductive organs. By extension, it was also a symbol of birth and regeneration. In a Christian connotation the regeneration can be taken to mean baptism. In early Roman times it became a symbol of resurrection during funeral rites——a meaning it carried over into early Christian art. Many of the pre-Christian meanings of the scallop were revived by the artists of the Renaissance. Finally, the shape of the scallop shell provides a complex, curving, occasionally angular outline, along with a ribbed surface that catches and holds shadows.

Which of these sets of meaning and characteristics explains the presence of the scallop motif at San Xavier? My suggestion would be: a shifting combination of most or all of them, possibly combined with others with which I am not familiar. And one must not neglect the possible importance of precedent—of a design simply being carried over from one building to another without much consideration of its specific meaning.

This very ambiguity and complexity of meaning strikes me as yet another characteristic of the baroque style. Things are not always what they seem to be. I have already mentioned that in San Xavier there are painted doors on the walls opposite real doors, paintings that imitate the effect of glazed ceramic tiles, and painted surfaces that resemble veined marble. This flirtation between reality and unreality is carried a step further by the realistic treatment of the sculptures. Flesh tones are carefully made to imitate real flesh. Draperies that appear to flow like cloth are actually carved from plaster or wood. This sense of ambiguity that comes from illusion as well as from possibly multiple meanings seems to be part of experiencing the baroque art and architecture of New Spain.

One final point should be made concerning the interior of San Xavier del Bac: its arrangement is by no means static. Older photographs prove that a few of the saints have been shifted from one niche to another. But the truly dynamic aspect of the interior operates on a seasonal cycle. In November the patronal statue of Saint Francis Xavier is taken down from its niche in the retablo mayor and placed in a small, portable shelter the size of a telephone booth. This latter is covered with fine-meshed gauze, to which are attached paper flowers. Here the saint stays until December 3, his day in the Roman Catholic calendar, and here he is visited by long files of devotees.

Later on in December, the church is decorated for Christmas. The angels flanking the triumphal arch are given special white gowns, and banners are placed in their hands. Commercial tinsel swags are hung across the nave of the church. A *nacimiento*, or "Christmas crib," made by a local O'odham carver is erected on an altar in the east transept. Other seasons bring other changes, apparently in perfect keeping with the overall aesthetic mood of the church interior.

The underlying aesthetic impulses behind the baroque style of eighteenth-century Mexico, then, appear to be as follows: dramatic contrast, especially between light and dark and plain and decorated surfaces; motion, represented in painting and sculpture and implied in the use of complex curved and broken lines; richness of materials, details, and meaning; and a certain sense of ambiguity. These organizational principles or rules affect the appearance of San Xavier del Bac just as surely as they affect the appearance of countless other churches, great and small, throughout New Spain.

It may well be that their influence extends even farther. Over the course of several years of investigating and documenting the contemporary traditional arts of southern Arizona's Mexican American population, I have come to the conclusion that much of this art follows the principles I have just described for the eighteenth-century baroque of New Spain.

Three Contemporary Mexican American Folk-Art Displays in Southern Arizona

In an attempt to demonstrate this thesis, I shall describe three folk-art ensembles which I documented in southern Arizona in the 1980s. Two are permanent, if changing; one was ephemeral. They are a front yard shrine in South Tucson, a grave marker in the Casa Grande Cemetery, and a low rider display at the Pima County Fairgrounds just east of Tucson.

Front yard shrines are an important feature of the landscape of those parts of Tucson occupied by Mexican Americans and by Yaqui Indians, who have adopted (and adapted) much of traditional Mexican culture. Some of these shrines are fairly simple free-standing *nichos* (niches) containing one or more Catholic holy images. Others, however, can become very complex indeed. For instance, one shrine in a front yard near the Yaqui chapel of San Martín de Porres on South Tucson's 39th Street is constructed in the form of a wishing well. (This phrase was used in describing the shrine by its maker, a Yaqui man who wishes to remain anonymous.) The base of the well (which is in fact a solid platform and not a well at all) is made of cement which has been scored to resemble bricks. The scored bricks are painted alternately green and white. On this base sits a white plaster shell or nicho containing a brilliantly painted statue of the Virgin. The nicho is edged with bits of red, black, and blue plastic tile. A cross surmounts a small projection on top of the nicho, with similar projections flanking it.

The nicho is shaded by a pitched, gabled roof, held up by four green wooden posts. The front edges of the posts are bevelled to create an undulating outline. The fronts of the posts are overlaid with black and white cruciform plastic tiles. The roofline is painted green and white. In the center of the gable stands a white wooden cross, overlaid with colored plastic tiles and bearing a red plastic heart in its center. Immediately below the cross on the gable end is an automobile decal featuring Our Lady of Guadalupe and crossed Mexican and American flags. The boards of the gable itself are painted white and have their ends rounded and adorned with small tiles. The shrine is decorated with tiny, flashing Christmas-tree lights; a string of larger, colored lights has been hung on the eaves of the house directly behind it.

Traditional Mexican American cemeteries often abound with grave markers which have been made or assembled by the families of the deceased.[10] One such marker is in the public cemetery at Casa Grande, in Pinal County, Arizona. When I visited the grave in 1984, it was surrounded by a raised cement curb. Within this curb, lying flat at its west end, was a commercially sand-blasted marker bearing the name and dates of the deceased (a woman) and an image of Our Lady of Guadalupe. Behind this commercial headstone, the head of the curb was backed by a low wall with a nicho at its center. Inside the nicho was a statue of the Virgin flanked by statues of angels and a small vase of artificial flowers and by statues of St. Anthony and St. Martin of Porres. On the rear wall of the nicho, behind the central Virgin, was an architectural setting consisting of two columns flanked by vertical volutes. A depiction of the Last Supper was painted on the low vertical wall below the nicho. Flanking the nicho were a statue of the Sacred Heart of Jesus, another Virgin, a small holy-water stoup, bunches of plastic flowers, a candle, a ceramic planter in the form of a cactus, and another small ceramic planter containing a cactus.

This assemblage is by no means static. The description above is based on slides taken in 1984. A slide dated 1982 shows a different arrangement of objects and reveals that most if not all of the statues

The yard shrine in South Tucson that is described in the text. In addition to the details of the shrine itself, note the string of colored lights on the adjacent house. The colors of the shrine are green and white. 1985 photograph by James Griffith.

had been repainted in the intervening period. When I revisited the grave in 1987, the following changes had taken place.

The headstone had been raised to a slant and propped against the low wall below the nicho, covering the Last Supper painting. Inside the nicho, which had been stripped of its columns and volutes, were a picture and statue of the Holy Child of Atocha, a rosary and a palm leaf cross, statues of St. Anthony and St. Martin de Porres, three angels (one wooden, one ceramic, and one a ceramic candle holder), a small glass votive candle container, two pots of artificial flowers, and a stuffed toy mouse wearing a sailor suit. Outside the nicho and flanking it were eight arrangements of artificial flowers (one made of sea shells) and a ceramic statue of the Holy Child of Prague.

I attended a Low Rider Happening at the Pima County Fair Grounds in 1982. One low rider car display was particularly striking. The car was painted a medium green with heavy metallic flake and some yellow inserts. Painted on the trunk was a scene of a car wash, with several (allegedly identifiable) cars and motorcycles in front. The left side of the car was jacked up off the ground and a mirror had been placed under the car to reveal that most of the metal underside had been chromed or freshly painted. Cheech and Chong appeared in the reflection, painted on the bottom of the gas tank. They were brandishing huge marijuana joints. On the edge of the open, left-hand door was painted a frog in a zoot suit. Miss Piggy languished seductively on the door of the glove compartment.

The interior of the car was upholstered in deep yellow pile. The steering wheel was small, made of chain link, and chromed. A built-in TV set occupied the space between the swivel-mounted bucket seats. Inside the hood, much of the engine was chrome-plated. The underside of the hood was upholstered in the same yellow pile used for the car interior. Beside the car, next to the display panel giving the names of the owner and the various artists who had worked on the project, stood a pedal-operated toy truck, painted and upholstered to match the low rider. It was occupied by a stuffed toy bear.

It should be clear what I am suggesting. The shrine, grave assemblage, and low rider display are all organized along lines which seem strikingly similar to the principles I have suggested for the organization of eighteenth-century Mexican baroque churches such as San Xavier del Bac. Let's run down the list once more. Motion—the implied

The grave marker in the Casa Grande cemetery that is described in the text. January, 1984, photograph by James Griffith.

A low rider car display at the Pima County Fair Grounds, August, 1982. The plaque at the left names the painters and upholsterers who worked on the car; behind it is a miniature pickup truck painted with a green metallic flake to match the car. Photograph by James Griffith.

motion of the car with one corner tilted up, the flashing colored lights, and the undulating supports of the shrine. Contrast—present on all three examples, which have both plain and decorated surfaces. Ambiguity—most evident, perhaps, in the shrine with its references to wishing wells, but present in the other examples too.

But the parallel with the Mexican baroque of the eighteenth century should be most obvious in the area of richness. Richness and elegance of material, with downright opulence in the case of the low rider display. Richness of color in all three examples. And most particularly richness of detail and of various kinds of meaning. The multiple meanings of "wishing well" and "niche with holy statue." The multiplicity of sacred images—Our Lady of Guadalupe; other Virgins, angels, and saints; the Last Supper; and the Sacred Heart of Jesus—brought together on the Casa Grande grave marker, along with such purely secular images as cactus planters. The presence at the grave site of a number of candles, each of which may well represent a distinct prayer on the part of an individual. The images of the car wash, Cheech and Chong, the zoot-suited frog, and Miss Piggy combined in the low rider display, apparently without the need for a thematically unifying device.

Each of these images, all of which come together in each instance to produce a remarkable impact, is a totally independent entity which has its own meaning and existence outside of the ensemble. Miss Piggy enhances the low rider display, but she has nothing to do with low riders in general. It is the same with the repertoire of sacred figures. Each has its own life and identity, but once in the ensemble, they add to the totality of that ensemble. In just the same way, the flowers, scallop shells, angels, and saints bring their own identity and meaning to the totality of the retablo mayor at San Xavier del Bac. They, too, in a sense, are just visiting.

These organizational features are not the only similarities between eighteenth-century baroque architectural decoration and contemporary Mexican American folk art in southern Arizona. One shrine in a Tucson yard is a miniature replica of an eighteenth-century-style baroque church,[11] another incorporates the *salamónicas*, or "twisted columns," which were so popular in seventeenth and eighteenth-century Mexico. Countless wrought-iron crosses in southern Arizona graveyards echo the curvilinear decoration that may be seen on the eighteenth century cross topping San Xavier's central dome.[12] These and other details are predictable results of living in proximity to a baroque church which was built by carriers of an earlier version of one's own cultural tradition. They have reentered the folk repertoire, or possibly have never left it, as discrete motifs. In the language of art history, they and their like can be labelled "neobaroque."

The same label can be used for those styles of Anglo American mainstream architecture that Spanish colonial details. Mission revival and baroque revival buildings have existed in Arizona for almost a hundred years. They seem to represent an attempt on the part of mainstream architects and builders to dramatize Spain's presence in this part of the United States. I have discussed this aspect of the neobaroque in more detail elsewhere.[13]

The three ensembles I have been discussing, however, seem to be a little different. They do not involve images taken from the baroque repertoire but rather seem to be organized along the same principles that the architects, planners, and artists of eighteenth-century New Spain used for their ensembles.[14] What is more, these principles seem to apply to the organization of other aspects of contemporary Mexican American life.

Two Socio-Religious Events

I attended a Yaqui wedding held in the mid-1980s just south of Tucson on the Pascua Yaqui Reservation. Even though the families involved were Yaqui, the events of the wedding ceremony were no different from the traditional Mexican weddings of the region. At the beginning of the ceremony, a group of hired singers and musicians played while the formally attired principals and their retinue marched down the aisle in procession. (The musical group was the one which usually played at Sunday Masses in that particular chapel and consisted of Yaquis, Mexican Americans, and an Anglo. The instrumentation included a violin, two guitars, a *guitarron*, and a *vihuela*.)

Mass started and continued up until the exchange of wedding vows. After that, several special elements were introduced into the ceremony, each one preceded by a statement from the officiating priest identifying the action and explaining its symbolism. These elements included the blessing and exchange of rings, symbolizing the fidelity of the couple to each other; the blessing and placing of the *lazo*, an outsized Rosary with two loops that were placed over the heads of the couple to symbolize their union within the Catholic religion; and the blessing and exchange of coins, symbolizing the couple's prayers for earthly security. Each of these discrete acts involved assistance from others in the wedding party; thus, each act created or strengthened ties between the newly wed couple and other individuals.[15]

At the end of the Mass, the bride, accompanied by her husband, placed her bouquet (which had previously been blessed) before an image of the Virgin. The wedding party then filed out of the church, posed for photographs, and signed the necessary documents before proceeding to a private home where a reception and several specifically Yaqui ceremonies took place.

The musicians played several times during the ceremony. Sometimes they were instructed to play specific songs that reinforced the meaning of the moment or added new layers of meaning, drawing on a combination of traditional Mexican and popular Anglo repertoires. Thus they played the mainstream "Wedding March" as the wedding party entered the church, a special song about wedding rings during the exchange of rings, a hymn to the Virgin during the dedication of the flowers at the end of the ceremony, and "La Marcha Zacatecas" as a recessional.

The other socio-religious event is a pre-Mass procession as it was planned and executed for the annual Tumacacori Fiesta in Tumacacori National Monument in the late 1980s. Tumacacori National Historic Monument is a small tract of land situated between Tucson and Nogales, Arizona, just east of Interstate 19. The Monument's most prominent feature and the reason for its existence is an unfinished nineteenth-century mission church. Tumacacori National Historic Monument's purpose is to preserve that church (along with two nearby ruins) and tell the story of Spanish mission activities in this part of northwestern New Spain.

Each year on the first Sunday in December, the Monument hosts the Tumacacori Fiesta. The event features traditional food, music, crafts, and dance from bearers of Mexican American, Tohono O'odham, and Yaqui cultural traditions. Inasmuch as a Catholic church is the central feature of the Monument, the fiesta always includes Mass at the old mission, often celebrated by the Bishop of Tucson or the Archbishop of Hermosillo, Sonora, Mexico. Before and after Mass there is a procession involving the clergy, the mariachis or other musicians who play for the Mass, various Indian religious musical and dance groups, and the Knights of Columbus.

In this particular instance, the Mexican American leader of el Grupo Cristo Rey, the musical group engaged to play at Mass, was helping with ideas for the organization of the procession. First would go the Yaqui Matachinis, a group of men and boys who perform contradances as an act of devotion to Our Lady of Guadalupe. In Yaqui tradition, they always lead a religious procession, blessing the ground with their music and dance. They (and their musicians playing violins and guitars) would be followed by Yaqui pascolas and a deer dancer, with their musicians which include violinists, a harper, and a flute and drum player. They in turn were to be followed by a group of young Tohono O'odham costumed for the traditional O'odham *chelkona* dance and carrying replicas of birds and clouds over their heads. Their singers, accompanied by a basket drum and rattles, would follow them. A Tohono O'odham pascola dancer, accompanied by his violin and a guitarist, came next. He was to be followed by the clergy and then by the Grupo Cristo Rey. The processional path would be lined by Knights of Columbus, saluting the Bishop with their swords and then bringing up the rear after the musicians had passed.

Each group, except the Knights, would be playing its own music, performing its own dances, and "doing its own thing," without reference to the others. The resulting procession (for things went pretty much as planned) was a sort of audible version of a baroque altarpiece—richly textured, filled with movement, and consisting of a large number of disparate elements, each complete and independent in and of itself, each endowed with its own layers of meaning. Like a high baroque altarpiece, the end result was rather overwhelming.

After Mass, an Anglo American woman approached the leader and told him that the mariachi of which he was a member sounded beautiful, but that it was a pity that "those other groups" were playing at the same time. The leader replied hastily and emphatically to the effect that the point of the whole procession—"our custom," as he put it, was to have everyone playing, singing, and dancing simultaneously.

Conclusions

I feel strongly that connections exist between the aesthetic or organizational principles underlying the twentieth-century objects and events which I have described and those which resulted in the baroque architectural assemblages of eighteenth-century New Spain. While the concept of surviving or revived knowledge serves perfectly well to explain the objects which I have described briefly as neobaroque, I believe that the materials and events I have detailed in this essay must be explained in a different way. To treat these modes of organization as direct survivals from the eighteenth-century baroque art style would require clear evidence of survival and transmission—evidence which may not be available. It seems much more likely that both they and the style of architectural decoration we call baroque are results of a sense of how things should go together that has been a basic part of Mexican culture since at least the eighteenth century.

It may have been in place much longer than that. I have seen sixteenth-century churchyard crosses in central Mexico that seem to be expressing many of the same organizational preferences. The outdoor cross at Atzacoalco in Mexico's Distrito Federal, for instance, is covered with the symbols of the Passion of Christ, carved in low relief. The crown of thorns is draped over the neck of the cross itself, and the image of Christ's face from St. Veronica's Veil is rendered in high relief at the crossing.[16] Both these features tend to anthropomorphize the cross or at least render its status as an object or as a being rather ambiguous. Further ambiguity is provided by gouts of blood which gush from nail holes in the cross.[17] At San Felipe de los Alzates in Michoacan, the Christian crown of thorns in the center of the cross surrounds a flat obsidian disc. This is thought by some scholars to be a survival of the reported Aztec custom of inlaying precious stones into idols in order to give them life.[18]

Such crosses as these, with their densely packed relief sculpture and ambiguous identity as artifact or being, are not alone in suggesting that the organizational preferences usually identified with the baroque style were in place in Mexican art a few decades after the Conquest. Over and over on sixteenth-century architecture there are densely packed portals, arches, and wall paintings which attest to the same set of organizational principles.[19]

And before the century of contact? Superficially it would seem that the masterpiece of Aztec sculpture known as the Great Coatlicue, currently on display in the Museo Nacional de Antropología e Historia in Mexico City, may have resulted from the application of similar principles. In fact, it may turn out that this deeply rooted aspect of Mexican culture, if indeed that is what it is, results from an all-too-familiar convergence between European and Mesoamerican cultural elements.[20] But that is far beyond the scope of this exploratory essay.

What I hope to have accomplished in the above pages is twofold. I have tried to point out, echoing such scholars as Irving Leonard,[21] that the organizational impulse of the baroque goes far beyond the details of a specific art style in a certain time and place—eighteenth-century Mexico. At the same time I have indicated ways in which it seems that the same aesthetic value system that produced the magnificent eighteenth-century churches that have so impressed generations of art historians and others appears to be still at work in what was once the northwest corner of New Spain.

A Few Final Words

What can be said in conclusion to this collection of disparate essays? Perhaps not much needs to be said; each essay stands alone as a treatment of a specific aspect of the rich folklife of the Arizona-Sonora borderlands. However, certain patterns emerge, and perhaps it is worth noting them once more.

In the first place, this is a region of strong continuities. Not only does Mission San Xavier del Bac still stand relatively unchanged since 1797, but also the organizational principles that governed its decoration are still powerful forces in the life of contemporary Mexican Americans in the region, two hundred years after the baroque went out of fashion in mainstream Mexican culture. Many other persistent aspects of regional culture—the making and use of cascarones, respect for the dead, reverence for the San Francisco image in Magdalena, devotion to non-canonical saints—are discussed in these essays.

But continuity does not imply a static existence. Cascarones have been made and used in the Santa Cruz Valley since at least the mid-nineteenth century, but today's cascarones differ from their predecessors in form, use, and meaning. El Tiradito is a part of life in Tucson just as it was in 1893, but its role (along with its appearance and location) has changed considerably. Horse-race corridos have been part of local culture for over a hundred years, but new corridos have replaced the older ones in the repertoires of singers and musicians.

Some of the changes that have taken place relate to the increasing immigration that is still an important regional dynamic. In Arizona, dominant Anglo American society has provided much of the impetus for change: by setting conditions, by wishing to participate in regional culture on its own terms, by reinterpreting items of local culture to fit its understanding and values. In some cases, a new meaning has simply been added to the traditional set; in others, the entire shape of the tradition seems to have been changed by Anglo participation.

Nor are the influences entirely from the north. In Nogales, Sonora, recent arrivals from other parts of Mexico have changed the ways in which people honor the memory of their dead. In the 1850s, the Black Christ statue in Tucson was associated with Our Lord of Esquipulas; today the Guatemalan connection seems forgotten and legends tie it and the Black Christ in Aconchi to Mexico City.

In addition to the realities of immigration, many of the essays reflect in one way or another the fact of the border. The cemeteries of Ambos Nogales illustrate a coming together of traditions from the United States and Mexico. The Magdalena glass paintings are created and sold in Sonora but used to a great extent in the United States. Leonardo Yañez' corridos have been recorded and sung on both sides of the border; one of Relámpago's races actually took place along the border fence.

But the border between the United States and Mexico is not the only cultural dividing line at work in this region. The very real borders between cultures: O'odham, Anglo, and Mexican American, Mormon and Gentile, miner and cowboy—all these lend their dynamics to the local folklife. The chapter on "The Mormon Cowboy," in addition to demonstrating ties to the occupational tradition of cowboy song and the fledgling national recording industry, reveals some of the dynamics between the occupational and religious communities of a part of Gila County that may on the surface look culturally monolithic.

Finally, the binational Pimería Alta cuts across more recent boundaries to remind us once more of the depth of many of our region's continuities. It is fitting that the Pimería be represented in this collection by the Magdalena glass painting, because the devotion to San Francisco is one of the strongest forces that still ties the region together.

Continuity and change, the coming together of cultures: these are the main themes of this collection of essays. Some of the traditions discussed here are strong; others, like "The Mormon Cowboy," seem to be on their way out. All contribute to the special flavor of the Arizona-Sonora border country, tying the region to other parts of the U.S.-Mexico Borderlands while at the same time demonstrating its historical and contemporary uniqueness.

These, then, are some of the themes that have engaged me over the past two decades of working as a folklorist in the Pimería Alta. What has always interested me—what I have been drawn to, often without realizing it—are places where two or more cultures come together. In addition, I am and always have been fascinated by the many ways in which "the more things change, they more they stay the same." The picture I see of this multicultural region is compounded equally of two important dynamics: continuity and adaptive change.

My view is on the whole an optimistic one. Where others might see cultural co-option by the dominant society, I find attempts to cope with alien materials in a new land and make them meaningful. Today's Pimería Alta is being flooded with immigrants from both north and south; I have hopes that at least some aspects of regional culture will survive this onslaught. The drug war and the attitudes it engenders are devastating the borderlands; I feel there is a possibility that some solution will be eventually found. It's not that I wholeheartedly embrace these hopeful predictions; it's simply that they seem more profitable than pessimism as starting points for action.

And much of my time here has been dedicated to that action. As a public folklorist I have lectured and produced educational radio and TV programs, organized and curated exhibitions, and organized an annual folklife festival, all with the aim of easing, however slightly, some of the tensions and misunderstandings that divide people. The essays reproduced here were written, as it were, in my "spare time."

I should make it clear that I did not choose the topics in this book because of any theoretical considerations or interests. I was first drawn to the material—art objects, legends, songs—because they engaged my interest on a very personal and usually aesthetic level. I experienced something, be it a cascarón, a performance of "el Moro de Cumpas," or a story about el Tiradito, and was drawn to learn more about it. After arriving at an understanding of the general shape of the tradition I was learning about, I became curious about the cultural dynamics the tradition seemed to display. "What's going on here?" is as basic a question as "what is this?", and I tried to answer both to the best of my ability. But my first and passionate engagement was always with the traditions and with the individuals and cultures who maintain those traditions.

I have placed myself in some of these essays for a simple reason: in many cases my presence has changed the traditions I was studying. Through displaying cascarones in public exhibitions, through inviting pajareros to demonstrate their skills on the National Mall and exhibiting their work in Arizona museums and galleries, through discussing el Tiradito in popular articles and on radio and TV programs, I have in some way altered all those traditions. It is therefore fitting that I factor myself into their study.

It should be obvious to the reader that this book is in no way a complete study of the folklife of the region I have chosen as my field of study. Another twenty years of work will doubtless produce essays on a host of different topics. Other folklorists will find other, equally exciting themes, other equally fascinating material. They will bring to this material different personalities, training, interests, and perceptions than mine. I long for their arrival.

Less obvious, perhaps, is the fact that each of the studies in the book is of necessity itself incomplete. In the first place, the cultures I have written about are living cultures, constantly changing and adapting to changing times. Not a single one of the customs and art forms I have examined is likely to remain the same for even a few years. All I have done is to try to present them as they were at a certain time.

The studies are incomplete in other ways as well. Between the first and final drafts of this book—a space of a year and a half—I have learned many details concerning my chosen topics. Each piece of information arrived fortuitously, without warning. I fully expect that process to continue. The essays I would write on these same subjects in five years' time would inevitably be different in many details from the ones in this book.

All of which simply goes to demonstrate that the work isn't yet done, that the answers are not yet all in, and that even the questions are in many cases imperfectly understood. It also provides an excellent excuse to stick around for a while longer, watching, listening, learning. For this is in deep ways my selected field of study, my chosen place to live. The late Van Holyoak, a cowboy from Arizona's White Mountains, made a statement about his part of the state that I cheerfully stole from him and have been using as my own for almost twenty years. "If there was any place I'd rather be, I would have gone there."

Notes

Introduction

1. Some of the ideas in this introduction first saw the light in James S. Griffith, "The Arizona-Sonora Border," in *1993 Festival of American Folklife* (Washington, D.C.: Smithsonian Institution, 1993).
2. Yaqui cultural history is set forth most recently by Edward H. Spicer, *The Yaquis: A Cultural History* (Tucson: University of Arizona Press, 1980). Muriel Thayer Painter, *With Good Heart: Yaqui Beliefs and Ceremonies in Pascua Village* (Tucson: University of Arizona Press, 1986), gives a wealth of details concerning the distinctive Yaqui ceremonialism as it was understood in Pascua Village in Tucson during the period 1940–1960.
3. Tucson was established in 1776 as a Spanish *presidio*, or military outpost. Some of the families who arrived in Tucson at that time are still resident in southern Arizona. See James E. Officer, *Hispanic Arizona, 1536–1856* (Tucson: University of Arizona Press 1987).
4. The commercially recorded còrridos concerning *el túnel* are: "El Túnel de Agua Prieta," by Alberto Urías, performed by Los Jilguerillos del Arroyo on *Todos los Corridos de 1991*, JGS-9024 (cassette), vol. 3, A-3; and "El Túnel de Agua Prieta" by Prisciliano Mondragón, performed by Los Rancheritos del Sur on *Los Rancheritos del Sur*, CCM-4006 (cassette), A-1.
5. Tom Miller, *On the Border: Portraits of America's Southwestern Frontier* (New York: Harper and Row, 1981), xi, xii.
6. A further account of Relámpago's career may be found in Chapter 7 of this collection.
7. Ralph Romero Jr. personal communication.
8. For Reyna, the jokes function within Texas Chicano society as a means of poking fun at recently arrived Mexicans who speak little or no English. This is fine as far as it goes, but doesn't explain the

fact that native English speakers tell them as well, at least in Arizona. See José R. Reyna, *Raza Humor: Chicano Joke Tradition in Texas* (San Antonio: Penca Books, n.d.).

9. This O'odham belief is discussed in a letter to John Collier, Commissioner of Indian Affairs, from Superintendent T. E. Hall of the Sells Agency, June 22, 1939. Original in National Archives, Pacific Southwest Division.

10. The devotion to a purely regional San Francisco in Magdalena de Kino is treated at greater length in James S. Griffith, *Beliefs and Holy Places: A Spiritual Geography of the Pimería Alta* (Tucson: University of Arizona Press, 1992), and in Chapter Two of this book.

11. Jay Ann Cox devotes a chapter of her dissertation to commercial "Sonoran cuisine" in Tucson. See "Eating the Other: Mexican Food in Tucson, Arizona," unpublished Ph.D. dissertation, University of Arizona, Tucson, 1993.

12. For excellent, recently published essays on the Southwest, see James W. Byrkit, "Land, Sky, and People: The Southwest Defined," *Journal of the Southwest* 34 (Autumn 1992), and Joseph C. Wilder, editor, "Inventing the Southwest," *Journal of the Southwest* 32 (Winter 1992). Marta Weigle and Peter White, *The Lore of New Mexico* (Albuquerque: University of New Mexico Press, 1988) presents the most complete summary to date of the folklore and folklife of New Mexico.

13. In 1991, I co-curated an exhibition of salsa labels with Jay Ann Cox at the University of Arizona Library. The preceeding paragraphs were adapted from the labelling of this exhibition. See also Cox, "Eating the Other."

14. Charles Di Peso, *Casas Grandes, A Fallen Trading Center of the Gran Chichimeca* (Flagstaff: Northland Press, 1974).

Chapter 1

1. An earlier version of this essay appeared as "Respect and Continuity: The Arts of Death in a Border Community," in the booklet of the same name, published in 1985 by the Southwest Folklore Center and the Pimería Alta Historical Society. I wish to thank both these institutions for their kind permission to use the materials. The original accompanied an exhibition by the same name which opened at the Pimería Alta Historical Society, Nogales, Arizona,

in October, 1985, and subsequently travelled through the state of Arizona courtesy of the Arizona Commission on the Arts.

2. For additional material on maquiladoras in Nogales, see Alan Weismann and Jay Dusard, *La Frontera: The United States Border with Mexico* (New York: Harcourt, Brace, and Jovankovich, 1986), 123–44; for an essay and photographs on working-class Nogales, Sonora, see Sterling Vinson, "Los Tapiros: Commentary and Photographs," *Journal of the Southwest* 33 (Spring 1991): 34–51.

3. A discussion of this aspect of Father Kino's legacy may be found in James S. Griffith, *Legends and Religious Arts of Magdalena de Kino*. Tucson: Southwest Folklore Center, 1988.

4. Death has long been considered an important focal point for traditional Mexican culture. See Octavio Paz, *The Labyrinth of Solitude* (New York: Grove Press, 1961).

5. Mexican American cemeteries in Arizona are described in Ann Hitchcock, "Gods, Graves, and Historical Archaeologists: A Study of a Mexican-American Cemetery in Harshaw," *AFFWORD* 3 (1973): 1–10, James S. Griffith, *Southern Arizona Folk Arts* (Tucson: University of Arizona Press, 1988): 35–41, and James S. Griffith, *Beliefs and Holy Places: A Spiritual Geography of the Pimería Alta* (Tucson: University of Arizona Press, 1992).

6. See Teresa Leal, "El Día de los Muertos," in *Respect and Continuity: The Arts of Death in a Border Community*, (Tucson: Southwest Folklore Center, and Nogales: Pimería Alta Historical Society, 1985).

7. For an excellent selection of Posada's calaveras, see Julian Rothenstein, *Posada—Messenger of Mortality* (London: Redstone Press, 1989), 122–47.

8. For a thoughtful discussion of el día de los muertos in contemporary Mexico, see María Teresa Pomar, *El Día De Los Muertos: The Life of the Dead in Mexican Folk Art* (Fort Worth: The Fort Worth Art Museum, 1987).

9. See Leal, "El Día de los Muertos."

10. Pre-Columbian antecedents are described in Alan R. Landstrom and Pamela Effrein Landstrom, *Traditional Papermaking and Paper Cult Figures of Mexico* (Norman: University of Oklahoma Press, 1986). See Griffith, *Southern Arizona Folk Arts*, 33–34, also James S. Griffith, "The Arizona Sonora Border," in *1993 Festival of American Folklife* (Washington, D.C.: Smithsonian Institution, 1993).

11. For pictorial evidence of the use of zempasúchiles in central Mexico, see Pomar, *El Día De Los Muertos*.
12. The baroque style in the Pimería Alta and its influences on contemporary Mexican American folk art are discussed in James S. Griffith, *Beliefs and Holy Places: A Spiritual Geography of the Pimería Alta* (Tucson: University of Arizona Press, 1992); and Griffith *Southern Arizona Folk Arts*: 5–9, as well as in Chapter 8 of this book.
13. Carol Edison, "Motorcycles, Guitars, and Bucking Broncos: Twentieth-Century Gravestones in Southeastern Idaho." In *Idaho Folklife, Homesteads to Headstones*. (Salt Lake City: University of Utah Press, 1985).
14. Alberto Suárez Barnett, "Funerary Styles of Nogales, Sonora," in *Respect and Continuity: The Arts of Death in a Border Community* (Tucson: The Southwest Folklore Center and, Nogales: The Pimería Alta Historical Society, 1985), 27–30.

Chapter 2

1. An earlier version of this essay was published in *New York Folklore* 8 (Winter 1982) under the title "The Magdalena Holy Picture: Religious Folk Art in Two Cultures." I wish to thank the New York Folklore Society for granting permission to publish this revised and updated version.
2. For a brief account of Eusebio Francisco Kino's life and of the discovery of his grave, see Charles W. Polzer, S.J., *A Kino Guide II* (Tucson: Southwest Missions Research Center, 1982).
3. For a more detailed discussion of the problem of the composite identity of the Magdalena San Francisco statue, of the legends concerning it, and of the regional devotion to San Francisco, see James S. Griffith, *Beliefs and Holy Places: A Spiritual Geography of the Pimería Alta*. (Tucson: University of Arizona Press, 1992), Chapter 3.
4. For more information on the Magdalena fiesta, see Henry E. Dobyns, "The Religious Festival," unpublished Ph.D. dissertation, Cornell University, 1960, Bernard L. Fontana, "Pilgrimage to Magdalena," *American West* 18 (Sept/Oct 1981): 40–45, 60, and Griffith, *Beliefs and Holy Places*.
5. James S. Griffith, "Accommodation and Renewal: Catholic Architecture of the Tohono O'odham Nation," *Folklife Annual 90*

(Washington, D.C.: The American Folklife Center of the Library of Congress, 1991); and Griffith, *Beliefs and Holy Places*, discuss O'odham Catholicism in greater detail.

6. David Santos, *David's Story: A Papago Cultural History Reader* (Sells, Arizona: Bureau of Indian Affairs, Papago Indian Agency, 1981).
7. Bernard L. Fontana, "Pilgrimage to Magdalena."
8. More detailed discussions of Tohono O'odham folk Catholic chapels are to be found in James S. Griffith, "The Folk Catholic Chapels of the Papaquería," *Pioneer America* 7 (July 1975): 21–36, Griffith, "Accommodation and Renewal," and Griffith, *Beliefs and Holy Places*.
9. Teresa Pomar, personal communication.
10. Lane Coulter and Maurice Dixon Jr., *New Mexico Tinwork, 1840–1940* (Albuquerque: University of New Mexico Press, 1990), 122–25.
11. Edward Leight, "Tinsel Paintings," exhibition catalogue (New York: Washburn Gallery, 1983).
12. Robert Quinn, personal communication, June 6, 1994.
13. The title of the exhibition, "Glittering Recuerdos," referred to the effects of the crumpled tinfoil and to the fact that many of the pictures include the word recuerdo, or souvenir. As an unintended result of this title, some Anglo Americans have assumed that recuerdo is a generic term for the frames. This is not the case. In Magdalena, I have heard the frames called *cuadritos*—little pictures—obviously a descriptive rather than an exclusive label.
14. The Tucson exhibition, "Magdalena de Kino: Pilgrimage and Religious Art," ran from May through November, 1988, in La Casa Cordoba, a division of the Tucson Museum of Art. An accompanying booklet was published, James S. Griffith, *Legends and Religious Arts of Magdalena de Kino* (Tucson: The Southwest Folklore Center, 1988).
15. Anastacio León's photograph, taken by Dr. Valenzuela, was on the cover of the Festival of American Folklife's 1993 program booklet, while a photograph of his late father appeared both in the booklet itself and on an interpretive sign at the festival.
16. Seri ironwood carving has been discussed by Scott H. Ryerson, "Seri Ironwood Carving: An Economic View," in Nelson H. H. Graburn, ed., *Ethnic and Tourist Arts: Cultural Experiences from the Fourth World* (Berkeley: University of California Press, 1976). I

know of no published discussions of Mexican-made imitations of Seri carvings. I have not yet visited the factory in Magdalena where some of these carvings are produced, although I know of its exist ence (Felipe de Jesús Valenzuela, personal communication, 1993).

Chapter 3

1. An earlier version of this paper was read at the annual meetings of the American Folklore Society in St. Johns, Newfoundland, Canada, in October of 1991. A still earlier and very much shorter version, "Cascarones: Southern Arizona's Dynamic Folk Art," was published as a one-page illustrated leaflet accompanying an exhibition of the same name at Tohono Chul Gallery, Tucson, Arizona, in February 1991. This present paper is a slightly modified version of an article that appeared in the 1994 issue of the *International Folklore Review.*
2. Brígida Briones, "A Carnival Ball at Monterey in 1829," *Century Magazine* 41 (November 1890-April 1891).
3. Mary Hallock Foote, "The Cascarone Ball," *Scribner's Magazine* 18 (August 1879): 614–17.
4. John G. Bourke, *On the Border with Crook* (New York: Scribner's Sons, 1891, reprinted Columbus: Long's College Book Co. 1950), 88. At about the same time, Tucson saloon-keeper George Hand noted in his dairy for January 31, 1875: "I closed up at 10 o'clock and went with Davis and took in the whole town. We brought up at a masquerade ball at the upper end of town . . . Bought a few cascarones for the girls." George Hand, Diary for 1875, unpublished manuscript on file at the Arizona Historical Society, Tucson.
5. Frederick Starr, *Catalogue of a Collection of Objects Illustrating the Folklore of Mexico* (London: Published for the Folk-Lore Society by Daniel Nutt, 1899).
6. Teresa Ruiz, personal communication to author, 1985.
7. Taped interview with Lou Gastelum and Virginia Yslas, Tucson, 28 January 1991. Arizona Folklore Archives 91-11/C-1.
8. See the discussion of *papel de china* in Chapter One. The possible prehispanic origins such work are important to many Mexican and Mexican American artists and craftspeople. One member of a Mexican American cascarón-making family in Tucson traces the roots of his art to Aztec times, when turkey eggs were used as storage vessels.

9. Notes from interview with Feliciana Martinez, Old Pascua Village, Tucson, Arizona, February 14, 1991, in author's files.
10. Notes from interview with Ernesto Quiroga, Tucson, Arizona, January 28, 1991, in author's files.
11. For a thorough discussion of the Yaqui Easter Ceremony as it is presented at what is now called Old Pascua Village in Tucson, see Muriel Thayer Painter, *With Good Heart: Yaqui Beliefs and Ceremonies in Pascua Village* (Tucson: University of Arizona Press, 1986).
12. Ernesto Quiroga interview, as above.
13. When I saw cascarones for sale for $6.00 each at Tucson International Airport in March, 1994, the saleswoman told me that they were "supposed to be good luck" when broken over someone's head. See also Note 17.
14. See "Bonkers," *Sunset Magazine* (March 1986): 112–13.
15. Letter to the author from Jan Wheeland, Portland, Oregon, January, 1991. On file with author. "Egg Bonkers" are produced by the N.L. Dickinson Company, P.O. Box 19412, Portland, Oregon, 97219, and were being sold in about 30 states "with mixed results" as of January, 1991.
16. Selected from a sheet of 40 Egg Bonker "Egg Yokes" sent to author by Jan Wheeland. Other sample "yokes" include: "What do you get when two eggs fight?—crackers," and "What do you call a philosophical egg?—an eggsistential."
17. With this sort of multicultural clientele in mind, cascarón maker Ángela Montoya (who does not herself speak or write English with any degree of comfort) had the following text written and printed as a handout:

Cascarones

The tradition of cascaron comes from Mexico where they add color, fun, and laughter to fiestas and carnivals. "Cascar" means to break. Each hand-decorated eggshell is filled with confetti.

Buy one and break it over the head of a friend. A surprise of blessings, magic and color fills the air around them.

Buy a bunch and put them in a vase, adding sparkle and festivity to any room. (Given to author by Angela Montoya, February 16, 1991. Original on file with author.)

Angela Montoya was born in California and raised in Sinaloa, Mexico, where she remembers seeing relatively simple, short-stemmed cascarones made for Carnival. She is currently a very successful Tucson cascarón maker, specializing in such characters as Pancho Villa, Adelita, Dick Tracy, Batman, the Ninja Turtles, and Bart Simpson. She also makes clowns, squirrels, skunks, rabbits, and snakes. A cascarón takes her about 20 minutes to make, and sells for about $2.00.

Chapter 4

1. An earlier version of this article was published as "El Tiradito and Juan Soldado: Two Victim-Intercessors of the Western Borderlands," *International Folklore Review* 5 (1987): 75–81. I also discussed victim intercessors at some length in *Beliefs and Holy Places: A Spiritual Geography of the Pimería Alta* (Tucson: University of Arizona Press, 1992).
2. Dorothy Perkins lists fourteen, see "Tales of the Wishing Shrine," unpublished paper on file at the Southwest Folklore Center of the University of Arizona Library.
3. See *El Tiradito—"The Wishing Shrine"* (leaflet), (Tucson: Tucson/Pima County Historical Commission, 1979).
4. A. S. Reynolds, "Legends of the Wishing Shrine," *Progressive Arizona* 5 (July 1927): 12.
5. Perkins, "Tales of the Wishing Shrine," 12.
6. Eduardo (Lalo) Guerrerro, personal communication.
7. J. S. Griffith field notes for May 5, 1982. On file at the Southwest Folklore Center.
8. Ronald W. Wogoman, "Collected Tales from Mexican-American Children; Tucson, Arizona," unpublished manuscript in the Southwest Folklore Center of the University of Arizona Library, 1972.
9. Alva Torres, "Torres' Living Room is Now a Movie Star." *Tucson Citizen* (January 23, 1990): B2. Interestingly enough, the application for El Tiradito's Historic Landmark status were drawn up by the late folklorist Byrd Howell Granger, then at the University of Arizona.
10. *El Tiradito—"The Wishing Shrine."*
11. Phoebe M. Bogan, *Yaqui Indian Dances of Tucson, Arizona* (Tucson: The Archaeological Society, 1925).

12. See untitled paragraph in the *Arizona Daily Star* (April 1, 1893): 4; George Berrel, Diary (1909), unpublished manuscript on file at the Arizona Historical Society, Tucson. The newspaper article describes a niche made of scrap tin and containing a cross and a candle; the shrine commemorates "the murder of a Mexican many years ago." The diary, kept by an actor who was visiting Tucson, describes a circular dirt enclosure filled with candles. This shrine commemorates a Mexican who "was killed, murdered on that spot." Each account mentions a "superstition" connected with the shrine; only the diary explicitly states that it is a place of petitions. Although there is no proof that either of these sites is connected with the present-day shrine, it seems highly likely. Both shrines are in the right general area of town.

13. Reynolds, "Legends of the Wishing Shrine."

14. J. S. Griffith field notes for December 10, 1983. On file at the Southwest Folklore Center.

15. St. Martin of Porres (1579–1639) was born in Peru as the illegitimate son of a Spanish knight and a Black Panamanian. He became a Dominican lay brother and was known for his humility and concern for the poor. He is patron of social justice and people of mixed race, see John Delany, *Dictionary of Saints* (New York: Doubleday, 1980), 477.

16. Griffith, *Beliefs and Holy Places*, 31–44.

17. Griffith *Beliefs and Holy Places*, 100–104; J. Frank Dobie, *Tongues of the Monte* (Austin: University of Texas Press, 1980), 160–65.

18. A photograph of the San Francisco statue at San Xavier del Bac, covered with milagros and other offerings, may be seen in Martha Egan, *Milagros—Votive Offerings from the Americas* (Santa Fe: Museum of New Mexico Press, 1991), 60. An excellent study of milagros in the Pimería Alta is in press: Eileen Octavec, *Gifts to the Saints: Milagros in the Arizona/Sonora Borderlands* (Tucson: University of Arizona Press, forthcoming).

19. This historical account is taken from José Manuel Valenzuela Arce, "Por los Milagros Recibidos: Religiosidad Popular a Traves del Culto a Juan Soldado," in *Entre la Magia y la historia: Traditiones, Mitos y leyendas de la Frontera*. José Manuel Valenzuela Arce, compilador (Tijuana: Programa Cultural de las Fronteras, el Colegio de la Frontera Norte, 1992), 77–84.

20. Helen Escobedo, *Mexican Monuments; Strange Encounters* (New York: Abbeville Press, 1989), 147.

21. Arturo Carrillo Strong, personal communication.

22. Prayer leaflet dedicated to Jesus Malverde, on file at the Southwest Folklore Center.

23. Kathleen L. Figgen, "Antonio Gil: Folk Saint or Folk Subversive?" Unpublished paper read at the annual meeting of the American Folklore Society, Philadelphia (October 1989).

24. C. O'Neill, "Saints." *New Catholic Encyclopedia* 12: 82–83 (Washington, D.C.: The Catholic University of America, 1967).

25. Alban Butler, *Butler's Lives of the Saints* (London: Burns and Oates, 1981) II: 28–9.

26. Griffith *Beliefs and Holy Places*: 114–15.

27. Jean-Claude Schmitt, *The Holy Greyhound: Guinefort, Healer of Children Since the Thirteenth Century* (Cambridge: Cambridge University Press, 1983), 22, 23. St. Martin, Bishop of Tours, died in 397 A.D. His day is the day of his burial, November 11.

28. Carol Sowell, "Prayer-Inspired Visions Draw Faithful to Fireplace," *The Arizona Daily Star* (28 February 1980): G-1.

29. Ray Pararella, "Mexican Village Holds Tightly to its Miracle," *The Arizona Daily Star* (18 April 1982): E-1.

30. R. H. Ring, "Some Customers Find Jesus Christ in Butcher's Picture," *The Arizona Daily Star* (2 May 1985): 2F.

31. In an earlier essay, I gave my opinion that El Tiradito seems to be secularizing. I have since modified my views. El Tiradito the site does seem, however, to have taken over much of the original importance of el Tiradito the person, and has become a multiple-use site in Tucson's multicultural society. See James S. Griffith, "El Tiradito and Juan Soldado: Two Victim-Intercessors of the Western Borderlands," *International Folklore Review* 5 (1987): 75–81.

32. Some accents have been added to the texts of the prayers, which otherwise match those of the original printed versions.

Chapter 5

1. An earlier version of this essay was read at the annual meeting of the American Folklore Society in Jacksonville, Florida, in October, 1992.

2. Paul M. Roca, *Paths of the Padres Through Sonora* (Tucson: Arizona Pioneers' Historical Society, 1967), 56–57.

3. Donald W. Page, "The Mexican troops' departure from Tucson, as recalled by Doña Atanacia Santa Cruz de Hughes and told Donald W. Page, May 12, 1929," typescript on file at the Arizona Historical Society, Tucson, 2, 5, 7.
4. James E. Officer, *Hispanic Arizona, 1536–1856* (Tucson: University of Arizona Press, 1987), 168.
5. Stephen F. de Borhegyi, *El Santuario de Chimayó* (Santa Fe: The Spanish Colonial Arts Society, Inc., 1956), 3.
6. Elizabeth Kay, *Chimayó Valley Traditions* (Santa Fe: Ancient City Press, 1987), 32.
7. For more information concerning the Santuario at Chimayó, see Kay *Chimayó Valley Traditions*. Yvonne Lange, "Santo Niño de Atocha: A Mexican Cult is Transplanted to Spain," *El Palacio* 884 (Winter 1978): 3–7, discusses the history of the devotion to the Santo Niño de Atocha in great detail. Briefly stated, the veneration of the Santo Niño de Atocha is a Mexican phenomenon, having had its origin in the mining town of Plateros, Zacatecas, where an image of the Christ Child got separated from the mother-and-child image of the Virgin of Atocha (a Spanish manifestation of the Virgin Mary) sometime early in the nineteenth century. Veneration of the image has since spread throughout many parts of Mexico, especially the northern mining country.
8. Tucson historian Frederick McAninch interviewed one elderly man who remembered visiting hot springs near the base of "A" Mountain, formerly called Sentinal Peak. Frederick McAninch, personal communication.
9. Page, "Mexican troops' departure from Tucson," 2, 5.
10. This occurred in September, 1934, and was part of a general move on the part of Sonora's government to destroy sacred images and convert churches to secular uses. The action must be viewed in the light of the religious conflicts that racked revolutionary Mexico in the 1920s and 30s. See James S. Griffith, *Beliefs and Holy Places: A Spiritual Geography of the Pimería Alta* (Tucson: University of Arizona Press, 1992), 50–51.
11. James S. Griffith, Field Journal for April, 1991. Sam Negri collected three narratives explaining the Black Christ at Aconchi. The first stated that the statue was sent to Aconchi from Esquipulas, Guatemala, to counteract the many witches that were at the time in Aconchi. The second is the story reported above concerning the attempted poisoning of the priest. The third tells of the statue,

then ordinary flesh color, being taken through Aconchi on its way to some other church. The statue refused to be moved from Aconchi and at the same time turned black, absorbing the sins of the people of townsfolk. See Sam Negri, "Enchanted Valley," *Tucson Weekly* 11 (13–19 April 1994). This theme of a statue refusing to be moved from its chosen location is mentioned in Chapter 2 in the context of the San Francisco Statue in Magdalena, see also James S. Griffith, *Legends and Religious Arts of Magdalena de Kino* (Tucson: The Southwest Folklore Center, 1988), 44.

12. Anonymous, *Know the Cathedral of Mexico.* Mexico, 1969, 17.

13. Quesadillas can vary in nature in different parts of the border country, although all contain cheese *(queso).* As served in Ímuris, a quesadilla consists of a thin slice of locally produced cow's cheese, melted between two small flour tortillas.

14. Taped interview with Cathy Giesy, August, 1992, on file at the University of Arizona's Southwest Folklore Center.

15. Letter to author from Francine Pierce, May 3, 1992.

16. Charles W. Polzer, "Legends of Lost Mission and Mines," *Smoke Signal* 18 (Fall 1968): 169–83.

17. Letter to author from Francine Pierce, May 3, 1992.

18. Letter to author from Francine Pierce, May 12, 1992.

19. Roca, *Paths of the Padres,* 162–4.

20. Anonymous, *La Catedral de Mexico.* (tourist guide) Mexico, D.F., n.d.

21. T. Philip Terry, *Terry's Guide to Mexico,* Hingham, Massachusetts, the author, 1943.

22. Stephen F. de Borhegyi, "The Cult of Our Lord of Esquipulas in Middle America and New Mexico," *El Palacio* 61 (December 1954): 387–401.

23. Mary Lee Nolan and Sidney Nolan, *Christian Pilgrimage in Modern Western Europe* (Chapel Hill: University of North Carolina Press, 1989), 209.

24. Conversation with Phillip Weigand, April 1994.

25. de Borhegyi, "The Cult of Our Lord of Esquipulas."

26. The Childrens' Shrine is discussed in some detail in Griffith (1992): 22–28.

27. Joyce Muench, "Shrine of the Three Babies," *The Desert Magazine* 6: 5 (March 1943): 13–15, and "Author Gives Source," *The Desert Magazine* 6: 8 (July 1943): 28. Muench's letter explaining her sources for the story is worth quoting in its entirety. She wrote it

after an anthropologist wrote the editors of *Desert Magazine* to complain that the O'odham versions of the story he had heard involved a flood and four children, Julian Hayden, letter to the editor, *The Desert Magazine* 6: 8 (July 1943): 26.

Dear Miss Harris:

   Indian legend and history alike were carried on many lips before it was put into writing and so subject to the eternal qualities of man's mind which never turns out anything quite the same when once it has passed through the filter of his own personal interpretation. But the essence of a legend is not so much in its details as in the truth about the people who treasure it, handing it down through their generations.

   My husband and I were informed about the presence of the Baby Shrine when we went through Casa Grande, Arizona. A very cordial gentleman there, a state senator, described it and located it for us, telling us the story as he had heard it. It was a delightful place and it was easy to believe that in this country where water is so necessary and so precious, that a drought would call for the greatest sacrifice people were capable of making.

   We went on to a nearby trading post and heard the same version of the story repeated there. We are aware of the version to which Mr. Hayden refers and which was mentioned in the March issue.

   I have had some scientific training myself and have the greatest respect for research and for those who conduct it. It is quite in keeping with such thinking to say about a legend that having studied all of the available material my own emotional constitution permits me to continue to enjoy the beautiful tale of a drought averted through the heroic sacrifice of children (three or four, it matters not to the tale) to save the tribe.

   Joyce R. Muench

28. Three children are sacrificed in a highly imaginative Anglo retelling of the story, Hector E. Stewart, *Indian Legend of the Desert. The Shrine of the Children* (Tucson: Arizona School for the Deaf and Blind, n.d.). On file with author. This is said to have been printed in the early 1920s (Otis Chidester, personal communication).

29. Ruth Woodman, letter to the editor, *The Desert Magazine* 6: 8 (July 1943): 28.
30. Dan Woods, "Legend Says Children Sacrificed," *Tri-Valley Dispatch* (24–5 October 1990): 3.
31. "Gold Placer of Quijotoa, Ariz." was written down in 1897 by Jose Lewis Brennan, a Papago Indian man who worked as an interpreter for ethnographers J. W. McGee and Frank Russell. The manuscript was collected by John N. Brinton Hewitt, and deposited with the Bureau of American Ethnology in Washington, D.C. It is now part of Manuscript No. 2325 in the National Anthropological Archives of the Smithsonian Institution. It was published as Jose Lewis Brennan, "Gold Placer of Quijotoa, Arizona," *Journal of the Southwest* 33 (Winter 1991): 459–74.
32. Pack Carnes, "A Folklorist's Perspective: 'Gold Placer' and the European Fairy Tale," *Journal of the Southwest* 33 (Winter 1991): 475–85, gives a detailed commentary on the story.
33. Some accents have been added to the texts of the prayers in appendices A and B, which otherwise match those of the original printed versions.

Chapter 6

1. An earlier version of this paper was read at the annual meeting of the American Folklore Society in Nashville, Tennessee, October, 1983. The paper was then published as Griffith, "'The Mormon Cowboy': An Arizona Cowboy Song and its Community," *JEMF Quarterly* 21 (Fall/Winter 1985, published 1990): 127–133. I wish to acknowledge the Center of Popular Music at Middle Tennessee State University, Murfreesboro, Tennessee, for permission to reprint this slightly revised version.
2. Harlan Daniel, Carl T. Sprague discography, in Glenn Ohrlin, *The Hell-Bound Train: A Cowboy Songbook* (Urbana: University of Illinois Press, 1973), 278–80. The song under discussion should not be confused with a bawdy song of the same title, also known in Arizona. In this other song, a young woman marries an unfortunate fellow whose "hobo would not stand." After he is tried and convicted by a Court of Ladies, she marries a Mormon Cowboy and is well satisfied. Guy Logsdon, coll. and ed., *"The Whorehouse*

Bells were Ringing" and Other Songs Cowboys Sing (Champaign: University of Illinois Press, 1989).

3. John I. White, *Git Along, Little Dogies: Songs and Songmakers of the American West* (Urbana: University of Illinois Press, 1975), 189–95.

4. Recorded by Carl T. Sprague, October 13, 1929. Transcribed from the reissue LP, *Authentic Cowboys and their Western Folksongs* (RCA Victor LPV-522.) Tune transcribed by John Fitch, University of Arizona.

5. Carl T. Sprague, personal correspondence, June 20, 1978. On file at the Southwest Folklore Center of the University of Arizona Library (83–16/5).

6. This and subsequent citations to Laws refer to G. Malcolm Laws, Jr., *Native American Balladry: A Descriptive Study and Bibliographical Syllabus*, revised edition (Philadelphia: American Folklore Society, 1964). In Laws' system, ballads are classified thematically by narrative content and/or by the ethnic or occupational group in which the ballad is thought to have originated or had currency in tradition. The identifying letter and number indicate the class or category (letter) and the individual ballad types (number). For example, the "B" section is devoted to "Ballads of Cowboys and Pioneers". B17 refers to "Tying a Knot in the Devil's Tail."

7. White, *Git Along, Little Dogies*, 117–25. Harlan Daniel (in Ohrlin, *The Hell-Bound Train*, 261) cites sixteen commercial recordings of "Tying a Knot in the Devil's Tail" made between 1930 and the early 1970s.

8. Hal Cannon, "Fame Price, Mormon Cowboy," unpublished paper read at the annual meeting of the American Folklore Society, Nashville, Tennessee (October 1983).

9. Ohrlin, *The Hell-Bound Train*, 158–51.

10. See, for example, "One More Ride" on the LP record *The Sons of the Pioneers* (JEMF 102).

11. The tapes were made on 2 August 1958, and 17 August 1958, respectively. It is interesting to note that there are slight but real differences between the texts.

12. FAC 188 and FAC II 112 in the Folklore Archives of Utah State University.

13. Barre Toelken, personal communication, November 28, 1983. On file at the Southwest Folklore Center of the University of Arizona Library (83–26/18).

14. *Folksongs and Ballads of Kansas, Sung by Joan O'Bryant* (Folkways LP 2134), and *American Ballads and Folklsongs* (Folkways LP 2338). "The Mormon Cowboy" does not appear on either album's list of titles.
15. Transcribed from a tape by Barre Toelken, November, 1983. The tape is now in the Southwest Folklore Center of the University of Arizona Library (83–26/C-18).
16. RCA Victor LPV-522.
17. Carl T. Sprague, *Cowboy Songs from Texas* (Bear Family Records LP, BF 15006). Recorded August, 1974, in Bryan, Texas. *Deseret String Band* (Okehdokee Records cassette, no number, 1981, also available on *The Deseret String Band* (Shanachie Records.)
18. The information in this paragraph comes from a tape-recorded interview with Blanche Hill, Tucson, Arizona, on file at the Southwest Folklore Center (80–5/R-1).
19. Ross Santee, *Lost Pony Tracks* (Lincoln: University of Nebraska Press, 1972), 179–201.
20. Blanche Hill interview.
21. Santee (1972): 200–201; Coyote Wolfe, comp., *Words for 30 Old Songs*, photocopy of a 34-page mimeographed booklet, n.d., in the Southwest Folklore Center of the University of Arizona Library.
22. The preceding material is quoted from correspondence and notes on file at the Southwest Folklore Center. This is the source for all Gila County information not otherwise credited. (83–26/6 through 83–26/17; 82–27/C-1).
23. Wolfe, *Words for 30 Old Songs*.
24. Cliff Edwards interview, 10 May 1984, J. S. Griffith field notes.
25. Blanche Hill interview; other identifications come from correspondence on file at the Southwest Folklore Center.
26. Notes to a telephone conversation with Mrs. Loretta Shepherd, 8 May 1982, on file at the Southwest Folklore Center (83–26/13).
27. The material in these two paragraphs comes from correspondence on file at the Southwest Folklore Center (83–26/C-17; 82–27/C-1).
28. Michael Korn, personal communication, January, 1984.
29. Thomas E. Cheney, *Mormon Songs from the Rocky Mountains* (Salt Lake City: University of Utah Press, 1981): #166, 144 ("None Can Preach the Gospel"); #38, 94 ("Echo Canyon"). Lester A. Hubbard, *Ballads and Songs from Utah* (Salt Lake City: University of Utah Press, 1961): #209, 399 ("The Handcart Song"). Cheney

gives an excellent discussion of Mormon folksong in his "Introduction to Mormon Folksong," pages 3–22.

30. Hal Cannon, personal communication, June 1984.
31. In his novelette, "Hit the Line Hard," Eugene Manlove Rhodes has one of his characters describe what is apparently "The Old Chisholm Trail" as ". . . a saddle song. That goes to a trotting horse." I am aware that other scholars hold other views on this matter; my interpretation is that some cowboys adapted their songs to horses' gaits and others didn't. Rhodes, who wrangled horses and cowboyed in southern New Mexico in the 1880s, apparently did. See Eugene Manlove Rhodes, *The Best Novels and Stories of Eugene Manlove Rhodes* (Boston: Houghton Mifflin, 1949): 371. See also Logsdon, *Whorehouse Bells*.
32. Thomas S. Johnson, "That Ain't Country: The Distinctiveness of Commercial Western Music," *JEMF Quarterly* 17 (Summer 1981): 75–84.
33. For the original text to "The Glory Trail," see Badger Clark, *Sun and Saddle Leather* (Tucson: Westerners International, 1983), 69–72. (Although Clark's full name was Charles Badger Clark, he signed his books "Badger Clark.") The poem also exists in oral tradition in different versions. Alternate traditional titles are "High Chin Bob" and "Way Up High in the Mokiones."

Chapter 7

1. An earlier version of this paper was read at the annual meetings of the American Folklore Society in Boston, October, 1988.
2. Bernal Díaz del Castillo, *The Discovery and Conquest of Mexico, 1517–1521*, trans. A. P. Maudslay (New York: H. Wolff, 1956): 38–39.
3. Mario Baeza, personal communication, August, 1983.
4. See Kathleen Sands, *Charrería Mexicana: An Equestrian Folk Tradition*. Tucson: University of Arizona Press, 1993.
5. For an introduction to horses and horse races as a corrido subject, see James S. Griffith and Celestino Fernández, "Mexican Horse Races and Cultural Values: the Case of los Corridos del Merino," *Western Folklore*, 47 (April 1988): 129-151.
6. "El Siete Leguas," in Gilberto Vélez, *Corridos Mexicanos* (Mexico: Editores Mexicanos Unidos, S.A., 1982), 272-73, deals with

Pancho Villa's horse, for example, while "Caballo Prieto Aza-bache," pages 300–301, describes the narrator's escape from Vil-listas on his obsidian black horse.

7. Keoki Skinner, "Back on Track: Mexican Town Revives Horse Races," Phoenix: *The Arizona Republic* (23 March 1987): B1.

8. For a discussion of the *valiente* as a corrido subject, see Américo Paredes, *With His Pistol in His Hand*. Austin: University of Texas Press, 1958).

9. Américo Paredes, *A Texas-Mexican Cancionero: Folksongs of the Lower Border* (Urbana: University of Illinois Press, 1976), 77–79. This corrido is also known as "Arnulfo Gonzales."

10. Griffith and Fernández, "Mexican Horse Races."

11. See also Vicente Acosta, "Some Surviving Elements of Spanish Folklore in Arizona," unpublished M.A. thesis on file at the University of Arizona Library, 1950.

12. Canciones rancheras are in many ways the equivalent of the Coun-try-Western music of the United States. They are songs with a rural setting, often dealing with love and its attendant pains and problems. They are aimed at rural dwellers and at urban, working-class Mexicans with rural roots, just as country music in the United States is aimed at a rural-turned-urban working class. The great composer of canciones rancheras was José Alfredo Jiménez; in many ways his career and works parallel those of Hank Williams, his counterpart on this side of the border. One of the conventions of the canción ranchera is that its performers dress in some form of charro costume. For an essay on ranchera music in contemporary Mexico, see Alma Guillermoprieto, "Report from Mexico: Sere-nading the Future," *The New Yorker* (9 November 1992): 96–104.

13. The information in the preceding paragraphs comes from inter-views with Ralph Romero Jr., November 23, 1982 and May 4, 1993. See also Sam Negri "Lore of Famous Horse Race Kept Alive in Film and Song," Phoenix: *The Arizona Republic* (Monday, December 13, 1982): B9.

14. Negri, "Lore of Famous Horse Race."

15. Horse color is considered by many horsemen in Mexico and else-where to reveal the horse's character. Mexican horse colors do not, unfortunately, correspond exactly to English and American horse color classifications. See Robert M. Denhart, *The Horse of the Americas* (Norman: University of Oklahoma Press, 1975): 324–28.

16. The information in the next two paragraphs comes from an interview with Trini Ramírez and Leonardo Yañez, 16 February 1989.
17. Ralph Romero Jr., "Relámpago," unpublished manuscript on file at the Southwest Folklore Center of the University of Arizona Library.
18. The information in this and the following paragraph comes from interviews with Ralph Romero Jr. on 23 November 1982 and 4 May 1993.
19. The biographical information on Leonardo Yañez comes from interviews with him on 27 January 1984 and 13 June 1988; also from José F. Medina, "'El Nano' Hizo Famoso al 'Moro'" Hermosillo, Sonora: *El Imparcial* (Tuesday, 31 March 1992), and "Murio 'el Compositor del Corrido,' Leonardo Yañez 'el Nano,'" *El Clarín*, Agua Prieta, Sonora (Tuesday, 12 March 1993); and Prof. Rodolfino Yañez Vargas, "Leonardo Yañez, 'el Nano,'" Hermosilla, Sonora: March 17, 1995. Privately distributed, copy on file at the Southwest Folklore Center, p. 3.
20. Text supplied by Leonardo Yañez, translated by James Griffith and Richard Morales. Punctuation and capitalization retained from Yañez's text; spelling and accents corrected.
21. Leonardo Yañez interview, 27 January 1984.
22. Mario Baeza, personal communication, August 1993.
23. *El Moro de Cumpas*, directed by Mario Hernández, produced by Antonio Aguilar, Producciones Aguila, S.A.
24. This process has been going on for a long time. There is in the Archives of the Southwest Folklore Center a text to "El Corrido de Toral," which describes the July 17, 1928 assassination of Mexican President Álvaro Obregón by León Toral and Toral's subsequent execution on 1 February 1929. The text, which was collected around 1935 from Rafael Montaño, a vaquero on Ronstadt's Las Delicias Ranch near Sasabe on the Arizona-Sonora border, is basically the same as that of a 21 February 1929 recording done in Chicago by the Trovadores Tapatíos. (Edward Ronstadt, personal communication; Hernández n.d.).
25. The information in the preceding two paragraphs comes from an interview with Trini Ramírez and Leonardo Yañez, 16 February 1989.
26. Robert C. Goss, *The San Xavier Altarpiece* (Tucson: University of Arizona Press, 1974), 75, 77.

27. The texts to Yañez's other horse-race corridos appear as Appendix A. There, punctuation and capitalization have been retained from Yañez's text, but spelling and accents have been corrected.
28. A list of Yañez's compositions on file at the Arizona Folklore Archives of the Southwest Folklore Center, including *canciones,* "songs," as well as corridos, appears in Appendix B.

Chapter 8

1. An earlier version of this essay was read at the annual meeting of the American Folklore Society in Albuquerque, New Mexico, in October, 1987. Descriptions of the three folk-art assemblages appear in James S. Griffith, *Southern Arizona Folk Arts* (Tucson: University of Arizona Press, 1988).
2. The name is bilingual, as was the custom for naming missions in the Pimería Alta. "San Xavier" indicates a dedication to St. Francis Xavier, while "Bac" (or Wa:k, as it is written in contemporary O'odham orthography) was and remains the native name for the village.
3. Bernard L. Fontana, "Biography of a Desert Church: The Story of Mission San Xavier del Bac," *Smoke Signal* 3 (1961) gives the best available historical treatment of San Xavier del Bac.
4. Richard Ahlborn, *The Saints of San Xavier* (Tucson: Southwest Missions Research Center, 1974), gives a photograph and description of each statue in the church. No comparable work exists as yet for the murals.
5. Manuel Toussaint, *Colonial Art in Mexico,* trans. and ed. by Elizabeth Wilder Weismann (Austin: University of Texas Press, 1967), 295–98.
6. Toussaint, *Colonial Art,* 298–302.
7. Elizabeth Wilder Weismann, *Art and Time in Mexico From the Conquest to the Revolution* (New York: Harper and Row, 1985): 44–55.
8. George Kubler, *Religious Architecture of New Mexico* (Chicago: Rio Grande Press, 1962).
9. My discussion of the various layers of meaning of the scallop shell is taken from Robert C. Goss, *The San Xavier Altarpiece* (Tucson: University of Arizona Press, 1974), 57–76.

10. James S. Griffith, *Beliefs and Holy Places: A Spiritual Geography of the Pimería Alta* (Tucson: University of Arizona Press, 1992), 115–22.
11. A photograph of this shrine appears in Griffith, *Southern Arizona Folk Arts*, 143.
12. A photograph of this cross appears in Marc Simmons and Frank Turley, *Southwestern Colonial Ironwork: The Spanish Blacksmithing Tradition from Texas to California* (Santa Fe: Museum of New Mexico Press, 1980), 166.
13. Griffith, *Beliefs and Holy Places*, 147–71.
14. It has been suggested to me by more than one person that the materials I have been discussing can be described by the term "kitsch." This may be true, but "kitsch" is a value judgement from the standpoint of late twentieth-century American high culture, and therefore neither describes nor analyzes the objects on their own terms. See also Griffith, *Southern Arizona Folk Arts*, 9.
15. The individuals acting in these support roles usually become *compadres* and *comadres* of the bride and groom, thus entering into a (theoretically) lifelong relationship of mutual support.
16. John Delany, *Dictionary of Saints* (New York: Doubleday, 1980), 569–70.
17. Elizabeth Wilder Weismann, *Mexico in Sculpture, 1521–1821* (Cambridge: Harvard University Press, 1950), 11.
18. Weismann *Mexico in Sculpture*, 13.
19. Elizabeth Wilder Weismann, *Art and Time in Mexico From the Conquest to the Revolution* (New York: Harper and Row, 1985), 90–150, provides a good place to start an examination of the sixteenth-century in Mexico.
20. Ramón Pina Chan, "Aztec Art and Archaeology," in Pedro Ramírez Vasquez, ed., *The National Museum of Anthropology, Mexico* (New York: Harry N. Abrams, 1968), 92, 96.
21. Irving A. Leonard, *Baroque Times in Old Mexico* (Ann Arbor: Ann Arbor Paperbacks, 1966).

Bibliography

Acosta, Vicente. "Some Surviving Elements of Spanish Folklore in Arizona." Unpublished M.A. thesis on file at the University of Arizona Library, 1950.

Ahlborn, Richard. *The Saints of San Xavier.* Tucson: Southwest Missions Research Center, 1974.

Anonymous, *La Catedral de Mexico.* Tourist guide. Mexico, D.F., n.d.

Anonymous, *Know the Cathedral of Mexico.* Mexico, 1969.

Arreola, Daniel and James R. Curtis. *The Mexican Border Cities: Landscape Anatomy and Place Personality.* Tucson: University of Arizona Press, 1993.

Berrel, George. Diary, 1909. Unpublished manuscript on file at the Arizona Historical Society, Tucson.

Bogan, Phoebe M. *Yaqui Indian Dances of Tucson, Arizona.* Tucson: The Archaeological Society, 1925.

"Bonkers." *Sunset Magazine* (March 1986): 112–113.

Bourke, John G. *On the Border with Crook.* New York: Scribner's Sons, 1891; reprinted Columbus: Long's College Book Co. 1950.

Brennan, Jose Lewis. "Gold Placer of Quijotoa, Arizona." *Journal of the Southwest* 33 (Winter 1991): 459–74.

Briones, Brígida. "A Carnival Ball at Monterey in 1829." *Century Magazine* 41 (November 1890-April 1891).

Butler, Alban. *Butler's Lives of the Saints.* London: Burns and Oates, 1981.

Byrkit, James W. "Land, Sky, and People: The Southwest Defined." *Journal of the Southwest* 34 (Autumn 1992): entire issue.

Cannon, Hal. "Fame Price, Mormon Cowboy." Unpublished paper read at the annual meeting of the American Folklore Society, Nashville, Tennessee (October 1983).

Carnes, Pack. "A Folklorist's Perspective: 'Gold Placer' and the European Fairy Tale." *Journal of the Southwest* 33 (Winter 1991): 475–85.

Cheney, Thomas E. *Mormon Songs from the Rocky Mountains.* Salt Lake City: University of Utah Press, 1981.

Clark, Badger. *Sun and Saddle Leather.* Tuscon: Westerners International, 1983.

Coulter, Lane and Maurice Dixon, Jr. *New Mexico Tinwork, 1840–1940.* Albuquerque: University of New Mexico Press, 1990.

Cox, Jay Ann. "Eating the Other: Mexican Food in Tucson, Arizona." Unpublished Ph.D. dissertation, University of Arizona, Tucson, 1993.

de Borhegyi, Stephen F. "The Cult of Our Lord of Esquipulas in Middle America and New Mexico." *El Palacio* 61 (December 1954): 387–401.

———. *El Santuario de Chimayó.* Santa Fe: The Spanish Colonial Arts Society, Inc, 1956.

Di Peso, Charles. *Casas Grandes, A Fallen Trading Center of the Gran Chichimeca.* Flagstaff: Northland Press, 1974.

Denhart, Robert M. *The Horse of the Americas.* Norman: University of Oklahoma Press, 1975.

Delany, John. *Dictionary of Saints.* New York: Doubleday, 1980.

Díaz del Castillo, Bernal. *The Discovery and Conquest of Mexico, 1517–1521.* Trans. A. P. Maudslay. New York: H. Wolff, 1956.

Dobie, J. Frank. *Tongues of the Monte.* Austin: University of Texas Press, 1980.

Dobyns, Henry E. "The Religious Festival." Unpublished Ph.D. Dissertation, Cornell University, 1960.

Edison, Carol. "Motorcycles, Guitars, and Bucking Broncos: Twentieth-Century Gravestones in Southeastern Idaho." In Louie W. Attebery, ed. *Idaho Folklife, Homesteads to Headstones.* Salt Lake City: University of Utah Press, 1985.

Egan, Martha. *Milagros—Votive Offerings from the Americas.* Santa Fe: Museum of New Mexico Press, 1991.

El Tiradito—"The Wishing Shrine" (leaflet). Tucson: Tucson/Pima County Historical Commission, 1979.

Escobedo, Helen. *Mexican Monuments: Strange Encounters.* Photographs by Paolo Gori. New York: Abbeville Press, 1989.

Fontana, Bernard L. "Biography of a Desert Church: The Story of Mission San Xavier del Bac." Tucson: The Tucson Corral of Westerners. *Smoke Signal* 3 (1961).

———. "Pilgrimage to Magdalena." *American West* 18 (Sept/Oct 1981a): 40–45, 60.

———. *Of Earth and Little Rain.* Flagstaff: Northland Press, 1981b.

Foote, Mary Hallock. "The Cascarone Ball." *Scribner's Magazine* 18
(August 1879): 614–17.

Figgen, Kathleen L. "Antonio Gil: Folk Saint or Folk Subversive?"
Unpublished paper read at the annual meeting of the American
Folklore Society, Philadelphia (October 1989).

Goss, Robert C. *The San Xavier Altarpiece.* Tucson: University of Arizona Press, 1974.

Griffith, James S. "The Folk Catholic Chapels of the Papaquería." *Pioneer America* 7 (July 1975): 21–36.

———. "The Magdalena Holy Picture: Religious Folk Art in Two
Cultures." *New York Folklore* 8 (Winter 1982): 2–4, 71–82.

———. *Respect and Continuity: The Arts of Death in a Border Community.* Nogales and Tucson: The Pimería Alta Historical Society
and The Southwest Folklore Center, 1985.

———. "El Tiradito and Juan Soldado: Two Victim-Intercessors of
the Western Borderlands." *International Folklore Review* 5 (1987):
75–81.

———. *Legends and Religious Arts of Magdalena de Kino.* Tucson: The
Southwest Folklore Center, 1988a.

———. *Southern Arizona Folk Arts.* Tucson: University of Arizona
Press, 1988b.

———. "'The Mormon Cowboy': An Arizona Cowboy Song and its
Community." *JEMF Quarterly* 21 (Fall/Winter 1985; published
1990): 127–133.

———. "Accommodation and Renewal: Catholic Architecture of the
Tohono O'odham Nation." *Folklife Annual 90.* Washington,
D.C.: American Folklife Center of the Library of Congress,
1991a.

———. *Beliefs and Holy Places: A Spiritual Geography of the Pimería
Alta.* Tucson: University of Arizona Press, 1992.

———. "The Arizona-Sonora Border." *1993 Festival of American Folklife.* Washington, D.C.: Smithsonian Institution, 1993.

———. "'Cascarones:' A Folk Art Form of Southern Arizona." *International Folklore Review* 9 (1994): 34–40.

Griffith, James S., and Celestino Fernández. "Mexican Horse Races
and Cultural Values: the Case of los Corridos del Merino." *Western Folklore,* 47 (April 1988): 129–151.

Guillermoprieto, Alma. "Report from Mexico: Serenading the Future."
The New Yorker (9 November 1992): 96–104.

Hall, T. E. Letter to John Collier, Commissioner of Indian Affairs, from Superintendent T. E. Hall of the Sells Agency, June 22, 1939. Original in National Archives, Pacific Southwest Division.

Hand, George. Diary for 1875. Unpublished manuscript on file at the Arizona Historical Society, Tucson.

Hayden, Julian. Letter to the Editor. *The Desert Magazine* 6: 8 (July 1943): 26.

Hernández, Richard. *The Mexican Revolution—La Revolución Mexicana—The Heroes and Events, 1910–1920 and Beyond.* Liner notes to Folklyric LP 9041/44, *The Mexican Revolution.* El Cerrito, California: Folklyric Records, n.d.

Hitchcock, Ann. "Gods, Graves, and Historical Archaeologists: A Study of a Mexican-American Cemetery in Harshaw." *AFF-WORD* 3 (1973): 1–10.

Hubbard, Lester A. *Ballads and Songs from Utah.* Salt Lake City: University of Utah Press, 1961.

Johnson, Thomas S. "That Ain't Country: The Distinctiveness of Commercial Western Music." *JEMF Quarterly* 17 (Summer 1981): 75–84.

Kay, Elizabeth. *Chimayó Valley Traditions.* Santa Fe: Ancient City Press, 1987.

Kubler, George. *Religious Architecture of New Mexico.* Chicago: Rio Grande Press, 1962.

Landstrom, Alan R. and Pamela Effrein Landstrom. *Traditional Papermaking and Paper Cult Figures of Mexico.* Norman: University of Oklahoma Press, 1986.

Lange, Yvonne. "Santo Niño de Atocha: A Mexican Cult is Transplanted to Spain." *El Palacio* 884 (Winter 1978): 3–7.

Laws, G. Malcolm Jr. *Native American Balladry: A Descriptive Study and Bibliographical Syllabus.* Revised edition. Philadelphia: American Folklore Society, 1964.

Leal, Teresa. "El Día de los Muertos," in *Respect and Continuity: The Arts of Death in a Border Community.* Tucson: The Southwest Folklore Center, and Nogales: the Pimería Alta Historical Society, 1985.

Leight, Edward. "Tinsel Paintings." Exhibition Catalogue. New York: Washburn Gallery, 1983.

Leonard, Irving A. *Baroque Times in Old Mexico.* Ann Arbor: Ann Arbor Paperbacks, 1966.

Logsdon, Guy, coll. and ed. *"The Whorehouse Bells were Ringing" and Other Songs Cowboys Sing*. Champaign: University of Illinois Press, 1989.

Martinez, Oscar J. *Border People: Life and Society in the U.S.-Mexico Borderlands*. Tucson: University of Arizona Press, 1994.

Medina, José F. "'El Nano' Hizo Famoso al 'Moro.'" Hermosillo, Sonora: *El Imparcial* (31 March 1992).

Miller, Tom. *On the Border: Portraits of America's Southwestern Frontier*. New York: Harper and Row, 1981.

Muench, Joyce. "Shrine of the Three Babies." *The Desert Magazine* 6: 5 (1943): 13-15.

———. "Author Gives Source." *The Desert Magazine* 6: 8 (July 1943): 28.

"Murio 'el Compositor del Corrido', Leonardo Yañez 'el Nano.'" Agua Prieta, Sonora: *El Clarín* (12 March 1993): 1, 4.

Negri, Sam. "Lore of Famous Horse Race Kept Alive in Film and Song." Phoenix: *The Arizona Republic* (13 December 1982): B9.

———. "Enchanted Valley." *Tucson Weekly* 11 (April 13–19, 1994).

Nolan, Mary Lee, and Sidney Nolan. *Christian Pilgrimage in Modern Western Europe*. Chapel Hill: University of North Carolina Press, 1989.

Octavec, Eileen. *Gifts to the Saints: Milagros in the Arizona/Sonora Borderlands*. Tucson: University of Arizona Press, forthcoming.

O'Neill, C. "Saints." *New Catholic Encyclopedia* 12: 82–83. Washington, D.C.: The Catholic University of America, 1967.

Officer, James E. *Hispanic Arizona, 1536–1856*. Tucson: University of Arizona Press, 1987.

Ohrlin, Glenn. *The Hell-Bound Train: A Cowboy Songbook*. Urbana: University of Illinois Press, 1973.

Page, Donald W. "The Mexican troops' departure from Tucson, as recalled by Doña Atanacia Santa Cruz de Hughes and told Donald W. Page, May 12, 1929." Typescript on file at the Arizona Historical Society, Tucson.

Painter, Muriel Thayer. *With Good Heart: Yaqui Beliefs and Ceremonies in Pascua Village*. Tucson: University of Arizona Press, 1986.

Paredes, Américo. *With His Pistol in His Hand*. Austin: University of Texas Press, 1958.

———. *A Texas-Mexican Cancionero: Folksongs of the Lower Border*. Urbana: University of Illinois Press, 1976.

Pararella, Ray. "Mexican Village Holds Tightly to its Miracle." Tucson: *The Arizona Daily Star* (April 18, 1982): E-1.

Paz, Octavio. *The Labyrinth of Solitude.* New York: Grove Press, 1961.

Perkins, Dorothy. "Tales of the Wishing Shrine." Unpublished paper on file at the Southwest Folklore Center of the University of Arizona Library, n.d.

Pina Chan, Ramón. "Aztec Art and Archaeology." In Pedro Ramírez Vasquez, ed., *The National Museum of Anthropology, Mexico.* New York: Harry N. Abrams, 1968.

Polzer, Charles W., S.J. "Legends of Lost Mission and Mines." Tucson: The Tucson Corral of Westerners. *Smoke Signal* 18 (Fall 1968): 169–183.

———. *A Kino Guide II.* Tucson: Southwest Missions Research Center, 1982.

Pomar, María Teresa. *El Día De Los Muertos: The Life of the Dead in Mexican Folk Art.* Fort Worth: The Fort Worth Art Museum, 1987.

Reyna, José R. *Raza Humor: Chicano Joke Tradition in Texas.* San Antonio: Penca Books, n.d.

Reynolds, A. S. "Legends of the Wishing Shrine." *Progressive Arizona* 5 (July 1927): 13–15.

Rhodes, Eugene Manlove. *The Best Novels and Stories of Eugene Manlove Rhodes.* Boston: Houghton Mifflin, 1949.

Ring, R. H. "Some Customers Find Jesus Christ in Butcher's Picture." Tucson: *The Arizona Daily Star* (2 May 1985): 2F.

Roca, Paul M. *Paths of the Padres Through Sonora.* Tucson: Arizona Pioneers' Historical Society, 1967.

Romero, Ralph Jr. "Relámpago." Unpublished manuscript on file at the Southwest Folklore Center of the University of Arizona Library, n.d.

Rothenstein, Julian. *Posada—Messenger of Mortality.* London: Redstone Press, 1989.

Ryerson, Scott H. "Seri Ironwood Carving: An Economic View." In Nelson H. H. Graburn, ed. *Ethnic and Tourist Arts: Cultural Experiences from the Fourth World.* Berkeley: University of California Press, 1976.

Sands, Kathleen. *Charrería Mexicana: An Equestrian Folk Tradition.* Tucson: University of Arizona Press, 1993.

Santee, Ross. *Lost Pony Tracks.* Lincoln: University of Nebraska Press, 1972.

Santos, David. *David's Story: A Papago Cultural History Reader.* Sells, Arizona: Bureau of Indian Affairs, Papago Indian Agency, 1981.

Schmitt, Jean-Claude. *The Holy Greyhound: Guinefort, Healer of Children Since the Thirteenth Century.* Cambridge: Cambridge University Press, 1983.

Simmons, Marc, and Frank Turley. *Southwestern Colonial Ironwork: The Spanish Blacksmithing Tradition from Texas to California.* Santa Fe: Museum of New Mexico Press, 1980.

Skinner, Keoki. "Back on Track: Mexican Town Revives Horse Races." Phoenix: *The Arizona Republic* (March 23, 1987): B1.

Sowell, Carol. "Prayer-Inspired Visions Draw Faithful to Fireplace." Tucson: *The Arizona Daily Star* (28 February 1980): G-1.

Spicer, Edward H. *The Yaquis: A Cultural History.* Tucson: University of Arizona Press, 1980.

Starr, Frederick. *Catalogue of a Collection of Objects Illustrating the Folklore of Mexico.* London: Published for the Folk-Lore Society by Daniel Nutt, 1899.

Stewart, Hector E. *Indian Legend of the Desert. The Shrine of the Children.* Tucson: Arizona School for the Deaf and Blind, n.d. On file with author. (Printing data and date attribution of "mid-20s" from Otis H. Chidester, personal communication.)

Suárez Barnett, Alberto. "Funerary Styles of Nogales, Sonora." In *Respect and Continuity: The Arts of Death in a Border Community,* pp. 27–30. Tucson: The Southwest Folklore Center, and Nogales: The Pimería Alta Historical Society, 1985.

Terry, T. Philip. *Terry's Guide to Mexico.* Revised and augmented edition. Hingham, Massachusetts: the author, 1943.

Torres, Alva. "Torres' Living Room is Now a Movie Star." *Tucson Citizen* (23 January 1990): B2.

Toussaint, Manuel. *Colonial Art in Mexico.* Trans. and ed. Elizabeth Wilder Weismann. Austin: University of Texas Press, 1967.

Valenzuela Arce, José Manuel. "Por los Milagros Recibidos: Religiosidad Popular a Traves del Culto a Juan Soldado." In *Entre la Magia y la historia: Traditiones, Mitos y leyendas de la Frontera.* José Manuel Valenzuela Arce, compilador. Tijuana: Programa Cultural de las Fronteras, el Colegio de la Frontera Norte, 1992.

Vélez, Gilberto. *Corridos Mexicanos.* Mexico: Editores Mexicanos Unidos, S.A., 1982.

Vinson, Sterling. "Los Tapiros: Commentary and Photographs." *Journal of the Southwest* 33 (Spring 1991): 34–51.

Yañez Vargas, Prof. Rodolfino. "Lonardo Yañez, 'el Nano.'" Hermosillo, Sonora: March 17, 1995. Privately distributed. In the Southwest Folklore Center of the University of Arizon Library.

Weigle, Marta, and Peter White. *The Lore of New Mexico.* Albuquerque: University of New Mexico Press, 1988.

Weismann, Alan, and Jay Dusard. *La Frontera: The United States Border with Mexico.* Photographs by Jay Dusard. New York: Harcourt, Brace, and Jovankovich, 1986.

Weismann, Elizabeth Wilder. *Mexico in Sculpture, 1521–1821.* Cambridge: Harvard University Press, 1950.

————. *Art and Time in Mexico From the Conquest to the Revolution.* New York: Harper and Row, 1985.

White, John I. *Git Along, Little Dogies: Songs and Songmakers of the American West.* Urbana: University of Illinois Press, 1975.

Wilder, Joseph C., Editor. "Inventing the Southwest." *Journal of the Southwest* 32 (Winter 1990).

Wogoman, Ronald W. "Collected Tales from Mexican-American Children; Tucson, Arizona." Unpublished manuscript in the Southwest Folklore Center of the University of Arizona Library, 1972.

Wolfe, Coyote, comp. *Words for 30 Old Songs.* Photocopy of a 34-page mimeographed booklet, n.d. In the Southwest Folklore Center of the University of Arizona Library.

Woodman, Ruth. Letter to the Editor. *The Desert Magazine* 6: 8 (July 1943): 28.

Woods, Dan. "Legend Says Children Sacrificed." Casa Grande, Arizona: *Tri-Valley Dispatch* (October 24–5 1990): 3

Index

Note: Photo citations are designated with **bold numbers**.

Aconchi, Sonora, 95
Agua Prieta, Sonora, 2; horse racing at, 3
Aguilar, Antonio: *El Moro de Cumpas* (movie) and, 187n23
Aguilar, José: at Ímuris, 88
Aguirre, Pablo, 127
Akimel O'odham (River People), 8
Alambrista, 3
All Saints' Day, 18
All Souls' Day, 18–22, 24–25, 27–28
Altar, **45**
Altar del Señor de Veneno (Altar of the Lord of Poison), 96–97
Altar de Perdón, 96
Altarpieces. See *Retablos*
Altar to the dead. See *Ofrenda*
Ambiguity, 159, 163
Ambos Nogales (Both Nogales): cemeteries of, 15, 17, 166; population of, 14. *See also* Nogales, Arizona; Nogales, Sonora
Angelitos/angelitas, 18–19
Anglo Americans, 1–2, 11; traditional cultures and, 8–10
Apaches, raiding by, 94
Archbishop of Hermosillo, Tumacacori Fiesta and, 161
"Arnulfo Gonzales," 186n9; couplet from, 126
Artesanos (craftspeople), 39
Artículos religiosos, selling, 41
Artificial flowers, 27, 46, 49, 57; making, 20–21, 28, 32–33; materials for, 29. *See also* Paper–flower arrangements
"Asesinato de Villa, El," 139

Atzacoalco, cross at, 163
Authentic Cowboys and Their Western Folksongs (LP), 113

Ballads, 3, 10–11; classification of, 183n6; corridos and, 123; cowboy, 110
"Ballads of Cowboys and Pioneers," 183n6
Baroque, 160, 163, 165; in New Spain, 149, 151–54; organizational impulse of, 164
Basques, 10
Bass, Sam, 121
Bellotas (*Quercus emoryi*), 39
Birdcatchers. See *Pajareros*
Birria restaurants, 14
Bishop of Tucson, Tumacacori Fiesta and, 161, 162
Bittick, Al: "Mormon Cowboy" and, 112, 119, 120
Black Christ, 98, 101, 166; devotional literature for, 102–7; narratives explaining, 91–93, 179–80n11
Black Christ of Esquipulas. *See* Señor de Esquipulas, el
Black Christ of Ímuris (*el Cristo negro de Ímuris*), 88, 89; explanatory narratives for, 91, 94–98
Blanco, Pedro: legend of, 77
Bogan, Phoebe, 71
Borders: cultural, 4–6, 13, 166; internal, 1–2; international, 2–6, 13
Borhegyi, Stephen de, 97, 98
Bourke, John: on cascarones, 57
Bóvedas, 31
Brennan, Jose Lewis, 182n31

Browne, Sam, 57
Butler, Alban: on St. Maria Goretti, 78–79
Butterfield Parkway proposal, El Tiradito and, 70, 71

Caballeros, 124
"Caballo Prieto Azabache," 186n6
Caballos famosos (famous horses), 125
Cajamarca, Peru: reverse glass painting in, 48
Calaveras (skulls), 19; political, 26
Camacho, Olga: murder of, 75
Cannon, Hal, 112, 118
"Cárcel de Agua Prieta, La," 139
Carnival, cascarones for, 56, 57, 58, 176n18
Carrera de recuerdo (race of memory), 131
Carroway, Shorty, 116
Casa Grande Cemetery, grave markers in, 154, **158**
Cascarones, **63**, 175n13; animal, 59; breaking, 55–56, 58; buying, 61, 65, 66; at Carnival, 56, 57, 58, 176n18; children and, 58, 59, 61, 64; at Christmas, 59, 60; complexity of, 58–60, 64–65, 165; courtship and, 58; cultural boundaries and, 60–61, 64–65; at Easter, 58; figurine, 59–60; at Hallowe'en, 59; Santa Cruz Valley–style, **62**; tradition of, 55, 175–76n17; Tucson-style, 64–65; Yaqui, **63**
Catalans, 10
Cataño, Quirio: statue by, 89
Cathedral Bakery. See *La Panadería Catedral*
Catholic Encyclopedia, 78
Cemeteries, 15–18; folk, 17–18; public, 29. See also Panteón
Chapel (Juan Soldado gravesite), **76**
Charros, symbolism of, 124
Chelkona (skipping and scrapping dance), 99, 162
Chicanos, 1
Children's Shrine, 10, 98–101
Chinese paper. See *Papel de china*

Christ: images of, 80; manifestations of, 89. *See also* Black Christ
Christmas: cascarones at, 59, 60; San Xavier del Bac at, 153–54
Chromolithographs, 41
Cinco de Mayo, 127; cascarones at, 65
Clark, Charles Badger, 185n33
Club Copacabana, 127, 131
Cobre tumbas, 17
Cocopah, 1
Cocóspera, 94
Colors, 33; horse character and, 186–87n15; richness of, 159
Colosio, Luis Donaldo, 36
Comadres/compadres, 189n15
Compradrazgo (co–godparenthood), 45
Confetti, 56, 58, 64, 65
Continuity, 165, 166–67
Copper Letter, Yáñez and, 140
Coronado National Memorial, Yáñez at, 140
Coronas, 21–22, **23**, 24; artificial, 27, 32–33; cost of, 32; foundation of, 33; making, 19–21, 27
"Corrido de Bacerac, El," 138, 139; text of, 144–45
"Corrido de Fronteras, El" 139
"Corrido del Guante, El," 136, 138, 139; composing, 131; recording, 140; text of, 141–43
"Corrido del Túnel," 140
"Corrido Panista," 139
Corridos, 10–11; ballads and, 123; composing, 124, 126, 165; horse–race, 126–27, 138–45, 165, 188n27; political, 139; symbolism of, 124–27
Coulter, Lane: on Mesilla Combed Paint Artist, 48
"Cowboy Jack," 112
Cowboy songs, 120; theme of, 121–22
Cox, Jay Ann, 170n13
Cristo negro de Ímuris, el. See Black Christ of Ímuris
Crosses, 51; "combed paint" style, **47**; baroque, 163; decoration of, 16; exhibition of, 50; forward–curving,

30; tending, 24; types of, 29–30; wrought–iron, 18, 21–22, 27, 30, 159

Culture, 10–11; borders between, 4–6, 13, 166; complexity of, 1–2, 9–10; contact of, 8–10; immigration and, 165–66; legend transmission and, 101; marketing, 9; Mexican American, 147, 165; regional, 4–6, 13, 14, 165

Dalhart, Vernon, 110
Day of the Dead (*el día de los muertos*), 15; celebrating, 18–19, 25–26
Dead, remembering, 28, 171n4
Dead man's bread. See *Pan de muerto*
Death Valley Days (radio program), 100
Decoration, 11, 151, 152
Deseret String Band, "Mormon Cowboy" and, 113, 118
Desert Magazine, Children's Shrine and, 99, 100, 181n27
Desert People. See Tohono O'odham
Día de los muertos, el. See Day of the Dead
Díaz del Castillo, Bernal, 124, 136
Dieciseis de Septiembre, 127; cascarones at, 65
Di Peso, Charles, 9
Dixon, Maurice, Jr.: on Mesilla Combed Paint Artist, 48
Dr. Joe (horse), 127
Douglas/Agua Prieta, 2
Drug war, devastation of, 167
"D–2 Horse Wrangler, The," 112

Easter: cascarones for, 58; Yaquis and, 71
"Echo Canyon," 120
Egg Bonkers, 64, 175nn15, 16
Ek–Chu–Ah, "The Black Lord," 98
El Capitan schoolhouse, dances at, 114, 118
El convento (convent, Tucson), 89
El Tiradito ("The Little Cast–away One"), 70, 165, 167; changes for, 72, 80, 81, 176–77n9, 178n31; legends about, 68–69; as multiple–use

location, 87; praying at, 71–72; protection for, 70, 71; shrine to, 68–72; as victim intercessor, 78, 80
Esquipulas, 97, 180n11; pilgrimage to, 89
Estípites, 148, 149
Estrada, Ignacio Castaneda: *pan de muerto* by, 25
Extremely Pious Three–Day Prayer to the Lord of Poison, 103–4

Festival of American Folklife (Smithsonian Institution), 50
Festivals/fiestas, cascarones at, 65
Fiesta del Presidio, cascarones at, 65
Fiesta de San Agustín, cascarones at, 65
Fiesta de San Francisco, 35, 36–38, 40; Anglos and, 8; O'odham at, 7–8
"Final de Dos Caballos, el," recording, 140; text of, 136–38
Fisk, Buck: "Mormon Cowboy" and, 112–13
Flood Children, 99, 100, 101, 102
Florists, 32; coronas by, 21, 27
Flowers. See Artificial flowers
Folk art, 28–29; Mexican American, 154–55, 157, 159–60
Folklore, 165, 167–68; cultural values and, 101
Folk–Lore Society of London, cascarones and, 57
Folkways, 113
Fontana, Bernard, 45
Frames, 38–39, 43, 52–54; exhibition of, 50; as folk art, 35; making/selling, 39, 41, 44; modern, 49–50; painting, 46, 48, 54; popularizing, 50; social/cultural complexity of, 51
Franciscans (Order of Friars Minor), 36, 88, 95
Fred Harvey Company, 9
Frisby, Florencio, 127
Frisby, Pedro, 127, 135

Gadsden Purchase (1853), 2, 88
Gallegos, Josefina: Black Christ narrative by, 91–92

Gardiner, Gail I., 111–12
Gastelum, Lou: cascarones by, 64
Giesy, Cathy: Black Christ narrative by, 92–93, 94, 101
Gil, Antonio, 78, 81
Glass paintings, 48–49, 50, 166; color from, 51
"Glittering Recuerdos—Glass Painting Traditions from Magdalena, Sonora" (exhibition), 50, 173n13
Globe Silver Belt, 115
"Gold Placer of Quijotoa, Ariz.," 101
Gomez, Tita, 77
Goodwin, F. H.: Tiradito narrative and, 68
Graham, George: "Mormon Cowboy" and, 116
Granger, Byrd Howell, 177n9
Grave markers: Anglo American approaches to, 27; decorating, 15–18, 23, 26, 28, 29, 31; as folk monuments, 16; Mexican American, 154, 155, 157, 158, 159; tending, 12, 18, 21–22, 24; visiting, 19
Great Coatlicue, 163
Guerrero, Lalo: Tiradito and, 69

Hallowe'en, 28; cascarones for, 59
Hand, George: diary of, 174n4
"Handcart Song, The," 120
Hayden, Julian, 181n27
Hernández, Mario: *El Moro de Cumpas* (movie) and, 187n23
Hewitt, John N. Brinton, 182n31
"High Chin Bob," 122, 185n33
Hill, Blanche Brittan, 117
Hill, "Teet," 117
Hinterglasmaleri (reverse glass painting), 48–49
"Hit the Line Hard" (Rhodes), 185n31
Hohokam, 10
Holy Child of Atocha, 43, 157
Holy Child of Prague, statue of, 157
Holy Family, 74
Holyoak, Van, 168; "Mormon Cowboy" and, 117–18

Holy pictures, 35, 39, 41, 46, 53, 54; contents of, 38; orientation of, 52
"Home Sweet Home," 114
Horse races: betting on, 135–36; corridos about, 126–27, 138–39, 141–45, 165, 188n27; popularity of, 125. *See also* Match races
Horses: color/character of, 186–87n15; famous, 125; symbolism of, 124–27
Hughes, Sam, 90

I'itoi (Elder Brother), 99
Immigration, culture and, 26, 165–66
Ímuris, Sonora, 88
Indio, el (horse), 138
Infante, Pedro, 127
Isaacson, Jacob, 27

"Jesse James," 121
Jesuits, 10, 88, 95
Jiménez, José Alfredo, 186n12
Johnson, Elizabeth: cascarones by, 64
Johnson, Thomas: on thematic focus/ western songs, 121
Jokelore, bilingual/bicultural, 4–5
Juan Soldado: chapel by grave of, 76; execution of, 73–74, 75; legend of, 72–75, 87; postcard of, 76; prayers to, 75, 81, 82, 83–84, 105; statue of, 73; as victim intercessor, 78, 79, 80

"Kaguama Topillera, La," 139
Kino, Eusebio Francisco, 10, 147; fiesta/ pilgrimage for, 7–8; at Ímuris, 88; Magdalena and, 36, 37
Knights of Columbus, 161; Tumacacori Fiesta and, 162
Korn, Michael: on western folk narratives, 119
Kubler, George, 152

La Panadería Catedral (Cathedral Bakery), *pan de muerto* from, 25
Laws, G. Malcolm: ballad classification by, 183n6

León, Anastacio, 54, 173n15; composite picture by, **43**; Festival of American Folklife and, 50; framed picture by, **42**
León, Jesús, 39, **40**, 49; crosses by, **47**; frames by, 44, 46, 54
León family, Jesús: crosses by, 53
León, Martín, 54
Leonard, Irving, 164
Lincoln, Abraham, 48
Lions Clubs (Douglas and Agua Prieta), horse races and, 130
"Little Joe the Wrangler," 121
Llorenz, Juan Bautista, 148
Lopez Portillo, President: Yañez and, 139
Lord of Poison. *See* El Señor de Veneno
Los Alegres de Teran, "El Moro de Cumpas" and, 139
Los Donneños, "El Moro de Cumpas" and, 139
Los Jilguerillos del Arroyo, 169n4
Los Rancheritos del Sur, 169n4
Lost Pony Tracks (Santee), on El Capitan dances, 114
Low Rider Happening, 157
Low riders, 154, 157, **158**, 159
Lukeville/Sonoyta, 2

McAninch, Frederick, 179n8
McGee, J. W., 182n31
Magdalena de Kino, 74, 79; fiesta/pilgrimage at, 2, 7–8, 35, 36, 44–45; frame manufacture in, 49–50
Malverde, Jesús, 77, 81; prayers to, 84–86; as victim intercessor, 78
Mano poderosa de Dios, la, (powerful hand of God), 43
Manuel, Frances: cascarones by, 60
Maquiladoras (assembly plants), 14
"Marcha Zacatecas, La," 161
Mariachi Conference, cascarones at, 65
Mariachis, 135, 162
Marigolds. See *Zempasúchiles*
Marmolerías, 16–17, 18, 22, 30
Martinez, Feliciana: cascarones by, 60

Martinez, Gilberto, 130
Matachinis, 162
Match races (*parejeras*), 124–27; cheating in, 125–26, 128; corridos about, 126, 140; negotiating, 125; verbal expressions concerning, 141. *See also* Horse races
Mausoleums, 17, 31
Mayes, Lyn, 116, 119
Mayo Indians, Fiesta de San Francisco and, 37
Memorial parks, 17. *See also* Cemeteries
"Merino Mentado, El," 126
Mesilla Combed Paint Artist, **47**; tin/glass crosses by, 48
Mestizos, 10
Mexican Americans, 1; culture of, 8
Mexican baroque style, 149, 154, 159; characteristics of, 151–52
Mexican food, 8, 9
Mission revival, 160
Mission Road proposal, El Tiradito and, 71
Mission San Xavier del Bac. *See* San Xavier del Bac
"Mojado Mafioso, El," 139; recording, 140
Mondragón, Prisciliano, 169n4
Montaño, Rafael, 187n24
Montoya, Ángela: on cascarones, 175–76n17, 176n18; cascarones by, 59, **62**
Morales, Juan Castillo. *See* Juan Soldado
Morales, Richard, 73
Moreno, Álvaro, 49; frames by, 41, 44; holy pictures and, 54; Magdalena and, 53
Moreno family, cascarones by, 60
Mormon community, songs of, 120
"Mormon Cowboy, The," 10, 123, 166, 184n14; as folksong, 120–21; investigating, 117–18; performing, 110; recording, 111, 112; social concerns and, 122; story line of, 112; variants of, 114, 115–16, 117–20; verses of, 110–11

Moro, el, **129**, 131, 138; popularity of, 130; race with Relampago, 127–28, 140

"Moro de Cumpas, El," 126–27; changes for, 135; performing, 167; popularity of, 123, 134–35, 139–40; recording, 139–40; text of, 133–34

Moro de Cumpas, El (movie), 129, 187n23

Moroyoqui, Gloria: cascarones by, **63**

Motion, 157, 159

Muench, Joyce Rockwood: Children's Shrine and, 99, 100; letter from, 181n27

Museo Nacional de Antropología e Historia, 163

Museo Nacional del Virreinato, 149

Naco/Naco, 2; volleyball games near, 3

Nameplates, 16, 31; common shapes for, 30

Nano, el. *See* Yañez Romo, Leonardo

Negri, Sam, 179–80n11

Neighborhood Youth Administration, 71

Neobaroque, 160, 162–63

New Spain: baroque architecture in, 149, 151–54; connections to, 162–63

Nichos (niches), 71, 153, 154, 157, 159, 177n12; decoration of, 16–17, 155; variety of, 30

"Nigger Tuck" ("Old Kentuck"), 116

Nogales, Arizona, 2, 14–33; growth of, 14

Nogales, Sonora, 2, 14–33; immigrants to, 14

Nogales Cemetery, 15; Jewish section of, 26–27

"None can Preach the Gospel as the Mormons Do," 120

Norteño Festival, cascarones at, 65

Norteño groups, 135

O'odham. *See* Tohono O'odham; Akimel O'odham

Objects Illustrating the Folklore of Mexico (Starr), 57

Obregón, Álvaro, 187n24

O'Bryant, Joan: "Mormon Cowboy" and, 112–13, 118–20

Ofrenda (altar to the dead), 25–26

"Old Chisolm Trail, The," 185n31

"Old Kentuck" ("Nigger Tuck"), 116

Old Spanish Days Fiesta, cascarones at, 61

Oliveros, Juan: Tiradito narrative and, 68

Olvera, Jorge, 97

Omnipresencia de Dios, la, (omnipresence of God), 41

Oración a la Ánima Sola de Juan Soldado (Prayer to the Solitary Soul of Juan Soldado), 81, 83–84

Oración a la Milagrosa Imagen del Señor de Veneno (Prayer to the Miraculous Image of the Lord of Poison), 105–7

Order of Friars Minor. *See* Franciscans

Our Lady of Balbanera, 46

Our Lady of Guadalupe, 41, 49, 54, 155, 159, 162; images of, **42**, 80

Our Lady of the Immaculate Conception, 150

Our Lord of Esquipulas. *See* Señor de Esquipulas

Page, Donald W., 90

Pajareros (birdcatchers), 35, 50, 51; social niche of, 39, 41

PAN. See *Partido de Acción National*

Pan de muerto (dead man's bread), 25–26

Panteón Héroes, 15

Panteón Jardin No. 1, 74

Panteón los Cipreses, 15

Panteón Nacional, 15, 22, **23**, 25, 26, 31, 77; commercial activity at, 28; entrance to, **20**

Panteón Rosario, 15, 31, 77

Papago Indians. *See* Tohono O'odham

Papel de china (Chinese paper), 20, 59, 174n8

Papel de seda (silk paper), 20

Paper–flower arrangements, 19–21, 45, 46. *See also* Artificial flowers

Parejeras. See Match races

Partido de Acción National (PAN), 139
Pascua Yaqui Reservation: Easter ceremonies at, 71; wedding at, 160–62
Pesqueira, Ignacio, 88–89
Piadoso Triduo al Señor del Veneno (Extremely Pious Three–Day Prayer to the Lord of Poison), 103–4
Pierce, Francine: Black Christ narrative by, 93–94, 95
Pima. *See* Akimel O'odham; Tohono O'odham
Pima Community College, 93
Pima County Courthouse, 71
Pima County Fairgrounds, low rider display at, 154, 157
Pinedo, Emilio, 130
Pomar, Teresa: on frames, 46
Ports of entry, listed, 2
Posada, José Guadalupe: calaveras by, 19
Potrero Trading Post, reverse glass paintings at, 48–49
Prayer to the Miraculous Image of the Lord of Poison, 105–7
Prayer to the Solitary Soul of Juan Soldado, 81, 83–84
Pre–mass procession, 161–62
"Prisoner's Song, The," 110
Progressive Arizona, El Tiradito and, 72

Quechans (Yuma), 1
Quiroga, Ernesto: cascarones by, 60–61, **62**, 65, 66

Ramas (branches), cost of, 32
Ramírez, Trini, 128, 130, 138
Recycling, 31–32
Relámpago, **129**, 130, 138, 166; popularity of, 131; race with el Moro, 127–28, 140
Religious processions, 161–62
Retablos (altarpieces), 149, **150**, 152, 159
Reverse glass painting. See *Hinterglasmaleri*
Reyna, José R.: jokes and, 169–70n8
Rhodes, Eugene Manlove, 185n31
River People. *See* Akimel O'odham
Rodríguez, Silvestre, 131

Romero, Rafael, Jr., 127, 128, **129**, 130, 131
Romero, Rafael, Sr., 131
Ruiz, Olga, 39, **42**, 49
Russell, Frank, 182n31

Sacred Heart of Jesus, 41, 49, 73, 74, 155, 159
Sacred Heart Parish Church, All Souls' Day and, 28
Saint Anthony, statue of, 155, 157
Saint Augustine's Cathedral, 71
Saint Francis, 79, 166; festival for, 7–8, 35, 36; image of, 165; power of, 37; statue of, 38, 74, 180n11
Saint Francis of Assisi, 36
Saint Francis Xavier, 150, 188n2; statue of, 36, 37, 41, **43**, 44–45, 46, 73, 90, 153
Sainthood, 78, 79
Saint James the Greater, 136, 139, 152
Saint James the Moor–killer, 152
Saint Joseph, 41, 88
Saint Maria Goretti, as victim intercessor, 78–79
Saint Martin of Porres (San Martín de Porres), 73, 154, 177n15; death of, 178n27; statue of, 155, 157
Saint Martin of Tours, story about, 79
Saint Theresa, images of, 80
Saint Veronica's Veil, 163
Salado, 10
Salamónicas (twisted columns), 159
Salpointe, Bishop: Tiradito narrative and, 68
Salsa, marketing, 9
"Sam Bass," 121
San Felipe de los Alzates, 163
San Francisco Xavier (Museo Nacional del Virreinato), 149
San Ignacio, Sonora, 91
San José de Ímuris, church of, 90
San Luis Río Colorado, Sonora, 2
San Pedro de Aconchi, Black Christ at, 95–96
Santa Cruz, Atanacia, 90
Santa Cruz Parish Church (Tucson), 102

Santa Fe Railroad, 9
Santa Prisca y San Sebastián, 149
Santee, Ross: on El Capitan dances, 114;
"Mormon Cowboy" and, 115
Santiago de Compostela (Saint James
the Greater), 136, 139, 152
Santiago Matamoros (Saint James the
Moor–killer), 152
Santiago y Nuestra Señora del Pilar de
Cocóspera (church), 94
Santo Niño de Atocha, 89, 179n7
Santuario de Chimayó, healing powers at,
89
San Xavier del Bac, 11, 16, 37, 74, **146,**
147, 148–49, 165, 188n2; baroque
style of, 149, 154, 157; at Christ-
mas, 153–54; facade of, 152; inte-
rior of, 152–54; painted doors of,
153; retablos in, **150,** 152, 159
San Xavier Fiesta, cascarones at, 65
San Ysidro, 91
Sasabe/Sasabe, 2
Señor de Esquipulas, el, 92, 98, 166;
crucifix of, 90; statue of, 89–90
Señor de Veneno, el (Lord of Poison),
91–92, 97; additional texts of, 102–
4; prayers to, 96, 102, 103–4, 104–
7; statue of, 96
Seri Indians, ironwood carvings by, 51
Severus, Sulpicius: St. Martin story and,
79
Shrines, 68–72, 78, 177n12; examining,
67; roadside, 46; yard, 154, **156,**
157
"Sierry Petes (or Tying Knots in the
Devil's Tail), The," 111–12, 183n6;
recordings of, 183n7
"Siete Leguas, El," 186n6
Silk paper. See *Papel de seda*
Silvas, Francisco: Festival of American
Folklife and, 50
Simon, Bill, 111
Socio–religious events, 160–62
Sonora: internal borders in, 1–2;
O'odham in, 2

Sprague, Carl T., 114, 115; "Mormon
Cowboy" and, 110–11, 113, 116–
19, 121
Starr, Frederick: cascarones and, 57, 58
"Streets of Laredo, The," 112
Sunset magazine, on cascarones, 64

Techitos (roofs), 17, 18
Terry's Guide to Mexico, 97
Tinsel painting, 48
Tin work, 48
Tío Juan (horse), 138
"Tío Juan, El," recording, 140
Tissue paper. See *Papel de china*
Todos los Corridos de 1991, 169n4
Toelken, Barre: "Mormon Cowboy" and,
112–13, 118–20
Tohono O'odham (Desert People,
Papago Indians), 1, 3, 11, 100; arti-
ficial flowers and, 49; cascarones by,
60; Catholicism and, 44; culture of,
8; Fiesta de San Francisco and, 37;
frames/crosses/boxes by, 51; frames
for, 44, 46, 50
Tohono O'odham Nation (Papago
Indian Reservation), 3, 7, 11, 148;
chapel altar at, **45;** Children's
Shrine on, 98
Toral, León, 187n24
Traditions, changes in, 165–67
"Trail to Mexico, The," 112
Trincheras, 10
Trovadores Tapatíos, 187n24
True Prayer of the Soul of Malverde, 84–
86
Tucson City Council, Tiradito narrative
and, 68, 71
Tucson Convention Center, 70
Tucson Department of Parks and Recre-
ation, 72
Tucson Festival, cascarones at, 65
Tucson Meet Yourself, 50; cascarones at,
65; Yañez at, 140
"Túnel de Agua Prieta, El," 139, 169n4;
ballads about, 3

Tumacacori Fiesta, 161; cascarones at, 65

"Tying Knots in the Devil's Tail." *See* "Sierry Petes, The"

Urías, Alberto, 169n4

Urquijo, Ángel, 131

Valenzuela, Chindo, 128, 135

Valenzuela, Felipe de Jesús, 50, 173n15

Valenzuela, Gilberto: "El Moro de Cumpas" and, 139–40

Velderrain, Juan Bautista, 148

Verdadera Oración del Ánima de Malverde, la, (True Prayer of the Soul of Malverde), 84–86

Victim intercessors, 67, 78–79, 80

Villa, Pancho, 139, 186n6

Vineyard, Jack, 116

Virgin, 74, 155; images of, 80; statue of, 96

Virgin of Atocha, 179n7

Virgin of Guadalupe, statue of, 71

Volto Santo of Lucca, 98

"Way Up High in the Mokiones," 185n33

Weddings: masses for, 160–61; Mexican, 160; Yaqui, 160–61

Wheeland, Jan: cascarones by, 64

"When the Work's All Done this Fall," 121

Williams, Hank, 186n12

Wills, Clarence: "Mormon Cowboy" and, 116

Wills, Hugh: "Mormon Cowboy" and, 116

Wishing Shrine. *See* El Tiradito

Wolfe, Coyote, 117; "Mormon Cowboy" and, 114, 115, 116

Woodman, Ruth C., 100

Wreaths: making, 19–20; ordering, 21

Wrought iron, 18, 21–22, 27, 30, 31, 159; painting, 33

Yañez Romo, Leonardo, "el Nano," 132, 187nn19, 20; ballads by, 10–11; corridos by, 127, 128, 131, 133–39, 141–45, 166; on match races, 125; recordings of, 139–40

Yañez Vargas, Leonardo, 139

Yaquis, 1, 2; artificial flowers and, 49; cascarones by, 60–61; ceremonialism of, 169n2; culture of, 8; Fiesta de San Francisco and, 37; frames for, 41, 46

Young, Bill: "Mormon Cowboy" and, 116

Young, Brigham, 116

Yuma. *See* Quechans

"Zebra Dun, The," 122

Zempasúchiles (yellow marigolds), 21, 23, 24; decorating with, 27–28